WAITING FOR THE APOCALYPSE

waiting
for the
apocalypse

a memoir of faith and family

VERONICA CHATER

W. W. Norton & Company

NEW YORK · LONDON

Bertrand Russell quote on p. 325 from *Principles of Social Reconstruction* (London: Routledge, 1997), p.115. © 1997 The Bertrand Russell Peace Foundation. Reprinted with permission.

"Does the Spearmint Lose Its Flavor": Words and Music by Billy Rose, Ernest Breuer, and Marty Bloom © 1924 (Renewed) Mills Music, Inc. Copyright Renewed by Emi Mills Music, Inc. and Double A Music Corp. All Rights for the U.S.A. Administered Jointly. All Rights for the World Excluding the U.S.A. Controlled and Administered by Emi Mills Music, Inc. All Rights Reserved. International Copyright Secured. Used by permission from Alfred Publishing Co., Inc.

For information about permission to reproduce selections from this book,
write to Permissions, W. W. Norton & Company, Inc.,
500 Fifth Avenue, New York, NY 10110

For information about special discounts for bulk purchases, please contact
W. W. Norton Special Sales at specialsales@wwnorton.com or 800-233-4830

Manufacturing by Courier Westford
Book design by Brooke Koven
Production manager: Anna Oler

Library of Congress Cataloging-in-Publication Data

Chater, Veronica.
Waiting for the apocalypse : a memoir of faith and family / Veronica Chater.—1st ed.
p. cm.
ISBN 978-0-393-06603-6 (hardcover)
1. Family—Religious life. 2. Catholic Church—Doctrines—History—20th century. 3. Vatican
Council (2nd: 1962–1965) 4. Chater, Veronica. I. Title.
BX2351.C5225 2009
282.092'2—dc22
[B]   2008043054

W. W. Norton & Company, Inc.
500 Fifth Avenue, New York, N.Y. 10110
www.wwnorton.com

W. W. Norton & Company Ltd.
Castle House, 75/76 Wells Street, London W1T 3QT

1 2 3 4 5 6 7 8 9 0

To my mother, who died while I was writing this book,
and to my father, who soldiers on

contents

Do not think that I came to bring peace on the earth; I did not come to bring peace, but a sword.

—MATTHEW 10:34

WAITING FOR THE APOCALYPSE

1

the smoke of satan

MIDNIGHT MASS has not yet begun. People are still trickling in
through the doors of St. Mary's Church, greeting each other, lighting votive candles, and locating a pew. They sluff off coats, store
their purses and canes, write checks in advance for the collection,
lower the kneelers, and settle in. If I peek through the lace of my veil
I can catch glimpses of the regulars without turning my head: the
obese lady in her feathered pillbox hat, the man with the waxed han-
dlebar mustache, the Winking Man, and Tall Miss Rose. The Pooles
are here. And the Guttos. And the Gurries. And the Dowds.

Also, many new faces. Modern people. "Progressives," Dad
calls them. Women who don't wear scarves, some of them in slacks
or miniskirts, men in everyday clothes, jewelry peeking out from
their chest hair. People armed with the new missal, the *Novus Ordo*
missal, circa 1970, boldly printed in English, with no scapular or
rosary in their possession. Vatican II people.

Some of them don't notice my family of eight taking up the
fifth pew, but some of them do. As they pass, their eyes flash with

recognition and quickly darken. We are the family that is making things difficult for Father Geary and Father Dunne. We are the stubborn traditionalists who won't modernize. We are the anti-revolutionaries.

My understanding of Vatican II goes something like this: Nobody died, or broke the law, or went to jail, but ten years ago, in 1962 (the year I was born), a meeting was called and it lasted three years, and the pope ordered the priests to "open their church windows wide to let in the fresh air." But instead, the Smoke of Satan entered, and muddled everyone's brains, making them modern and sinful and prone to divorce. And now Catholics everywhere were behaving like Protestants, which was only one step away from being atheists, which was no different from being Communists.

Dad took Vatican II very seriously and told us about it over dinner, and what he said about it wasn't one bit good, as I could tell by his unhappy face and angry tone, and by the way he slammed down his fork and wiped his mouth hard on Mom's linen napkin, and by all the strange, harsh-sounding words he used.

"Vatican II . . . Ecumenical Council . . . Vatican II . . . Masonic infiltration . . . Vatican II . . . heresy . . . Vatican II . . . snow job."

When Dad told us about Vatican II, I pretended to get what he was saying and agree absolutely, because when a person talked with such vehemence you didn't want him to have to repeat himself. But also because Dad was a policeman and looked so strong and handsome in his California Highway Patrol uniform, and carried a .357 Magnum in his holster, and had one tan arm and one white one from driving with an arm hooked out the window of his patrol car, and because of the lovable oddity of having one leg shorter than the other, requiring him to wear a shoe insert. And because when he played the harmonica, he had a way of curling over the instrument with his shoulders and head, and stomping his foot, and frowning, and huffing into the mouth organ, and I didn't want him to ever stop doing that, ever. I pretended to understand when he used words like "ostpolitik" and "pontificate" and "ex-cathedra" as if they were everyday words like "soap," "paint," and "elephant" because I wanted him to think I was on his side. But honestly, I didn't get what the big deal was. I mean, church was church, no matter how you sliced it.

Mom, who "hated politics" and never had much to say about Vatican II outside of the kitchen, suggested to Dad that he wasn't making things clear for our young minds, and Dad sighed and made a helpless gesture, and said, "Well, there's no other way of explaining it!" and Mom shrugged, and instead of showing him how, asked, "Who wants seconds?"

It's no wonder that it was Mom, and not Dad, who eventually clarified Vatican II for me.

"Sister Mary Margaret wore the shortened veil at mass today," she said one day after church. "I always thought she of all the nuns . . . I don't know. I guess I thought she'd hold out."

Thanks to Mom, I was able to put the Vatican II puzzle together. Sister Mary Margaret's jazzy new shoulder-length veil: Vatican II. English words instead of Latin: Vatican II. No scarves on ladies' heads: Vatican II. The altar facing the congregation instead of facing the crucifix: Vatican II. Standing at the communion rail instead of kneeling: Vatican II. The wafer in the hand instead of on the tongue: Vatican II. The Handshake of Peace: Vatican II.

"And I only got three 'Hail Mary's' from Father Geary in confession," she added. "He used to give at least ten."

Shorter penances: Vatican II.

"My class got new catechisms today," I said, trying to put a fresh spin on Vatican II. "The pictures are much more colorful. The angels' wings look real. I like them."

"Well, I won't have that progressive propaganda in this house," Dad said. "I'm going to talk to Father Geary, and give him a piece of my mind."

"Mimi Rendler says maybe we can be altar girls," Terry ventured.

"Nonsense," Mom said.

"But St. Matthew's has altar girls," Terry said.

"That doesn't make it right."

Terry and I exchanged disappointed glances.

Altar girls: Vatican II.

"Mom, why can't I watch *Sesame Street*?" Nick asked one Saturday morning.

"Because it teaches children to be socialists."

Sesame Street: Vatican II.

At St. Timothy's in San Mateo, Father Schmidt broke the Holy Rosary in half and threw it on the ground, saying, "The rosary is outdated. I'd rather read a dirty book." So we left St. Timothy's and we joined St. Gregory's. Then we walked out of St. Gregory's and joined St. Matthew's. Then we left that church, and Dad went on a parish hunt, searching the entire Bay Area for a single church that stuck to the old ways. Each church disappointed him more than the last. There was no more denying what had happened to the Catholic Church. Before Vatican II you couldn't find a church that didn't say the Tridentine Mass. Now you couldn't find one that did.

And then he came across St. Mary's in San Jose, which was part of the German National Parish (meaning it was "on a longer leash from the diocese"). Father Donovan, who wasn't German but Irish, came from the old country and had no time for progressives. He said the Tridentine Mass in Latin and followed the 1962 edition of the *Missale Romanum*. Relieved, Dad stopped looking.

But the Smoke of Satan slowly began creeping in through the

windows of St. Mary's. First, progressive priests started mixing with the traditional ones. Then new missals arrived in crates at the rectory. New catechisms arrived at the school. Father Dunne began holding the New Mass. It drew large numbers. Father Donovan's Old Mass hardly drew anyone beside my family (the Arnolds), the Dowds, the Gurries, the Guttos, and the Pooles. The diocese gave a warning to Father Donovan to use the vernacular like the rest of the parish. He ignored them. Finally, the diocese gave him an ultimatum. If he didn't conform to Vatican II, they would retire him.

Father Donovan's response was swift and final. He died.

We were living in the age when the prophecies of Fatima would be fulfilled—the time of the Holy Chastisement. Progressives didn't place much weight on the prophecies of Fatima, but if you knew your Catholic faith you understood that the Virgin Mary's apparitions at Fatima were the most significant event of the century and directly related to Vatican II and the modernization of the Catholic Church.

It happened back in 1917, in Portugal. Our Lady visited three shepherd children, Lucia, Jacinta, and Francisco, as they tended their sheep in a cove called the Cova da Iria, close to Fatima. Descending from the sky, she was "more brilliant than the sun, shedding rays of light clearer and stronger than a crystal glass filled with the most sparkling water and pierced by the burning rays of the sun," said Lucia, the oldest. Hovering over a shrub, Our Lady spoke to Lucia, and gave her Three Secrets to share with the world. The First Secret was a detailed vision of hell, where "poor sinners" go. Lucia would describe this vision as a "great sea of fire [filled with] demons and souls in human form, like transparent burning embers, all blackened or burnished bronze, floating about in the conflagration . . . amid shrieks and groans of pain and despair." The Second Secret was that if people didn't pray and make reparation for their sins, "Russia would spread her errors throughout the world and many nations will be annihilated." Russia's errors, Dad explained, meant Communist totalitarianism—the biggest threat to Catholicism that existed. This was happening faster than you could imagine. By the time I was born, the Communists had already infiltrated half the world. Now they were in North Vietnam, and spreading to the south. America was fighting them, but losing. Losing the war overseas, and losing our resolve at home. It was only a matter of time before the war of ideologies came to a head in our own homeland.

The Third Secret, though, was the clincher. It explained everything. Or *would* explain everything if the Vatican weren't suppressing it. Even though Lucia had clearly instructed Pope John XXIII that Our Lady of Fatima wished for it to be revealed to the world by 1960, he'd refused to reveal it. And Pope Paul VI after him had refused also. And here it was 1972, and the secret was still resting in a sealed envelope in a locked vault in the Vatican. The reason for that, both popes told waiting Catholics everywhere, was that the world was "not ready." However, the truth was far different. And if you were on the ball you knew that both popes had refused to reveal the secret because it prophesied the Second Vatican Council, which had opened the doors and windows of the Catholic Church to communism, allowing Lucifer himself within the walls.

Meaning that the world was teetering on the brink of the Holy Chastisement: an apocalypse so huge that entire nations would be *annihilated*, as promised by Our Lady of Fatima. "When you see a night illumined by an unknown light," Lucia said, "know that it is the great sign that God gives you that He is going to punish the world for its crimes."

Dad said that by "annihilated" Our Lady meant a lot of things, but he didn't go on to list those things, except to say that one of its meanings was "obliterated"—another word that lacked the imagery of meaningful speech.

My older sister Terry, who was twelve, and had read the entire collection of Albert Payson Terhune dog books, and knew a lot about suffering and hardship, said the word "annihilated" was just a stylish way of saying "majorly creamed."

"Floods and famine and asteroids falling from the sky will be the fun part," she said across our dark bedroom one night. "What *I'm* dreading is the plague. Flies crawling all over people's rotting, stinking bodies . . . starving dogs eating limbs off babies who are too weak to beat them off, and vultures gathering in hoards, their beaks dripping with blood, to fight with the dogs over someone's maggoty guts . . . tapeworms invading our stomachs because we are forced to eat cow manure and drink polluted water. That's what *I'm* dreading."

Progressives called people who believed in the prophecies of Fatima "prophets of doom." But we were not prophets. We were simply True Catholics. And as True Catholics, our job was to pray hard enough and loud enough to consecrate Russia to Our Lady's Immaculate Heart, and stop the flood of communism so that the world would return to the One Holy Catholic and Apostolic Church. Personally, I worried that living in California—practically on the other side of the planet to Russia—might be a disadvantage in terms of proximity, but Terry said it was all the more reason to pray harder, louder, and more often. Because if we failed to accomplish this, if we failed to convince Russia to return to God, the Holy Chastisement would come and we would all die in a ghastly and hideous and gruesome way.

Sitting in my pew, I am not thinking about the Smoke of Satan, or communism coming to America, or bombs dropping, or vultures eating people's maggoty guts. It's enough to handle just being here so late at night, and taking it all in. I am thinking about how the church is light and dark at the same time, and how that must be a special talent for this building because what other building can do that? Candles glow in half-moons like tiny setting suns. Shadows ripple like the unlit portion of the sea, shape-shift, engulf, and dissipate. The stained glass windows have turned off their pictures and gone as black as the night behind them.

I am also thinking about the taste and texture of a dry Cheerio and how it turns to mush in my spit, and about how my dress scratches at the neckline and whether I'd be able to quietly tear off the lace without Mom noticing, and how the curve of my back doesn't quite match the curved back of the pew, and about whether it's too early to dig up Fred, my parakeet who died last summer, and share his skeleton at school. And how dark it must be in that shoebox grave . . . how very, very dark . . . in that dark . . . shoebox grave. And then I stop thinking altogether.

This happens to me a lot in church. As the minutes go by, my thoughts start to wander, my legs stop swinging, and my eyes begin to blink. Soon afterward, my lungs forget to inhale more than the smallest sips of air—just enough to keep me alive—and all the thoughts in my head evaporate like water in a dog's bowl on a hot summer day. I'm afraid of what this implies—that I am not an especially good Catholic. And this worries me on a daily basis. How am I going to live an exemplary life and die in the state of grace and go straight to heaven if I am not a good Catholic? And how am I going to be canonized like my favorite saint, Joan of Arc, if I can't get through a single prayer without daydreaming?

Luckily, Mom, always alert behind her cat-eye glasses, keeps me on my toes. Leaning forward, she rattles her rosary—which is her way of saying, *Wake up, sleepyhead! Use the time to pray!*—and I make a quick sign of the cross and force the rosary into my head,

choosing the Sorrowful Mysteries (even though I should be saying the Joyful Mysteries) because they are slightly more interesting. I offer up the rosary for our current pope, Pope Paul VI (even
though he might turn out to be the anti-pope because he is pro—
Vatican II), and for the poor souls in Purgatory, and for unbaptized
babies, and for starving people in Africa, and for the Communists
in Russia who are plotting to take over America. But no sooner do
I get to the first "Hail Mary" than it happens again: my hands go
limp, my jaw sags, my eyes droop, and my mind dehydrates in the
heat of an invisible sun. And as usual, no prayers get said by me
for anyone.

I AM revived at midnight by the ear-tickling sound of little brass
bells from the direction of the altar and I look up. There is Father
O'Brien, massive in his giant stiff robes and tall arched hat, gliding
up to the altar like the Holy Ghost in the flesh. And now the congregation stands in slow motion, moving like a colossal creature
waking up from its century-long nap.

I stand too, and Terry stands beside me. Terry has silky blond
hair that falls to her waist, breasts pointed like two sugar cones,
glasses that she only wears when there are no cute boys around,
and clear blue eyes that can see far beyond her twelve years to
the adventures that await her. To Terry, life is full of romance. At
night she turns on her flashlight and reads aloud from *The Lady of
Shalott*, and her voice trembles with emotion and grows hoarse and
frail and eventually falls silent, because the Lady of Shalott isn't
the only one trapped in a tower. Terry is trapped in a tower, too,
even if it is imaginary, and Alfred Lord Tennyson surely must have
had her in mind when he penned his tale more than a century ago
way back in England.

I stand beside the Lady of Shalott, flat-chested and a head

shorter, with a tangle the size of a tennis ball sticking out the back of my wavy blond hair. I don't place a lot of hope in poets or romantic adventures. The kids at school call me "Scrawny Ronnie," and I know the name suits me. My kneesocks have holes in the heels. Little crescents of raw pink peek through where my shoes abrade the skin. Rubber bands hold up my socks, squeezing pink rings into the skin around my calves. I've just discovered ringworm under my bicep for the second time and am worried about showing it to Mom for fear of the rigorous rubbing with alcohol I'll get.

Facing the congregation, Father O'Brien makes a fanfarish sign of the cross, throwing his hand out wide on a loose-hinged wrist, a gesture that makes applause seem necessary. But I don't clap. I stare with a stern, serious face as Father O'Brien holds his hands out wide and sings a lugubrious psalm that lingers around a single note, and the choir sings an equally doleful psalm back. And when that is over, I pause expectantly along with the rest of the congregation until it remembers it has to sit, and then does, slowly lowering itself with a sigh, like an exhausted, overweight beast onto its bed of polished wood.

And the mass has formally begun.

On the other side of me, Nick and Danny, seven and eight, squirm and bounce and twitch, twisting and roiling their legs as if they're running in air. I don't believe that in all their years of attending mass my brothers ever touched a pew. If they did, they'd have missed something, and that would be tragic, because if there is something lost, Nick and Danny are the ones to find it. Foremost, my brothers are treasure-seekers, scavengers of the world's lost things. And that requires them to hover just a millimeter above all surfaces, their eyes darting around all the dark places where no one else bothers to look. Nick and Danny never see the view straight ahead where the light is good. They aren't interested in what can be seen. They're interested in what lurks in the shadowy crevices. Money, a comb, a pocket knife, a whistle, a pen, a Tootsie Pop, a lighter, a crayon, a dollar bill, a five-dollar bill, a hundred-dollar bill—you never know what you might find. They believe in chance. Chance that has to be snatched quickly and run away with before the opportunity is gone.

Beyond Nick and Danny sits Mom with the babies: Vincent, who is three and mentally retarded, and Jennifer, who is two. Jennifer rocks back and forth against the pew—a habit she takes with her everywhere, that if left unchecked usually advances to full-scale head-banging. Mom hands her a single Cheerio every minute or so to stave off the next phase, and extends one to Vinny every so often, too. Vinny is usually content with sucking his thumb but can require some creative handling when he reaches his limit of tolerance. He may or may not respond to a Cheerio, or a stern look, or a shoe pulled off and handed to him, or some lap bouncing. If those measures fail, Mom will wrap the rosary around his neck and let him chew the beads. No child, as far as she knows, has ever been strangled by a rosary.

A HIGH MASS is a fancy kind of mass, with a lot of extra ceremonies, and prayers made longer by the singing of them. Father O'Brien will sing the *Kyrie* and draw out each syllable, changing the notes and maybe adding some new ones, and the choir will send it back twice as long, and then the congregation will have its turn. Mom and Dad sing the *Kyrie* extra loud because the *Kyrie* is part of the traditional mass, and they savor it for that reason.

Most of the time the *Novus Ordo* mass is sacrilegious, so Mom and Dad don't participate in the liturgy. While the rest of the people in church are following the new missal word for word in English, Mom and Dad are following the old missal in Latin. So when

Father O'Brien and the rest are saying, "I confess to Almighty God, to blessed Mary ever Virgin," Mom and Dad are saying, "Confiteor Deo omnipotenti, beatæ Mariæ semper Virgini."

Around us, people pretend not to notice that the parents of the family in the fifth pew are speaking the old rite. And Mom and Dad pretend to be participating in the same way as everyone else. But it's a clumsy act. A controversy is raging in the form of two languages. It's like a war, but it's not a war. It's a battle of ideas. And those ideas represent the heart and soul of the believer. And even though we treat each other with courtesy outside the church, inside we are engaged in linguistic self-defense: two sides convinced they are right.

For the reading from the Epistles Father O'Brien steps up to the pulpit, opens his large black Bible, and turns the pages. You'd think that when it came to the Bible, written practically when Catholicism began, all Catholics would be in agreement. But that is not true. The Bible has been rewritten dozens of times and in dozens of different languages, and except for the correct Douay Rheims version, all have been tampered with by the grubby hands of the enemies of the Church. So since Father O'Brien is probably not using the Douay Rheims Bible, but the King James Bible, which even the Protestants use, it's doubtful that we are hearing the correct version of the Epistle. Even so, you have to go along with it and kind of hope that it is close to true.

Finding his page, Father O'Brien raises his eyes and looks out over the congregation as a ship's captain would gauge the weather on the horizon, and when he sees that it is fair, he lowers his glasses into their permanent groove, clears his throat, and begins to read the Truth. Tonight, the letter of Paul to Titus, 2:11–13: "For the grace of God that bringeth salvation hath appeared to all men, Teaching us that, denying ungodliness and worldly lusts, we should live soberly, righteously, and godly, in this present world; Looking for that blessed hope . . ."

I listen to the Epistle for about . . . four seconds. Epistles can be tedious, and very difficult to absorb. I worry that I don't have the mind for them. Most of the time I understand them about as well as a dog understands a rabies shot. Once, when I told Mom this, she said, "You don't have to understand it. You just have to have faith." Mulling this over, I took it to mean that the *understanding* of words was not as important as the *saying* of words, and that was fine with me.

After the Epistle comes the reading from the Gospels. Tonight, the Gospel of Luke, 2:1–14: "And it came to pass in those days, that there went out a decree from Caesar Augustus, that all the world should be taxed. And all went to be taxed, every one into his own city. And Joseph also went up from Galilee, out of the city of Nazareth, into Judaea, unto the city of David, which is called Bethlehem . . ."

After the Gospel comes the Homily. If I focus hard I can usually find a little bit of sense in the Homily, but it's a strain. Instead, I spend long minutes picking out scents, like cat hairs from a sweater. The honeyed odor of burning beeswax . . . the blended aroma of women's hairspray and men's cologne . . . the rush of pine when somebody somewhere slams a door . . . and of course, the bully of all smells, frankincense, which rises continuously from the altar boys' thuribles in little white clouds and floats head-high, engulfs your senses, and eventually drives away all the finer scents.

And I set my sights on communion. At least during communion there is some movement, and even a change of scenery. That's when the altar boys ring their little dinner bells, calling guests forward, and the congregation sighs and stretches and stands up to slog in slow procession toward the communion rail. And that's when I get to look around and see what everyone is wearing, and watch the toddlers make a run for the candles, and the mothers chase them, and the old people unfold themselves from their sitting positions to lean on canes or walkers or their tired, crooked spouses, and I get to peek at the lady with elephantiasis of the foot who hoists her leg out in front with every step. And that is when my family and I will make a small scene at the communion rail by putting out our tongues instead of our hands, and everyone else will pretend not to notice that we are sticking to our pre–Vatican II principles.

I set my sights on communion, knowing that I have still have to get past the Handshake of Peace. The Handshake of Peace is the most awkward part of the mass, and the reason for this is that we don't give one. Dad says handshakes are fine when you run into someone in Sears or Kmart, but what's fine *outside* of church is not necessarily fine *inside* of church. And that's what the Vatican II people don't understand. They want to blend church and fun. And church should definitely not be fun. It should be as serious as a funeral, which is what it is, after all: a funeral for Jesus who is dead on the Cross, not some kind of social gathering. But how do you explain this to someone who is smiling and holding out their hand and saying with twinkly eyes, "Peace be to you"? It would take too long, and they still might not understand, so instead of explaining it you do the unthinkable: you clasp your hands together and close your eyes and pretend they aren't there. And there is this frozen moment when the parishioner's hand is hanging out there, and the parishioner is suspended like a trapeze artist in midair with no hand to grasp and save him from a fall, and you just have to let him fall. It's unfriendly, it's antisocial, and it's embarrassing. But if you're going to help the fight against the progressives, you've got to be impolite. And that's the difficult thing about religion. It makes you do things you wouldn't ordinarily do.

Waiting for the dreaded Handshake of Peace is like waiting for a tetanus shot. You can't think of anything else with it hanging there. It gets in the way of everything, and with every passing moment your anxiety over what to do about it grows, until you just want to get the pain over with. I worry about the handshake through the Introit, I worry about it through the *Gloria*, I worry about it through the Nicene Creed. It's only during the Rite of Peace, when Father O'Brien turns to the congregation and says, "The peace of the Lord be with you always," that I stop worrying. It's time for the handshake. I hold my breath and close my eyes and bow my head and weave my fingers into a tight ball. I am not here. I am invisible. I am nobody. A small, insignificant child. Not worth noticing. Definitely not worth giving a handshake to.

I feel a tap on my shoulder. Tilting my head, I crack an eye and peek at Terry. Her head is bowed so low her hair is covering her face like curtains. I look forward and see a lady smiling and holding out a hand to me in friendly way. "Peace be to you, little girl," she says. This hasn't happened before. The parishioners usually know better.

I glance at Mom. Her head is bowed and her eyes are squeezed shut. I glance at Dad. His face is closed, eyes tight, chin on his chest. Danny's and Nick's eyes are closed, too, although their lids are fluttering. My whole family is oblivious to my situation. I give the lady an anxious smile. A charge of heat rushes to my face. A daring takes hold. I lift my hand. "Peace be to you," I say with hardly a sound. And she takes my hot, sweaty hand in her smooth, cool one, and shakes it. Then she turns back around as if nothing bad just happened. I look at my hand. I wonder what I've done. Was that a sin? Will I have to go to confession? But how can I confess the handshake, when Father O'Brien told us to do it?

I am struggling with this dilemma when the altar boys ring

their bells and everyone rises for Holy Communion and the trip to the altar rail is such a relief it's almost worth the wait, with Father O'Brien placing the wafer on our tongues and saying, "The body of Christ," in the new way, instead of, "Corpus Domini nostri Jesu Christi custodiat animam tuam in vitam æternam, Amen," in the old way. Then communion is quickly over and we are back in our pews where we started.

Now would be a good time to end the mass, in my opinion. But Father O'Brien doesn't feel that way. Stepping up to the podium, he surveys the congregation and turns the pages of his book for another reading. This time it is the Last Gospel, which is a misnomer because it turns out to be not the Last Gospel at all, but the penultimate Gospel. Having experienced many high masses, I have come to realize that Christmas Mass never comes to a real end, since no one says, "The End." Rather, it makes a show of ending while in fact dragging on and on. Somehow there is always one more prayer of some kind, requiring the tedious refilling of incense burners, the ringing of bells, the singing of more antiphons, and the saying of more prayers.

On Christmas, this added ceremony is called Benediction, and it lasts another quarter of an hour, at the end of which Father O'Brien takes a slow tour of the church, cruising up and down the aisles for Asperges, dipping his sprinkler into his bucket and flinging holy water at all the people, and the altar boys swing their thuribles, slowly, and we kneel, we stand, we cross ourselves, we genuflect (a quick kneel), we stand, we sit, we stand, and the final minutes elongate into hours, the hours into decades, the decades into eons. How I manage not to burst into tears of mortal agony I don't know. But at long last, moments before my slow and painful death from excruciating boredom, the organist plays the opening notes of *Adeste, Fideles*, the congregation begins to sing on a note two octaves too low for my voice, and Mom stands up, crosses herself, and regretfully closes her missal.

Adeste, Fideles! I bellow the song rather than sing it, partly out of a sense of triumph and partly because I can't reach the note. Our pew looks like a scene from a refugee camp. Vinny is slouched in a corner, asleep with his thumb in his mouth. Jennifer is sprawled beside him. Cheerios dot the pew, crumbs are scattered everywhere, coats, purses, rosaries, and missals litter the pew and kneeler. Danny and Nick are leaning into each other, spittle in the corners of their mouths, their cheeks pink from tiredness. Terry stretches with a look of catlike satisfaction on her face.

And it is the real End.

2

praying for russia

To LOOK AROUND, you wouldn't think the Chastisement is coming. Myrtle Avenue is a happy place to live. Sunshine sparkles on the dew-laden grass. Finches chirp in the juniper tree. Airplanes rub their white chalk lines across a blue chalkboard sky. The world is normal. We are normal. Anyway, what is normal? Normal is events repeating themselves so often they can't happen any other way. Normal is Mrs. Pringle answering the door in her black slip and squinting an eye over the cigarette that dangles from her strawberry-red lips. "Ya wanna play with Wendy?" she says. "Well, ya can't. She's busy. Come back tomorrow." Normal is Marvin Sheptow thundering away at Tchaikovsky on his piano and leaving his doors and windows wide open to showcase his extraordinary talent but never exiting the house for fear someone will see him. Normal is Mr. Koch doing push-ups on his fingers and toes on the sidewalk at the crack of dawn, and Mrs. Koch drinking Screwdrivers in a pink tennis skirt by their swimming pool. And it is Noreen Poole parking and reparking her yellow Cadillac with the tailfins in her driveway four times, leaning hard on the gear shift like she's working a submachine gun, and checking all the mirrors to get her mile-long car dead center.

Normal is our peppermint-pink house in a neighborhood of matching houses the colors of saltwater taffy—lemon-lime, pineapple, tangerine, cherry, and banana—with their matching front lawns and friendly neighbors who leave their oscillating sprinklers running all day just in case some kids want to run through them. On our front porch is a welcome mat made of plastic grass with its own plastic daisies, and a hydraulic aluminum screen door purchased from Sears Home Improvement Center that swings open with a hiss and closes by itself in three gentle stages. Rimming our front lawn, a white picket fence gleams like freshly polished teeth, and beyond the lawn a sidewalk unrolls itself like a bolt of white satin to take you straight to Paul Moore Park, where you can swing high enough to see over the Little League baseball game all the way to St. Mary's School.

Inside the house, Mom is fresh and clean and trim in her starched cotton blouse, fitted skirt, and low-heeled shoes. She is the prettiest mom I know—except for Mrs. Poole maybe, who wears a mod leather skirt and false eyelashes and who always looks top-notch even though she is divorced. Mom has dark hair ratted in a heart-shaped bob and full lips that don't quite cover her buck teeth and sharp green eyes that don't miss a trick from behind her cat-eye glasses. Dad likes to joke that Mom was created from the rib of Our Lady of Angels in the Garden of the Fifties, and not even the entire force of the women's liberation movement can change her. Mom's response to this is, "You'd better believe it, Buster," as if Dad is testing her resolve to see if she just might give in to the other side after all   which she definitely won't. Mom has no interest in what those braless feminists have to offer. In fact, she'd like to know what kind of cryin'-out-loud waste of time self-actualization is, anyway, and what she would want with a man's job. "Like I don't have enough to handle right here in front of me without running off to join a plumber's union or a truck driver's union, or good grief, competing with a man for the job of a police *person* of all the confounded things." If you ask Mom what she *is* interested in, she'll tell you: children that do as they're told, a plenary indulgence on All Souls Day, affordable shoes, low taxes, the GI Bill that allowed Dad to take college courses, allegiance to God and country, and getting away with traffic violations by flashing her own CHP badge (a small replica Dad brought home from headquarters for just that purpose).

Anyway, what has the women's lib movement got to offer that she doesn't already have? She keeps a clean house, free from dust and mold. She cooks nutritious meals and serves them before we are even hungry. She schedules regular doctor appointments for us even though we are perfectly healthy, and regular dentist appointments even though so far none of us has a single cavity. Weekday mornings she flicks on the lights at exactly seven-fifteen a.m. and sings, "Good morning, it's a lovely morning. Good morning, what a wonderful day," no matter what the weather is like, and helps us get dressed in our school uniforms—blue knee-length skirts, white blouses, and blue ties and sweaters—and is backing out of the driveway in our green 1964 VW Bug (a car Mom admits is a *little* small for our family of eight but one that we keep because Dad loves it) in plenty of time to get us four oldest to St. Mary's School for the Pledge of Allegiance at eight-thirty. And then she is waiting out front at two-thirty while we sing "Holy God, We Praise Thy Name," with the engine idling and the babies sitting loose in the front seat, and beeps the toylike horn and shouts, "Come on, kids! Hop to it! I don't have all day!" And when we've squeezed in and are gripping the looped handles, she grinds the Bug into first and our heads jerk back with every gear shift as she drives out of the downtown district with all its stops and go's to the more spread out suburbs, where there's plenty of room to make a U-turn if you accidentally pass by a garage sale. And by the time she's pulling onto Cherry Avenue, she's thundering out her long stream of orders about what needs to be done before anything else, and hasn't yet taken a breath when she pulls up at our house on Myrtle Avenue and we're climbing over each other to get out of the car and barreling up the walkway, ". . . and I don't want any lunch boxes or sweaters left in the car and you're to hang your sweaters *in the closet* and fold your uniforms and when you take off your shoes don't throw them in two directions, and Danny put your shirt in the hamper, it's filthy, and wash your hands all of you, and I want all your homework finished and *in your book bags* and ready for school tomorrow before you go out and play, and Ronnie brush that hair of yours I can't stand the sight of it *one minute longer!*"

At six, Dad breaks from his patrol shift on Highway 17 and drives home for dinner. As he nears the house he bleeps his siren and parks his squad car sideways in the driveway as if he's just fishtailed right out of the fast lane at the scene of a shoot-out, and he sits in the car for a minute to scribble his break time into a tiny spiral notebook with a mechanical pencil, then calls Rita the dispatcher on the mobile unit to advise her of his location, saying the words we've all learned by heart: "San Jose, 24/7 . . ." (*Go ahead, 24/7*) "I'm going code 7 at the Myrtle Avenue residence . . ." (*Copy that, 24/7*). Then he rises slowly from the driver's seat like a man-sized balloon inflating, hoists up his trousers with their rattling handcuffs, and strolls to the front door, heel, toe, heel, toe.

When Mom hears the bleep, she shouts from the stove as she scrapes the sloppy joes onto the plates, "Terry set the table Ronnie put the babies in their high chairs Danny pour the milk Nick put out the napkins, let's go, move it, Dad's home!" and the noise in the kitchen is deafening for a whole minute as we scramble for the table, put down place settings, yank out the chairs, and take our seats.

All is quiet when Dad enters the house. His broad shoulders fill the doorway, and his badge flashes its seven blades individually, and his hand rests on his .357 Magnum as he surveys the scene before him. His black hair is short and wavy and combed smooth, and his blue eyes twinkle like cut diamonds reflecting a clear sky. He is the handsomest dad on the block, if not the handsomest man in the world, and we catch our breath at the sight of him, and our six hearts palpitate with pride and each of us hopes to be the one who will get to give him a foot rub for a dime. Pulling out his chair, he lowers himself in, and sighs happily, taking in the cool air. "It's a furnace on Seventeen," he says. "Cars overheating every mile on the upgrade. You wouldn't believe the backup." And Mom shakes her head and clamps her lips as if she told those drivers "time and time again" to pack extra coolant and "as usual no one bothered to listen." She takes a can of Pabst Blue Ribbon from the fridge, pours it into a frosty glass, and sets it down in front of Dad, and he takes a long thirsty slug, his Adam's apple bobbing like a buoy on a rough sea, and when he licks his lips and says *Ahhhh!* Mom looks satisfied, and slides into her chair at the end of the table, and we all bow our heads, make the sign of the cross, and say Grace together with eight mumbling, uneven voices.

"Blessusohlord—n—thesethygiftswhichweareaboutto-receive—fromthybounty–throughchristourlor—damen."

When dinner is over, Dad gulps down another Pabst, then strolls back out to his patrol car, curls into the driver's seat, calls in to Rita, *San Jose, 24/7, 10–8 (Copy 24/7),* and drives into the sunset of 17 where the backup is unbelievable. And then Mom bathes the babies and dresses them in their jammies as Danny and Nick clear the table and Terry and I wash the dishes and we all make our school lunches, and then it's rosary-round-the-bed, and lights out before we are even the slightest bit sleepy. Terry goes to sleep in the bed Father Donovan died in, which Dad bought from a rummage sale at St. Mary's (a creaky iron twin bed with miniature scrolls along the headboard), and even though I am a little envious of this, I am also extremely grossed out by it, to tell you the truth.

And life is good. If hell opens its gates and spills out Satan and his army of demons, Dad will take his .357 Magnum from his holster and shoot them, shouting for us to take cover. And if a demon should escape the bullets, Dad will swing his leaded spring billy club with just enough snap of the wrist to bend it midair and double the force of the impact. And if more demons come, he'll perform his special Judo flip—a move that puts the opponent's strength to the defendant's advantage—and lock the demon in handcuffs and shove him into the backseat of his patrol car behind the wire barrier where the doors are locked and have no handles, and drive him off to the station to book him. And after he's successfully shot or disabled or arrested all the demons that have dared to attack, Mom will shake her head and say, "For cryin' out loud. How many times did I tell them not to come around here?" and she'll continue to cook meals that feature one serving each of meat, starch, and vegetable, and take her place at the opposite end of the table, and we will continue to live peacefully on Myrtle Avenue, and ride our bikes to Paul Moore Park, and watch *Looney Tunes* on Saturday mornings, and there will be no more threat of hell breaking open and mass annihilation.

NORMAL IS VINCENT being different from everyone else on the planet. Mom brings him to the hospital for tests to see why he sticks his tongue into the air like a dog facing the wind, and why his eyes Ping-Pong back and forth, and why at the age of three he hasn't learned any words. We all go with her to Kaiser Hospital and sit in the examining room and watch the doctors place their stethoscopes on his chest between the strings of his scapular (which Mom refuses to remove in case Vincent dies while it's off). They peer through a light into his eyes, ears, and mouth, and measure his skull and hammer at his reflexes and take blood samples and X-ray his brain. Vincent is patient with the doctors. He doesn't squirm under their cold hands or try to grab their instruments. He doesn't even cry when they slide the needle into the tiny vein in his arm. There is Danny bouncing nervously on his toes and almost peeing his pants at the sight of the needle, but Vincent just sits there with a sweet smile staring across the room at us, happy to have us there. Maybe Vincent's patience is part of his medical condition. The doctors murmur together and flip the pages of their books and nod. They ask Mom how many martinis she drank when she was pregnant, and Mom frowns and says, "Don't be ridiculous, only a few," and they ask her did she do any jumping jacks or other exercises during her pregnancy, and she says, "Do you mean calisthenics? What do you think I am, some kinda women's libber?" So there are more tests, and more murmurings, and just when it seems we might as well move in and take up permanent residence at the hospital, the doctors tell Mom what he's got. Or what he hasn't got. "No precedent . . . chromosome five . . . genetic blueprint . . . medical first . . . The Vincent Syndrome."

Mom crosses herself. She knew it: a gift from God. An angel sent from heaven. An *innocent*. She doesn't need a doctor's prescription for innocence. She picks Vinny up in her strong arms and says proudly, as if the doctors weren't there, "I could have told those doctors you were one of a kind and saved them all their tests.

God broke the mold when He made you, didn't He, Bean Bag? Oh yes He did." Now when people see Vinny's eyeballs boinging back and forth as if they were touching something hot and see his tongue wagging out and hear him cry like a kitten, Mom can say, "He isn't dangerous. He's got the Vincent Syndrome. The only known case in the world."

There are definitely benefits to being an innocent, instead of a guilty, which is what I probably am, and Danny, too, who gets blamed for everything even when he's asleep. When you're an innocent, you get to be in a book just like the *Guinness Book of World Records*, and whoever else gets your syndrome will have to put their name under yours in smaller print and use your name for what they have. And Mom will love you with a special love that is all your own because you were flown down from heaven in the arms of the angels themselves and given as a gift to your family. When you're an innocent, you get whatever you want. All you have to do is reach for it and say *Aaah* and nobody will think you're spoiled. You don't care about TV or toys or candy or any of the things other kids are so worked up about, because you are happy inside yourself. You are satisfied with one cookie and don't even think of asking for more. You don't mind being served last at the dinner table because it doesn't matter if your food comes now or later. You go to bed without complaining and get up without complaining because you enjoy being asleep and awake equally. And you are happiest in the place most kids hate the most: the bathtub.

Vinny likes water so much he climbs into the empty bath with his clothes on and waits for water to magically rise. When he does this, Mom strips him and fills the tub, and Vinny opens his palms and flaps them on the top of the water like a wingless duck trying to lift off from a pond, as his pointy tongue reaches far out for the flying drops, and his wide-set green eyes gape at the wet fireworks sparkling in the air. He splashes. Stops. Tastes. Splashes. Stops. Tastes. Mom can leave him in the tub for an hour and do house-work and check on him through the door and not worry about her innocent drowning, since God would never take an innocent with-out a good reason. "Look at the baby boy who just loves his bath. Yes he does! Oh yes he does!"

Another benefit to being an innocent is that when you die, your soul will advance straight to heaven faster than that of a martyred saint. No time in Purgatory for bad behavior, since innocents are incapable of willfully committing a sin. Vincent embodies the purity of a newly baptized soul, and Dad says if you look real close you can actually see a halo suspended over Vincent's head. I not only see the halo, I can feel it. Whenever I'm near Vincent my skin feels warm, as if it is bathing in the graces of Vincent's purity. Either that, or I just love him so much I get a fever from it.

The most enviable part of being an innocent is that you get to live with Mom and Dad for the rest of your life in your childhood home. Mom says that even though the rest of us kids will grow up and get married and move to different places and get jobs and have families of our own, Vinny will stay with her and Dad forever. Years will pass, and new presidents will be elected, and fashions will change, and Vinny will still be right there on Myrtle Avenue, splashing in the bathtub, his face alight and his tongue stretched out to catch the wet stars. Life couldn't be better than that, so I wonder why I feel strangely sad whenever I think of it.

I WOULDN'T SAY the Pooles are normal, and that's what I like about them. Everything about the Pooles is the same as us, only backwards, beginning with their lemon-yellow house three doors down that mirrors ours like a Looking-Glass House. In our house, the furniture is heavy, solid, rounded around the edges, and indestructible. You can tip over the tables to make forts, hide behind the couch, pile chairs on top of chairs, and make good use of the cushions. In the Pooles' house, the table and chairs are lightweight and perched on narrow legs that taper to points, not at all conducive to building structures, with corners so sharp that if you catch a shin on one you will bleed. In our house, the walls are hung with paintings of the Sacred Heart of Jesus, Our Lady of Fatima, St. Joseph, some family photos, and a large country landscape. The Pooles' walls and tables are decorated with objects that tease: masks you can't wear, musical instruments you can't play, glass fruit you can't eat, and brightly colored ashtrays that tempt you to smoke even though you're not allowed to. Our dog, a German Shepherd named Chema, has good house manners, and knows when it's okay to bark. The Pooles' dog, a mutt named Hobo, barks like a maniac when you ring the doorbell and races through the house as if a dozen rabbits were on the loose.

Just like her house, Mrs. Poole is the opposite of Mom. Our Mom shouts orders like an army captain and uses a wooden spoon on our behinds for back talking. Mrs. Poole asks her kids to do their chores with a hesitant whisper that reminds you of Marilyn Monroe, and cries real tears if they don't listen. And they don't listen very often, so Mrs. Poole cries a lot, and the chores never get done. Our mom dresses in clothes she can change a tire in, climb a ladder in, run and crawl in, and rescue a child from a burning building in. Mrs. Poole wears clothes that seem to make walking a chore, and would surely cause her injury if she were caught in a high wind. But there's a reason for high fashion. When you see Mrs. Poole walking down the street, you think that any moment a limo will pull up and drive her straight to Hollywood, where a famous director will make her his leading lady, because there is no injustice bigger than that much glamour going to waste.

Like their mom, the Poole kids are the opposite of us. The oldest daughter, Teri—spelled with an exotic *i* instead of a common *y*—is in the sixth grade and will "take shit from no one." Teri cuts up old dresses and sews triangular flares into her bellbottom jeans and wears socks that have toes and a vest with a fringe that falls to her knees. She's the kind of girl who smokes the cigarette butts she finds under the bleachers at the baseball diamond, and flips the bird at boys that whistle at her, and sings "Jesus Christ, Superstar, Who in the world do you think you are?" knowing full well she's taking the name of God in vain. Once Teri said to Danny, "You think you're hot shit in a champagne glass, but you're not. You're cold diarrhea in a Dixie cup," and I laughed until I got a cramp in my stomach because there is nothing funnier than an older girl calling your kid brother cold diarrhea. Tami, ten, is only slightly less exotic than Teri. She wears her long black hair in two braids, Indian-style, and has brown, rectangular glasses, and stands hip-out with her skinny white arms akimbo in a way that makes her look like a cutout doll. Everyone says Tami's a priss, but she doesn't care because that just means she's smart. While everyone else is riding bikes and climbing trees and rolling down the grassy hill at Paul Moore Park, she is playing Bank on the foldout table in her bedroom, counting out fake money, and using words like "checking account" and "overdrawn" as she serves her stuffed animal customers. Behind her glasses her dark eyes fix on you, and slowly bore into you, giving you that special chill that only real X-ray vision can give.

Dixon is my age, and as far as I'm concerned, not quite human. He is male, but not a generic boy. He's a mysterious cross-species of boy and animal: the kind who uses words like "butt-ugly," "snotweed," and "cheese-weasel" with obvious pleasure over the texture of their sounds. He'll say, "Want a Hertz donut?"

and I'll say, "Okay," and he'll twist my arm behind my back and say, "Hurts, don't it?" and he'll laugh. I try to keep my distance from Dixon in case he carries something contagious, but that's hard to do because he shares a room with Michelle, who is the youngest Poole and my best friend. Michelle has soft brown eyes and perfectly feathered hair and a funny, snorty kind of laugh that makes everyone else laugh when they hear it. Her number one talent is painting rainbows with watercolors. She can paint a rainbow flawlessly on any surface, like on her bedroom wall, and on her dresser drawer, and on the tops of her tennis shoes, and on her school Pee Chee folder. Her number two talent is macramé, which can be boring to watch but is worthwhile in the end because sometimes she gives away the projects that don't turn out right, and you could be the lucky new owner of a not-completely-perfect plant holder or belt.

The Pooles are traditionalist Catholic, too, and go to St. Mary's School and St. Mary's Church. When Mrs. Poole comes over to stand by our air conditioner and drink cocktails, Dad talks to her about Vatican II and the Holy Chastisement, and Mrs. Poole agrees with everything he says by nodding her head and whispering, "Gosh . . . I mean *really* . . . Isn't it terrible?" But I get the feeling that Mrs. Poole agrees with everything Dad says because he says it so convincingly, and that if Dad wasn't around to inform her about Vatican II, she'd be fine with the *Novus Ordo* and the Handshake of Peace, and so would Teri, Tami, Dixon, and Michelle.

IN THE SUMMER, the Arnolds pile into the Bug and the Pooles pile into their Cadillac and we drive in convoy over the Santa Cruz Mountains to Sea Cliff Beach, which has a long, flat white strip of sand perfect for sunbathing, and medium-sized waves for body-surfing, and an old ship at the end of a pier that you can fish from—

if you're inclined to fish, which we aren't, because that would waste good beach time.

Steering the car with her knee, Mom digs through her handbag with both hands, fishes out her rosary, crosses herself, says, "For the conversion of Russia," which is her signal for the rest of us to grab our rosaries, and starts praying out loud:

Inthenameofthefatherandofthesonandoftheholyghostamenibelievein onegodthefatheralmightycreatorofheavenandearth. . . .

Mom has a prayer for every hour of the day and every occasion, and she enforces the saying of these prayers by crossing herself and shooting us an on-your-marks-get-set-go glance. The Daily Offering in the morning. The Act of Contrition for times of temptation. Prayer to My Guardian Angel when in danger. The Memorare at times of doubt or faithlessness. Intercessions to keep us in the state of grace. Ejaculations for sudden spiritual needs. And the Spiritual Communion when we're sick and can't make mass. But the prayer for any and *all* occasions is the rosary. If there is ever an unfilled slot of time, Mom will pull out her beads, in public or private, make the sign of the cross, implement the glance, and start praying, and we'll follow suit or suffer grave consequences the nature of which we can only guess. To Mom, there is never an inconvenient time to pray for Russia, and no shame in doing it openly, whether you are sitting in a hospital waiting room, standing in line at the grocery store, weaving through traffic, or waiting for a solar eclipse to begin. And the half-hour drive to the beach is the best time of all to get in a rosary or two.

And so I grab my beads from my pocket and add my voice to the other atonal voices meeting in prayer over the putter of the engine, but it's hard to concentrate on the mysteries when the car smells like Coppertone and your legs are sticking to the vinyl seat and your bathing suit is wedging into your crack, and the Pooles are in the Cadillac behind you with the music blaring and some of the kids doing headstands in the backseat and Mrs. Poole driving at such a slow speed that Mom has to downshift to keep pace with her. And it's a drag that it takes twice as long to say the rosary because of all the interruptions. Mom has the kind of eyes that can watch you in the rearview mirror and still see the road, and she doesn't miss a beat when your thoughts start to wander or a fight breaks out for space in the backseat.

Hail Mary, full of grace—Terry, take that thing out of Jennifer's mouth before she chokes—*who art in heaven hallowed be*—Ronnie, that's enough pushing, keep your hands to yourself—*kingdom come thy will be done on earth*—and that goes for you too, Danny, there's enough room for both of you—*our daily bread and forgive us our trespasses*—Nick, get off the floor and pay attention to the rosary—*and lead us not into temptation but deliver us*—for cryin' out loud, Noreen is stuck behind a sixteen-wheeler again—*from evil*—go ahead and pass him, Noreen, for goodness' sakes, don't just sit there!—*Amen.*

At Sea Cliff, Mom and Mrs. Poole lounge at the picnic area, talking and picking at Chex Mix and pouring something pink from a thermos into paper cups, and never once come down to the shore to wade or even wet their feet—the point of a beach for mothers is that they can spend the whole day having fun and not have to shout at kids. Every so often they'll shade their eyes and scan the ocean for us, but they don't worry. They know we won't drown out there unless God decides it's our time. And if He does, then there's not much they can do about it anyway. When it's your time, it's your time. It doesn't matter where you are if God is ready for you. You could be sitting on a couch reading a book. Or sleeping. Or playing Parcheesi. Or walking along the sidewalk. Or talking on the telephone. Or going to the bathroom. God doesn't need a dangerous condition to strike you dead. Anyway, if worst comes to worst we can say the Act of Contrition in the amount of time it will take to drown, so at least our souls are safe. And let me tell you, it's a big comfort knowing your soul is safe when you're bobbing on a two-dollar air mattress a quarter mile out beyond the waves, where the giant purple jellyfish billow softly with the slow surge of the tide, and vast tracts of seaweed coast by like small, slippery continents, and low-flying pelicans skim by at hyper speed, and a harbor seal occasionally pops up, its spotty gray skin and bald head and empty black eyes looking at first glance like the skull of a drowned person risen up from a watery grave with a look that says, *Let me tell you what I've seen*—although no words come.

Teri Poole, who stays on the sand to watch Jennifer and Vincent, says that the harbor seals are there to warn you of the presence of sharks. She also says that if you drift farther out than the bow of the ship, you won't come back because that's where the great white sharks patrol for stupid kids on cheap plastic rafts that don't honor the harbor seals' warning. I believe Teri, but I also don't since Teri can be "full of shit." Once I traveled so far out that I could see the fishermen standing on their decks (from the shore you could barely make out the tiny silhouettes of the fishing boats) and hear their milewide shouts and see them moving around on their boats doing the things that fishermen do. It was an extra comfort to know that there were real people carrying on with their business out there in the ocean miles from land just like you.

When you're out at sea you're more alone than anywhere else on the planet, so you can practically have a conversation with God. Out there, your breathing becomes pronounced and your skin luminous and your heartbeat audible and the flat table of water actually invites you to talk, almost as if the ocean were God's own big eardrum. Being out at sea is a little bit like being in church only better, since you have all of God's attention and don't have to share it with hundreds of other people, and you get to say whatever is on your mind instead of reading the words in a missal. *Dear God,* you might start out. *Thank you for the sunny weather and for the slightly warmer inch of water on the surface of the ocean, it feels so nice. And please don't let me get stung by a jellyfish or stuck in the seaweed or run over by a speedboat. And please make Mom cook barbecued hamburgers, but not the kind mixed with powdered onions. And make Terry stop being so mean to me. And, oh yeah. Please don't let the sharks get me, since I'm way out here in shark territory and I've already seen two seals. Through Christ, Our Lord, Amen.*

When you lie with your ear pressed to the inflated pillow on your flotation device, your arms dangling in the water, and the cold water rolling onto your pillow and tickling your ear, you can get hypnotized by the rhythm of wave-water slapping against the underside of plastic and echoing within the compressed air of the mattress. It's better than any kind of music I know. *Shloosh. Plumpk. Shloosh. Plumpk. Shloosh. Plumpk.* And if you close your eyes against the glare of the white sun, you might even fall asleep, like Terry did (or *said* she did, although I don't believe her, since you can never completely go to sleep when you've got to keep one eye open for shark fins at all times), and catch the tide that takes you all the way to Hawaii.

Out there you might last about an hour before you get bored or hungry or scared, and then you've got to work really hard to get back in, using your hands like oars and digging them down into the blue-green water to propel your raft forward and make your way back to land. If the ocean is in the mood to toy with you by pulling you back out, it might take you an hour or so to get close enough to catch a wave and ride it in, but it'll be worth it because then you'll be surrounded by everyone asking questions, and you can brag about how far out you went this time, and how many harbor seals warned you, and how many shark fins circled you, and how your raft sprung a leak and you could see the bubbles coming up from below (even if you didn't), and everyone will tell you how lucky you are to be alive and how you'd better not tell Mom you were in shark territory with a leaky raft. And then you can find yourself a nice quiet spot away from the hole-diggers and Frisbee throwers where the heat purls upward in gentle, wiggly waves, luxurious to breathe, and feel happy to be alive after your brush with death. You can slather baby oil all over your body and feel your body temperature rise two degrees a minute as you lie on your piping hot towel and listen to KFRC on your transistor radio, and feel the tingle of your skin as it broils a dark red under the shimmering sun. And, trust me, you will sigh a prayer more eloquent and moving and sincere than any you've ever known, and it doesn't even require you to kneel.

WHAT'S NORMAL FOR the rest of us isn't normal for Dad, and Dad tries to explain this to Mom over and over again since she apparently doesn't understand. At night, when we're in bed, I can hear him explaining it to her behind their bedroom door, his voice a muffled bark like a dog trapped in a box. Every so often a word punches through the wall, and it's usually a word I recognize, like "Vatican" or "progressives" or "Fatima." During the day, he follows Mom around the house as she does her housework, a reporter of grievances giving a mobile oratory to his audience of one. As Mom folds laundry and puts the dishes away and vacuums and empties the trash cans and polishes the furniture, Dad tells her about what he just read in *The Remnant Magazine* and asks her if she can believe the things that are printed in there. Mom's response is always the same: "I know, Lyle. I know. I don't like it any more than you do." But she keeps on vacuuming and scrubbing and doing laundry, and that really gets Dad's goat.

"One of the greatest crimes in the history of mankind is happening right here, right now, in our own lifetime, and what are we doing about it? Are we taking up arms like they did in the Crusades, and defending the Holy Catholic Church? Are we marching in the streets demanding that the Vatican expose the Third Secret of Fatima? Six hundred thousand soldiers died for Abe Lincoln in his war over the Union. Twenty million died because of World War I. *Sixty* million died because of World War II. Where are the people defending the Catholic Church? I'll tell you where we are. We're shopping, and barbecuing, and paying our bills on time, and watching TV, and mowing the lawn, and going to the beach as usual, because we've got our lives to live, right? Let the Second Vatican Council destroy the Church that Our Lord gave to his apostles. We aren't going to rock the boat. Why should we? Life is good! Anyway, we don't have any fight in us. We want to buy more Hostess Twinkies!"

I gather Mom is listening to him because I hear the *I know, I know* sound, but apparently she doesn't fully get what he's saying because Dad has to turn up the volume to drill his point home.

"And since we're not fighting the war, we might as well join the hippies in the Haight-Ashbury and celebrate the leftization of the world by drinking Kool-Aid mixed with LSD and having bed-ins and waving peace signs and singing, 'Power to the People.' At least then we'd be doing something. Because I don't think I can stand doing nothing anymore."

It's hard to hear the cartoons when Dad is explaining the hard facts to Mom and sounding slightly accusatory, as if Mom were to blame for everything and had a lot of explaining to do. If my mind were a pie chart, it would be divided into thirds: one third worried about Mom, one third worried about Dad, and the last third not worried one bit, but convinced that Bugs Bunny is the wisest and funniest creature that ever lived.

"Why do I love carrots, anyway? There's not much meat on them. They're kinda dry, too. But I love 'em. I LOVE 'EM . . . I LOVE 'EM! . . . I LOVE 'EM! I LOVE 'EM! I LOVE 'EM!!"

"They bastardize the Tridentine Mass, they kick out the devout priests, they open their arms to Communists, and who cares? Not us. We've been numbed by modernity into a moral coma, anesthetized by relativism, made fat and lazy with junk food, and diverted by baseball, and rock 'n' roll . . . and . . . and . . . *cartoons*."

When Dad says "cartoons" it comes off like a swear word, and he flings his hand toward the TV as if it were a steaming pile of puke, and I shrink and pretend that I'm bored with TV, too—that Bugs Bunny is just a diversion, and not really that funny at all.

"Are you hearing me, Marty? Or am I just talking to myself?"

And Mom says, "I hear you, Lyle. I hear you," and shuts off the vacuum and coils the cord and stores the machine in the closet and looks at her watch, and says, "I've got to take Vinny to his eleven o'clock doctor's appointment. Do you need me to pick up some new razor blades?"

PART OF DAD's problem is family life. He isn't cut out for it. The noise, the routines, the interruptions in the bathroom, the dirty diapers left to soak in the toilet, the toys underfoot, the constant accumulation of pets, the relentless comings and goings of neighborhood kids, the phone calls from teachers, the household appliances breaking down. It drives him crazy. He can't concentrate with family life impinging on his time.

Of course, Dad doesn't say these things outright. He's studying political philosophy at San Jose State University and stacks his textbooks on the kitchen table and types his papers there and gives Mom his thoughts on the rise of bureaucratic middle management after the French Revolution and how it led to the failure of the Catholic Church to lead nations as Mom sweeps the floor and wipes the sticky jam off the table around him. But Mom isn't fooled. She gets what Dad is *really* saying, and says, "I think you should build yourself a study in the backyard. It would be better for everyone if you had a quiet place to read."

She's given up on Dad being helpful around the house, anyway. As she points out to Mrs. Poole often, and within hearing, he isn't handy like her father, who could replace the air, oil, and fuel filters in the car, build a set of shelves, and wash the dog all before ten in the morning. The one time Dad tried to fix something was when the washing machine gave out in the middle of a heavy load. "It's stuck on the wash cycle," Mom had said, pointing to the dial. "It won't go into spin." Dad had kicked the offending appliance. "Why do you want it to spin?" Mom stared at the man who should, by nature, dominate the machine. "It's part of the process. Look. *Wash, Rinse, Spin.* It removes the water from the clothes." "Oh. Well, that shouldn't be too hard to fix." Dad took out his tools, unscrewed the side panels, the back panel, and other irrelevant parts, then yanked off a hose and flooded the garage with laundry water. And that was the last time Mom relied on him for household maintenance.

Dad can't operate a can opener. He can't cook an egg or make a peanut butter and jelly sandwich. He can't scare away the boogieman, or soothe a crying baby, or tell a story without bringing in world history. All he can do is talk about Vatican II and the world history that led up to it, and she's sick and tired of hearing about all that.

Of course, Mom doesn't say these things outright. She looks

at Dad with a knowing smile and crosses her arms and loves him with the kind of unconditional love you feel for a child who is having a temper tantrum, and decides it's better to have him *out* of the way than *any other* way.

"I've been saying it for years. You need a place of your own."

"Good," Dad says. "Okay."

"Fine, then. Do it."

"I will."

"Great."

And the next day Mom tells Mrs. Poole, "So Lyle begged me to let him build his study, and I finally gave in. I figured it's better to have him *out* of the way than *in* the way, if you know what I mean."

And for the next several weeks, men come and go with their toolboxes. They measure out the dimensions, hammer pine stakes into the lawn, string twine, dig a square pit, and pour the foundation. You can actually see Dad's mood lifting with each new phase. It lifts as Uncle Joe frames it. It lifts again when Bud Huss wires it. And it lifts even higher as different friends insulate it, side it, and roof it. It lifts so high that when it's finished, Dad does the chicken dance all around the backyard, flapping his wings and kicking out his white hairy legs in their shorts, looking more like a chimpanzee than a chicken.

That evening, as we all stand around the backyard admiring it, Mom says, "You need a sign over the door." And Dad says, "By gosh, you're right," and disappears into the garage and runs a power tool for a long time. I expect the sign to say *Keep Out* or *No Trespassing* or *Private Property*. But when he finally comes out of the garage, what he nails up over the door isn't that kind of a sign. It's a sign to remind you of why the cabin was built in the first place. The sign reads: *Womb*.

3

dubious friends

ONCE THE WOMB is built, Dad begins to spend all his spare
time in it. On weekdays he comes home from his patrol, pockets a
pack of Camel straights, grabs the wine bottle, and doesn't come
back in the house until past bedtime. On weekends he leaps out of
bed, intercepts the coffeepot, and heads straight for the Womb,
staying there all day. Mom takes him a plate of hot food like a saint
visiting a hermit in a cave, hands it through the door, and goes
back to get it when he's done.

If Dad is in the Womb, Mom says, don't bother him. And she
means it, because she doesn't bother him either. Things in the
house can break, short out, plug up, explode, catch fire, jam, flood,
crack, or melt, but no problem is big enough to necessitate breaking Dad's concentration with a complaint. When the dishwasher
begins to leak during the rinse cycle, Mom slides a cookie sheet
beneath it to catch the water. When the garbage disposal stops
turning, she scoops the junk out by hand. The backyard fence is
yawing at a forty-degree angle as if being blown down by a high

wind and she bolsters it with a two-by-four. The '55 Ford Wagon that Dad bought to supplement the Bug dropped its rusty tailpipe somewhere on Brokaw Road and now gargles out its exhaust in violation of California Vehicle Code 27150. Mom doesn't mention it. If she gets pulled over, she'll flash Dad's badge.

In the daytime, Dad casts a bright figure in the doorway of the Womb where a shaft of sunlight serves as a reading light. As evening falls, his figure darkens to a murky silhouette, backlit by a single cone of lamplight, smoke layered above his head, the red button of his cigarette blushing like a brake light when he takes a drag. At night, my bedroom window projects the glow from the Womb onto the white wall over my bed and I lie awake watching the ghostly movement of Dad's shadow and listen to the fitful dance that his fingers tap out on the Underwood typewriter, pausing with him at the *ding* of the bell, mentally slamming back the carriage, and joining him again in his stumbling box step.

The Womb is where Dad keeps track of the Communists' advance across the globe. If you have any doubt where the action is taking place, you have only to go into the Womb and take a look around. On a giant world map hanging over his desk, tiny colored pins bearing flags mark the various hot spots and areas of resistance. As the Vatican sells out the Catholic Church to communism, bishop by bishop, parish by parish, priest by priest, the pins multiply and change position and color. The pins, needless to say, are as plentiful as flies on roadkill, leaving only the ocean and Antarctica vacant—although they will probably crowd up too if you wait long enough. On either side of the map hang two large photographic prints. On the left, poised proudly on an emerald-green hill, its turrets pointing into a blue cloudless heavenly sky, a medieval castle in France overlooks a gentle rolling valley of farms and vineyards. On the right, its ash-caked windows cracked and boarded and its tall chimneys belching black pollution into an oily sky, an industrial factory in East Berlin squats low amidst the filth that it created. It doesn't take much in the way of brains to know that the castle represents the Catholic Church overseeing the glorious age of Christianity before Vatican II, and the factory represents the Catholic Church selling out to communism after Vatican II.

The bookshelf is choking from more than it can hold. If you skim the titles you will get an idea of the complex ideological warfare in which the world is engaged: *The Great Sacrilege* by Fr. James Wathen; *The Grapes of Wrath* by John Steinbeck; *War for the World* by Major General Thomas A. Lane; *Brave New World* by Aldous Huxley; *Fahrenheit 451* by Ray Bradbury; *Liberalism Is a Sin* by Dr. Don Felix Sarda y Salvany; *Our Lady of Fatima* by William Thomas Walsh; *The Screwtape Letters* by C. S. Lewis; *Nineteen Eighty-Four* by George Orwell; *The Miracle of Lourdes* by Ruth Cranston; *Thus Spake Zarathustra* by Friedrich Nietzsche; and *The Exorcist* by William Peter Blatty. Thumb through the stack of *Time* magazines and you can see photos of American soldiers under fire from Russian-built artillery in the hands of the Viet Cong. Then see more photos in those same magazines of Nixon and Kissinger shaking hands with the Russian Communist leader Leonid Brezhnev and clicking glasses with Mao Zedong, whom Dad calls "mass killer *par excellence*." On a corkboard, a comic from the March issue of the *National Review* shows Nixon wearing a Mao suit and standing in front of a full-length mirror as a haberdasher fits him. "So far, so good," Nixon says. "Now, as a sop to the conservatives, how about a narrow tie?"

On hot days, when the rotary fan whirs at its post in the doorway, magazine articles that Dad has Scotch-taped to a wall from *Triumph* magazine and *The Remnant* wave up and down in the passing breeze. Look up, and you'll find the three shepherds of Fatima staring steadily out at you from their gilded picture frames. Look up higher, and Our Lady of Fatima, her outspread hands shedding light, oversees the entire downfall of humanity. Stand directly in the center of the Womb, and you can look at the three-dimensional world itself: a giant globe on a brass stand, with a gyroscopic mount, and a handy numerical guide for easy longitudinal and latitudinal reference that allows you to better visualize the exact location of and distance between the countries the Red Army have conquered so far, as well as the ones they are about to take over.

"East Germany," Dad will say, pointing to a small brown splotch in the middle of Europe, "Czechoslovakia . . . Poland . . ." His finger will follow a slow, serpentine trail eastward. "Hungary . . . Romania . . . Albania . . . Bulgaria," and loop up, circling a large, empty-looking area. "The fifteen countries of the Soviet Union," and loop down, creating a figure eight, "China," and creep over to some small projections: "North Korea . . . North Vietnam . . . South Vietnam . . . Laos . . . Cambodia," and arch back around to the west, "Afghanistan . . . Iraq . . . Syria . . . Lebanon," and fall south, "Egypt . . . Ethiopia . . . Mozambique . . . Rhodesia . . . Angola . . . Congo," and farther west, where the sunlight will fall on the more familiar side of the planet, "Uruguay . . . Chile . . . Bolivia . . . Peru. . . . Nicaragua . . . and Cuba." He'll pause. "And soon"—that's when his finger will circumscribe the whole of the United States and Canada and finally land on California—"they'll be here."

At night, when the house is silent, I can almost hear the echoes of marching boots touching down on California soil, resounding over Santa Clara County as the Red Army besieges Sunnyvale, Cupertino, Saratoga, Milpitas, closes in on San Jose, and finally converges on our own neighborhood, growing louder as they turn down Hillsdale Avenue and Foxworthy Avenue, their gray uniforms standing out against the candy-colored background of suburban tract homes, their boot heels clomping like drumbeats off the pavement, crashing through hedges and vines and flowerbeds and decorative fences. I can hear them advancing up Cherry Lane, spreading out on Overlook Drive and Myrtle Avenue, invading the Kochs' house, the Sheptows' house, the Osborns' house, and the Pringles' house, turning them all into rotten stinkin' commies, kicking down the Pooles' front door, deaf to Hobo's panicked barking and Teri's cussing and Mrs. Pooles' whispered complaints, coming up our walkway, yanking open the hydraulic screen door, smashing the holy water font, tearing down the pictures of the Sacred Heart of Jesus and Our Lady of Fatima, and asking everyone they meet: "Are you for us, or against us?"

I worry that Dad is taking on too much. Sometimes he forgets to shave. Or he leaves out a false tooth. Or his hair sticks out at excited angles. When he leaves the Womb, he often has a puzzled look on his face as if he's been trying to find the solution to a difficult math problem that no one has ever successfully worked out. Sometimes he is thinking so hard about the problem, he'll stub the same toe on the same step he stubbed it on the day before.

"Son of a . . . In the name of . . . Jeeeee . . ."

When Dad stubs that toe the cusswords fight to come out, and his face grows red from clenching his teeth to lock them in, and sometimes he works so hard at holding back the words he'll step on a toy or knock over a plant, which makes him even madder and have to fight harder not to break the Third Commandment. But the thing that maddens him most is the evening news.

"Oh! This really takes the cake!" he'll storm from his easy chair as Mom works in the kitchen. "Here's Nixon, running off to shake hands with Mao Zedong in China, and then racing to give a hug to Brezhnev in Moscow, and making stupid policies that are killing our soldiers by the thousands in South Vietnam, and here's

Kissinger *decontaminating* American foreign policy from religion right under our very noses, and abortion going to the Supreme Court, and what's the top story mesmerizing the country? The baseball season might be delayed because of a strike. The country is going to the dogs, but God forbid we should miss a baseball game. I've never felt so ashamed in all my life."

I don't like the news because it gets Dad upset, which gets Mom upset, which gets Danny upset, which causes him to lash out at Nick, which makes Nick cry, which convinces Mom that it's late (no matter what time it is) and that we should all just go to bed. Instead of the news, I wish we could watch *Love American Style* or *The Sonny and Cher Show* or *Laugh-In* like the Pooles get to watch, and sit around gut-laughing at the telephone operator lady with the nasal voice who insults callers; but I don't ask to watch those shows because Dad says no. If there is anything Dad hates, it's *pointless comedy TV*. For Dad, the only shows worth watching are shows about real issues. He keeps his eye out for them on *NBC's Saturday Night at the Movies*, and when a good one comes on, he turns out the lights and joins us on the couch and explains the movie to us the whole way through, and it's never what you think. Most horror movies pretend to be about horror but are actually about something else, like *The Blob*, which is about the *Novus Ordo* devouring and ingesting Christian civilization; or *The Day the Earth Stood Still*, which is about the world's resistance to the truth about Fatima; or *Them!*, which is about the Communists' invasion of society; or *Invasion of the Body Snatchers*, which is about the takeover of the conservative individual by the soulless modern masses. When this film comes on, Dad writes a note on a scrap of paper that says: *Body Snatchers, 8:00, Channel 2!* and sends Danny running to the Pooles' house to deliver it.

My favorite film of all time is *The Wizard of Oz*, and even though Dad explains what it's really about, I just like the story.

"*The Wizard of Oz* has some good messages. The clicking of the heels is very metaphysical. It means that the intellect is at the top of the human hierarchy of character. It forms the will. And then there is the scene when Glenda appears in a sphere of light. That scene came right out of Fatima, which took place twenty-two years before *The Wizard of Oz* came to the movies. Also good are the flying monkey demons, which show how the Russians are bad. That part is pure brilliance."

Every so often you come across a movie that is a clear-cut, factual drama torn right out of the pages of history and needs no explaining. The film *A Man for All Seasons*, which is about Sir Thomas More opposing King Henry VIII's divorce from the queen, got Dad so excited that he saw it twice in the theater and then took us all to see it so we could memorize the scenes and act out his favorite parts for twenty-five cents. Terry was best at it. "I will not give in, because I oppose it . . ." she would say in her perfect English accent, and Dad would begin counting the coins from his pocket. "Not my pride, not my spleen, nor any other of my appetites . . . but I do . . . *I*."

Another factual film, *The Song of Bernadette*, came on TV one Sunday in 1972, and when Mom saw it listed in *TV Guide* she bought a stack of TV dinners so we could all watch it at dinnertime.

The Song of Bernadette is a true story about a saint who was visited by the Virgin Mary in a grotto outside of her town near Lourdes, in France. When Bernadette told the priest of the village about her visions, the priest wanted a miracle to prove her story. So Bernadette requested one from the Virgin, who commanded her to *drink from the spring*. Since the ground was hard and dry, Bernadette dug into the dirt in search of an underground spring while people mocked and laughed at her. But a few days later a miraculous spring began to gush from the hole, and the water began to heal blindness, paralysis, and even putrid diseases of the flesh— and continues to heal even to this day.

I'd seen the film once before, and was prepared for Mom's tears at the end when Bernadette has her last vision and dies, but this time something else happened. A silent tension filled the room as the credits rolled across the screen, and the silence seemed to generate from Dad's side of the room. It felt like an anticipation of some kind, but for what I couldn't say. The moment was ripe for something—a fight, a lecture, a temper tantrum? Mom wiped her eyes with a tissue, and we all sat very still.

And then Dad said, "It's pointless."

"What do you mean?" Mom asked.

"This charade we're playing."

"What charade?"

"The American Dream charade. Happiness. Wealth. Security. It's all a hoax. It doesn't exist."

"We don't have it so bad."

"Exactly. In fact, we've got it pretty darn good. But don't you see? That's the problem. We've got it so good we don't notice that we're compromising. We're selling our souls to comfort."

"It all depends on how you look at it."

Dad stared unseeing at the credits on the screen. "Well, the way I look at it, we're stuck in the pit of mediocrity. We've got to climb out of this hole. Take a chance. Roll the dice. See what else there is. Get out of here. Try living somewhere different for a change. Move someplace where people think like us." He looked at Mom and his eyes sparkled with the revelation. "Lourdes, Marty.

We should move to *Lourdes*." It was as if the answer to all of life's problems were contained in that one word.

Mom smiled as if he'd said something funny, and Dad stared back. I didn't know, but Mom must have felt the prick of dread, because her voice was full of it when she finally said, "Lourdes."

"I could join their police force."

"Oh, Lyle. Don't be ridiculous."

"I'm not being ridiculous. We could do it. What's stopping us?"

"We're not *French*."

"So what? Is there any law against Americans living in France? French people live *in America*. Think about it. Lourdes is a polyglot community. People make pilgrimages there from all over the world. English is the most common language. They're bound to need English-speaking officers."

"But you don't speak French."

"I could learn by immersion."

"You? Learn French?" Her smile stretched wide, uncovering her splendid teeth.

"I could do it."

Mom chuckled. "Even if *you* could, I'm pretty sure *I* couldn't."

"Sure you could. We all could."

"Lyle, you don't just suddenly decide to pack your bags and move to France. Be realistic."

"I'm being *totally* realistic, Marty. People immigrate into America all the time. Who's to say people can't emigrate *out*?" Dad's voice had notched up a decibel, and his eyes were shiny orbs of light as if he were having his own vision of Our Lady. With a face like that, Dad seemed invincible. "I could send away for an application and get headquarters to write a letter of recommendation for me and mail it to the chief of police at Lourdes. They'll take one look at my background and hire me, guaranteed."

Mom looked away, already half-conquered. "Well, I don't see the point. Whatever happens in the States is bound to happen elsewhere, even in France."

"Come on! France is the birthplace of Joan of Arc! It gave the world generations of kings and knights to fight in the Christian Crusades! France is *perfect* for us."

As always, I was torn between Dad's passion and Mom's practicality. Like Mom said, you couldn't just pack your bags and move somewhere else, could you? And what was the point of moving to another country when the blob would eventually dominate the whole world? But then again, wouldn't it be nice to live close to the miraculous waters?

Terry said, "I think it's a great idea."

I said, "Me, too."

Dad said, "See, Marty? The kids think it's a good idea. Let's have a vote. All in favor of moving to Lourdes raise your hands."

We all raised our hands, including the babies, and Dad turned triumphantly to Mom, who sighed and shrugged. It was clear she didn't really believe Dad would actually do this crazy thing. But it didn't hurt to egg him on a little. "Well, then. Good luck."

Now that Dad had his solution, he went right out to the Womb and composed a letter to the chief of police in Lourdes asking for a job with their police department. He listed his experience: eight years in the Marine Corps, one year at San Quentin, five years at the San Mateo County Sheriff's Office, and seven years at the California Highway Patrol. He stapled together his résumé, his college transcript, a letter of recommendation from Captain Arnold Zinc, put about twenty stamps on the envelope, and went right out to the post office. When he returned home, he was carrying a shopping bag with an audiocassette tape inside. For weeks afterward a woman's crisp singsong voice accompanied the tapping on the Underwood.

Excuse me, Miss. May I borrow your pen?

Pardonez-moi, Mademoiselle. Est-ce que je peux emprunter votre stylo?

Dad waited for an answer from France. A month went by, and then another week, before it finally showed up. Mom held up the letter up when Dad walked in from the garage. The look on her face showed some humor, but there was worry there, too. What if Dad pulled it off?

"I can't imagine what you think is going to happen," she said.

It was a Saturday morning and Mom had just put pancakes on the table and Dad had been working the speed bag and was flushed, his white T-shirt so sweaty you could see his scapular and St. Joseph's medal through it. Ripping open the envelope, he unfolded the letter, and frowned as he read it out loud, trying to make out exactly what it meant.

> *Dear Monsieur Arnold,*
> *Thank you for the gentleman's inquiry. The French police department must always require a good police officer. One respects the American law system. One is sure you are a police-man of best quality. But in France one must hire police officers who is French, and himself attended the French academy. In Lourdes we thinks California is a lovely place, and myself I would like to visit Hollywood. We wishes you the best of luck, and sincerely hopes you have better luck in another country.*

Dad was disappointed. He couldn't believe Our Lady didn't want him to go to Lourdes. It seemed like such a great idea. He looked at Mom, and his face and shoulders drooped.

"Where is my Catholic utopia?" he asked. "Where is it, if not in Lourdes?"

Mom didn't have the answer to that, and with a lost-puppy look that made you want to pat him on the head, Dad plodded off to the Womb. Moments later, the sound of Merle Haggard's voice drifted across the yard, bewailing with Dad how hard life is when you're a workingman with the blues. With the smallest look of I-told-you-so on her face, Mom heaped a plate with pancakes and brought it out to him, while we all sat at the table wondering what we were going to do.

DAD CONVERTED TO Catholicism at the age of nine when his friend Dave invited him to Sunday mass at Holy Rosary Church in Edmonds, Washington. On that day, Dad said, he watched a row of nuns, their heads bent in prayer, rise in sync and file up the aisle for communion. That sight made his heart swell with joy, and when he went home, he told Grandma, "I want to be a Catholic." The result of that visit to the church was four conversions: Dad's, his mother's, his eleven-year-old sister Judy's, and his Grandma Smith's (who went on to take the monastic vow of the Third Order Secular). Dad did not, however, manage to convert Grandpa (nobody told Grandpa what to do), until Grandpa was on his deathbed in 1980. And then Dad won him over, too—bringing the tally to five conversions.

Mom was, as she puts it, a "cradle Catholic." As a kid, she went to school at Our Lady of Angels in Burlingame, run by the Capuchin Franciscans and taught by the Sisters of Mercy. She read only books approved by the Catholic Church. She saw only movies rated A by the Legion of Decency. She wore her scapular and medal all her life, even in the shower, and never skipped her daily rosary. So when it came to her Catholic duties, Mom was incapable of defaulting. It would be easier to cut off her own hand. She didn't like what St. Mary's was up to either, she told Dad, but she didn't know what to do about it. St. Mary's was all we had.

Dad didn't feel that way. There was plenty you could do about it. First he stopped volunteering on bingo night. Then he stopped giving at the collection. Then he stopped sitting in the pews, and only stood at the back with his hands folded in front of him. It was getting so that pretty soon he'd be standing outside the front doors, or maybe just not coming at all.

Mom continued attending PTA meetings, lit candles for the priests, took Terry and me to choir practice and Danny and Nick to altar boy practice, volunteered at the church cake sales and bingo nights, sat with us in the pews, and wrote checks for the collection. It was the checks that bothered Dad the most.

"How can you give money to the collection when you're giving it straight to the *Novus Ordo*?" he carped on the way home after mass.

"I'm not going to go to mass and not contribute."

"What do you think the church does with the money you donate?"

"Maintenance, utilities, salary. The usual."

"But you're funding the progressive movement."

"I'm funding the priests. Vatican II isn't their fault. They're just doing as they're told by the diocese."

"You can't make excuses for the priests. The priests have free will. They don't have to follow the diocese. Father Donovan didn't."

"And look what happened to Father Donovan. Not every priest can do what he did."

"They can if they want to!"

"*Novus Ordo* priests have to eat, too."

"I refuse to pay one cent to the Catholic Church. I just can't do it."

"I can."

"Then you're a hypocrite."

"That may be true, but I have to contribute if I'm going to receive the sacraments."

"That means you're buying the sacraments!"

"Then I'm buying the sacraments."

"You can't buy the sacraments!"

"I can if I don't have a choice!"

"We *do* have a choice. If every Catholic stopped writing a check, what kind of a message do you think that would give the Vatican?"

"I'm not going to boycott the sacraments."

"Would you boycott them if they weren't valid?"

"I guess I'd have to."

"Well, chances are they're not valid."

"But we don't know that for sure."

"St. Thomas Aquinas said that if you alter even one word, you alter the *sense*, and if you alter the *sense* you alter the *meaning*, and if you alter the *meaning* you invalidate the *form* of the transubstantiation. Well, Paul VI didn't just alter a few words, he mutilated the entire liturgy."

"But the sacraments might still be valid. We don't know for sure."

"Are you saying that words have no meaning?"

"I'm saying the words may be close enough to make the sacraments valid."

"In the Middle Ages they'd have slaughtered the heretic who took the liturgy into his own hands."

"I know. But we don't live in the Middle Ages. We live in modern times. And God is challenging us for reasons that we can't understand. I don't like it any more than you do."

"But how can you go on putting money in the collection basket?"

"You follow your conscience, and I'll follow mine."

Their arguments lasted the entire drive home, and continued as Dad parked in the driveway, turned off the ignition, and unlocked the front door, and we hung up our coats in the closet, and Mom put her missal and rosary on the table, and went about her day.

"Your actions are an expression of your will!" he said, following her from room to room. "If you contribute money, you're expressing your approval of the *Novus Ordo*."

"To them, maybe. But not to me."

"Your logic is flawed, Marty. Can't you see your logic is flawed?"

"Then it's flawed."

As usual, I found Dad's side hard to disagree with. Words had meaning. Paul VI had changed Christ's words from "my blood shall be shed for *many*" to "my blood shall be shed for *all men*." That pretty much changed everything in terms of meaning (ignoring the fact that women weren't mentioned at all). However, I also agreed with Mom. You couldn't say for a certainty that changing *many* to *all men* invalidated the substance of the Holy Eucharist. If you knew for sure, that would be one thing. But if you didn't know, and wanted to go to church and receive the sacraments, you should go ahead and do it, and you should put money in the collection basket and hope you were doing the right thing. It was all very confusing, and their arguments didn't solve anything, and all I could think was, *Where is the Chastisement? And why is it taking so long? If it would just come, then all the churches and schools will be blown up, and then there won't be anything left for Mom and Dad to argue about. And then we can all have some peace.*

THE CHASTISEMENT DIDN'T come that year as expected. Instead, Harry Doten came. When Dad overheard the words "Vatican II" spoken loudly at the wedding reception of a friend, he wandered over to hear what the hubbub was about. The man talking was Harry Doten, and what he was saying came as a complete surprise to Dad: that Vatican II was *a conspiracy between the Communists and the Freemasons to bring the Catholic Church to its knees*, and that the suppression of the Third Secret of Fatima was *a coverup of the fact that Vatican II was an inside job*. Dad could barely contain his excitement. His hand extended, he introduced himself to the stranger and spent the rest of the day in rapturous dialogue with the man. And a few days later, Harry and Gail Doten and their three oldest sons came to dinner at our house. Banned from the table because of space, we kids sat on the kitchen floor and ate tacos and watched the action like fans at a soccer match. Harry's Vatican II monologue would get the ball rolling, and then Dad would intercept the ball and get his own monologue going and pass the ball back to Harry, who would run with it for a while and then pass it back to Dad, and before you knew it they would score a goal.

"Considering that Archbishop Bugnini, the author of the New Mass, was a Freemason," Harry would say, "and that the Freemasons' anti-Catholic objective is to form the modern, liberal state . . ."

". . . You'd think people would put two and two together about the New Mass," Dad would say, "and realize that there is a diabolical, anti-Catholic animus behind the liturgical changes."

Harry was a short, smiling man with a cue-ball head, tortoiseshell glasses, and a breezy suit jacket that he wore over a crisp Oxford shirt, and Gail was an elegant woman with a platinum blond bob, silk scarves, wooden bracelets, and a flowing dress that trailed a long river of flowery scents, and the reason that Harry and Gail looked so rich was because they were rich. Harry was an entrepreneur who'd torn down a block of condemned warehouses and built an open-air carnival called The Fun Spot, where people came to play pinball, ride the bumper cars and Tilt-O-Whirl, listen to the mariachi bands, and wander among booths filled with arts and crafts. The Fun Spot had made the Dotens a fortune, and if you had any doubt about the size of the fortune you had only to look at Harry's big rich man's smile.

Harry showed his teeth a lot, and they were edged with silver. He showed them to Mom, who handed him a snifter of brandy, and to Dad, who leaned forward to accept the flame of his silver lighter. And he showed them to Mrs. Poole, who arrived looking chic and sexy in a tight cashmere top with crystal buttons, red, white, and blue spiked heels, and a jazzy quilted skirt that was several inches shorter than respectable. And he showed them to Vinny, who tried to taste the flavor of smoke in the air, and to Jennifer, who trustingly climbed onto his lap, and to the rest of us, who milled around the kitchen just to be near these strange new people. Harry's smile was contagious, because everyone who saw it seemed compelled to smile back. Especially Dad, who seemed grateful to have a reason to smile these days.

But the smiles always changed into frowns, and did so that night when Dad opened the June issue of *Triumph* magazine. "Listen to this, Harry," he said. " 'The only hope for those who oppose the anti-Christian revolution is the formation of a new anti-revolutionary international that will address itself simultaneously to the Christian reconstruction of the social order and to the struggle necessary to halt and defeat the enemies of Christ.' What I want to know is if such a thing as an anti-revolutionary international exists."

"If it existed, I'd know about it," Harry said confidently.

"Well, if it ever comes into existence, it's a conspiracy I want to be in on," Dad said.

"Me, too," said Harry.

Harry was the most connected traditionalist Dad had ever encountered, so Dad told him about his failed Lourdes scheme. "I was dead-set. I thought that if an anti-revolutionary international was anywhere, it might be there . . . in *Lourdes* . . . I don't know. It seemed like a really good idea at the time. I even learned some French."

Everyone laughed, Mom the loudest. But Harry stayed strangely serious.

"Lourdes is a tourist trap," Harry said. "You don't want to go there. Crowds, buses, invalids lining up in wheelchairs, gift-shops, street vendors, inflated prices. You got the right idea, Lyle, don't go to Lourdes. Go to Fatima. It's possible there's an anti-revolutionary movement there. Our Lady of Fatima promised that the dogma of faith would always be kept in Portugal, didn't she? What other guarantee do you need?"

The room was quiet. Dad stared at Harry, and Mom stared at Dad.

"Fatima!" Dad said.

"Heck, I'd go if I could," Harry said. "But I can't. Not now. Not with The Fun Spot doing so well. I'd be crazy to liquidate now when I'm getting ready to expand and charge for parking."

"I don't know," Dad said, relaxing a little. "The police force in Fatima would probably want me to graduate from the Portuguese police academy or something silly like that."

"Forget policework, Lyle. It's a dead end. You can do better than law enforcement. I'll tell you what. Go to Portugal, and we'll set something up together. Do some business."

"Like what?"

"I don't know . . . leather goods, sheep's wool, folk art. Find something they make in Portugal and export the stuff to me. I'll sell it at The Fun Spot. Trust me. It's a no-brainer."

"You think so?"

"Think so? I *know* so."

There was something about rich people that made you stop and listen and see things their way, and we were all listening.

"I know a Carmelite priest from Chicago, Father Marcello, who's been living in Fatima and saying the daily Latin mass for a parish there for years. I'll give you his address. Write to him. He'll tell you how great it is there."

"Gosh, Harry. You may be onto something."

The mood in the kitchen lifted again. The air conditioner hummed like an old factory, churning out a damp, metallic-smelling chill, the glasses clinked, and the cigar smoke gathered in a cloud at the ceiling and spilled its gray overflow into the living room, hallway, and bedrooms. Soon Dad pulled out some of his cop stories—like the one about pulling over a Baptist minister for going only five miles over the speed limit (he only ticketed Protestants), and giving him an "attitude pinch" (a ticket for whining), making the minister late for his Sunday service—and laughed harder at the stories than anyone.

DAD ONCE SAID he had experienced two callings in his life: the first was when he converted to Catholicism. The second was when he found out about the visions at Fatima. At the latter time, he was a Marine on board a Landing Ship Tank (LST) outside the

Philippines. He'd joined the Marines as a way to stay out of prison. After years of fighting, drinking, larceny, and vandalism on the streets of Seattle (he'd been in two "feral groups," as he called them, the Zunks and then the Marquis), he realized he had tendencies to becoming a professional criminal, walked into a recruiting office two days after his seventeenth birthday, and signed up. It was while he was aboard the LST that a Catholic from New Orleans named Ferdinand, who slept in the bunk across the way, started talking about the Fatima visions. Dad was intrigued. Excited. He wanted to know more. Shortly after, while on R&R, he dropped into a British military PX to buy a paperback book and chose *The Deliverance of Sister Cecilia*, the story of the Communist takeover of Czechoslovakia in 1948 as told by a Czech nun. Reading that book, Dad had an "explosion of faith." It was not by accident that things had happened the way they had. He went outside to smoke a cigarette and look at the stars. He understood communism. He understood "Russia's errors" and the meaning of Fatima. He said to himself, "Things are different now." He began to prepare for the Apocalypse.

"Everyone into the living room," he said to us one night shortly after Harry's visit. "Family meeting."

The table erupted with chairs and bodies, and we raced to the living room and packed the couch with our bodies. Dad stood solidly in the center of the room, legs apart, arms crossed over his broad chest, chin square. Mom leaned in the doorway holding a dishtowel, looking like a co-conspirator.

"Kids . . . You understand that the Catholic Church has abandoned you and placed your everlasting souls in peril?"

We nodded our heads.

"And you understand that the Catholic Church is leading the world toward the Chastisement?"

We nodded again.

"Good. And you understand that America is at the forefront of the progressive movement and that the American Catholic Church is declining at a rapid rate?"

We nodded again.

"And that we are living in a time of history that demands action?"

My heart had started to clippity-clop as if it knew something I didn't and was trying to get my attention. I glanced at Terry, wondering if she could hear my heart beating. Her eyes were softly sparkling.

"Knowing all this, would you agree that we can't stay in America any longer?"

We nodded again, but slowly.

"You remember how I tried to get transferred to Lourdes, and it didn't work out because that wasn't the will of God and Our Lady? Well, I realize now that Lourdes was the wrong place. But I know where the right place is." Now he glanced at Mom, and Mom came to him and slipped her arm around his waist.

"We're moving to Portugal," Dad said, smiling. "Where Our Lady promised *the dogma of faith will always be kept*. Portugal is the only place that will survive what's coming."

"Is Portugal anywhere near Hawaii?" I asked.

Dad laughed. "Nowhere near it."

"Where *is* Portugal, Dad?" Danny asked.

"Go get the atlas!" Dad said.

Danny shot off to the Womb and got the atlas, and we surrounded Dad as he opened it and slowly turned the pages past Africa, North America, South America, Australia, the British Isles, and China. He stopped on Europe, and pointed to a brown blotch of earth that was stuck to the edge of Spain.

"There it is. The Old World in all its glory. No traffic, no billboards, no drug peddlers. Just slow living, the old Catholic way."

"Are we going to live in Fatima, Dad?" I asked.

"You bet. Or as close to it as possible."

Whenever his spirits were high, Dad would pull out his harmonica and play a song, like "Waltzing Matilda," or "Lili Marlene," or "Grandfather Clock." Now he leaned back in his faded red velvet armchair and played a new song he just taught himself. It was the theme song from *The Godfather*—a film he'd gone to see with Harry Doten. It was an ominous, mournful song, and Dad played it with heart.

Sitting on the floor by Dad's feet, I listened to the song with a bottoming-out feeling. We were leaving America. That meant we were leaving our pink house on Myrtle Avenue with its big front lawn and white picket fence and juniper tree. And we were leaving Paul Moore Park and St. Mary's School and the Capitol Drive-in and Sea Cliff Beach. And we were leaving the Pooles.

Terry put on her glasses, leaned over the map, and carefully articulated the names of towns in the country we were adopting, none of which sounded the least bit appealing.

"Cataxo. Burinhosa. Abuxarda," she said. "I don't know, but I'll bet the boys are cute there."

I looked skeptically at the tiny country. "It sure is small," I said, my voice betraying my disappointment. "It's not even half the size of California."

"It may be small," Terry said in a sophisticated tone meant for Dad, "but I'll bet it's rich with ancient history."

She selected the *Po-Pr* volume from the *Encyclopaedia Britannica* and we pored over pictures of girls and women wearing embroidered aprons over brightly colored skirts. Again, my eyebrows lifted in a worried arch and my mouth twisted critically low.

"They sure do wear a lot of ruffles," I said. "And look at those pompoms. I don't care if that is the style there. I'm not going to dress like that."

"You're so right," Terry said. "Jeans and T-shirts have far more class than a *millennium* of tradition."

She turned to the food section. "*Caldeirada a Moda de Guincho* is a staple dish dating back centuries, made with white fish, mackerel, potatoes and onions." She looked concerned but refused to be defeated. "Well . . . we'll just have to get used to it."

4

dispose of all your worldly
possessions and follow me

ON THE DAY Dad turned in his badge at CHP headquarters, he came home and did the chicken dance, his thumbs hooked in his armpits, elbows flapping, legs kicking, handcuffs rattling, and billy club flopping. The chicken dance was Dad's own dance. It was a dance of unrestrained glee. The chicken dance meant that you were no dumb cluck, that you'd outwitted the fox, and let that be a lesson to all foxes. It also meant that if there was one thing as important as the One True Catholic and Apostolic Church it was a sense of humor.

It had been a long time since Dad had done the chicken dance, and it filled the house with light. Gathering around him, we clapped to keep the unrestrained glee going. The more we clapped, the more Dad leaped and flapped and kicked and jangled. Every kick seemed to bunt away his cares. No more backups on Highway 17. No more evening news. No more flagged pins crowding the map. No more letter writing on the Underwood late at night. No more arguing with Father Dunne over the New Catechism. No more charades. No more hypocrisy. No more progressives. And, hey, come to think of it, no more broken dishwasher, drippy shower faucet, tipping fence, or Vehicle Code violations. We were leaving it all—*all!*—behind. We were starting a totally new life where everything—*everything!*—would be different. We were going to a country where Catholicism was a part of the fabric of society, not a recreation you reserved for Sundays; where tradition was respected and unchanged; where the true dogma of the faith began at the top, with the Catholic Constitution, and trickled down through society like water over rock, cleansing, shaping, purifying.

Dad said it was so, and so it must be.

In the Womb he wrote a letter to Harry's contact in Fatima, Father Marcello, announcing our impending arrival and declaring his eagerness to join Father Marcello's traditionalist parish. Father Marcello, who must have sensed he didn't have much time, responded quickly. Mom handed Dad the airmail envelope. Dad delighted in the fifty centivos stamps that pictured mounted medieval knights carrying swords and shields against backgrounds of olive-green, dark gray, and russet-orange, took out his miniature broadsword letter opener to slice the seam, pulled out one thin page, and read the contents out loud.

Casa Beato Nuno
Fátima, Portugal
September 10, 1972

Dear Lyle,
You seem to be determined to come to Portugal, and quickly.
But what will you do once you get here? Instead of coming
here lock, stock, and barrel, with all the costs of transporting
a family, etc, why not come yourself first, and see how things

are? Portuguese is not an easy language for a foreigner. Several
families have come here with more or less your same ideas, but
couldn't stay. Others have gone through a several years period
of adjustment; others are wondering if they can (or should) stick
it out. I do feel with you in your fears for your children in the
present American atmosphere; but it's not so easy to say that
moving will solve the problem. If I were you I would consider
your move carefully.

God bless you all, in union of prayer and sacrifice with Jesus
and Mary, Amen.

Father Marcello

"That doesn't seem very encouraging," Mom said. "Maybe he's
right. Maybe we shouldn't rush this . . ."

"He has to downplay it," Dad said, his disappointment apparent
on his face. "Otherwise he could start a mass exodus. He doesn't
want that to happen. He could have all kinds of nuts knocking on
his door."

Dad filed the letter and wrote to another contact of Harry's who
lived in Fatima, Alma Brewer from Kansas. Alma, the mother of
ten, also wrote back immediately.

Dear Lyle,
I was delighted to get your letter. When we started looking for
a safe, moral place about six years ago, we decided on Portu-
gal because of Fatima. However, Mary didn't really promise
safety—just that "the truth will be kept in Portugal." We
decided that the truth was better than nothing, and worth the
sacrifice. But things have not been easy. After six years, my
husband Leroy is still working in Kansas and we are still
$6,000 behind the 8 ball!!! The best job in Portugal pays $150

a month. Not enough to make a living. Still, we are looking for
land to buy with our "no money" as a means of survival and
independence: land, water, and potatoes. The American price is
ten times that of the Portuguese, but with Our Lady's help we
will get around that. Quite frankly, all of us are complaining
of the cold. Right now, the Portuguese use <u>no</u> heat, and it gets
down to 21 degrees F. at night. We use butane, but that takes
the oxygen out of the air and cannot be left on at night. You are
welcome to come for a visit. Our house is 14th century, meaning
the walls are wet, but we do have electricity and running water.

    Sincerely, Yours in Christ,
    Alma Brewer

"Their walls are wet?" Mom said. "That doesn't sound very healthy."

"That's normal in the Mediterranean," Dad said. "I'm sure the walls are dry in summer."

"Butane has a foul smell."

"Apparently it's a very efficient way to heat."

"I think a family needs more than water and potatoes to survive."

"That's just an expression. For gosh sakes, Marty, stop being so negative!"

Dad filed the letter away. A hoarder of information, Dad never threw a relevant piece of paper out. He placed it into a file that went into a sleeve that went into a drawer that grew so tight with paper it was a struggle to pull the file out when it was needed. The newest file was labeled *Portugal* in his tiny, windswept scrawl, and had lately grown fat with articles about the Portuguese wars against the Communists in Angola, Mozambique, and Guinea, along with page upon page of typed or handwritten notes on Portugal's history.

1. *1910: King Manoel II overturned—Portugal becomes Republic*
2. *1910–1926: three revolutions a year*
3. *1926: Salazar given reins, de facto dictatorship*
4. *1961: anti-Communist wars begin in African colonies*
5. *1968: Salazar replaced by Marcelo Caetano, Roman Catholic*

Included in the Portugal dossier was the following article cut out from the *San Jose Mercury News*, folded thrice, and unmarked by comment:

Sunday, October 1, 1972
Portugal Economy Hurting
By E.S. Corbett
The London Observer

The financial strain of the long drawn out wars in Africa is pushing Portugal's balance of payments into the red.

A deficit for 1972 or 1973 is a distinct probability judging from the present trading trends. . . .

The abundance of cheap labor that once attracted foreign investors to Portugal no longer exists and Portuguese goods are becoming increasingly less competitive abroad. . . .

Agriculture moves from crisis to crisis and bears little relation to changing habits and times. Thus milk, cheese and meat, which are regarded as staple foods in modern society, are in permanent short supply.

In defiance of the din that must have been clamoring out caveats in his subconscious, Dad set off to Ace Hardware and returned with a *House for Sale* sign that he hammered into the front lawn, a gallon of off-white paint that he rolled over the gray band of dirt made by our six pairs of sweaty hands in the hallway, and a bolt of fresh screen that he used to reface the screen door. Alternately whistling and humming, he bolstered the fence posts, replaced the garbage disposal, oiled the door hinges, and patched the cracks in the stucco. He secretly found a home for our dog, Chema, and arranged for the new owners to take him away when we were at school. When friends dropped in to check on his progress, Dad insisted they take away items they could use. "Want a Ping-Pong table? It's got a lot of life left in it." He had an old wooden boat on the side yard. "It's yours. Honestly, you'll be doing me a favor if you haul that thing out of here." A neighbor had recently converted their garage to a family room. "Need a sofa for the family room?" Dad asked. "It's only good for naps at this point, but you're welcome to it." They took it. The candy-striped swing set rolled away in the back of a pickup truck.

With the shedding of property, all the old silly songs Dad used to sing to us when we were toddlers came tripping off his tongue as he tapped his foot and clapped his hands:

> *Does your chewing gum lose its flavor on the bedpost overnight?*
> *If your mother says don't chew it do you swallow it in spite?*
> *Can you catch it on your tonsils? Can you heave it left and right?*

From the Womb he'd shout for Mom across the yard, and Mom would rush out with a ball of twine or a roll of packaging tape or a box or a trash bag or whatever it was he needed, and then rush back into the house to hold conference with Mrs. Poole over the worth of her possessions.

Surrounded by boxes labeled *Noreen*, *Garage Sale*, *Purple Heart*, and *Dump*, Mom and Noreen stood with perplexed expressions on their faces as they tried to wrap their minds around the dilemma at hand. How did one liquidate a life's worth of assets? How did one dissolve one's presence in a place? Mom was a saver of things, not a thrower away. To dispose of an entire household of items she would later need in Portugal defied common sense. Mrs. Poole empathized deeply. She'd spent the better part of every summer with Mom trolling the local garage sales and accumulating the objects every family needs to survive—and at a bargain. Even though she stood to inherit such valuables as Mom chose to discard, Mrs. Poole couldn't bear to see Mom lose a single item. Wandering through the obstacle course of boxes, they both picked things up and put them back down, reasoning against parting with anything that still had a use.

"You can't get rid of *that*," Mrs. Poole would say when Mom held up her crystal candy bowl. "Wasn't it a wedding present?"

"You're right," Mom would say. "I love this bowl."

"No . . . not your ice cream scooper. It works so *well*."

"Do you want these place mats?" Mom would ask, flipping through a dozen plasticky prints of Canadian winter landscapes.

"Oh, for gosh sakes, keep them," Mrs. Poole would reply. "They hardly weigh a thing."

Pulling things out of cupboards, examining them for functionality, and putting them right back, Mom and Mrs. Poole agreed with each other on every count.

"I'd better hang onto this colander," Mom said. "It's got this great wooden handle that doesn't heat up."

"You should keep this bread knife. It could be really expensive to replace. And this manual ice crusher. I have one and it's so handy."

In our room, Terry and I walked in little circles bumping into each other as we crossed paths. Our job was to label all our stuff with prices for the garage sale, and we were in a crisis of uncertainty over what our belongings were worth. Terry's art supplies, horse models, horse posters, and books were all critical to her happiness. My board games, puzzles, and sticker books represented the building blocks of my character. I might as well put my heart and brain into the box. An eerie silence grew with the increasing hollowness of our drawers. Every so often Terry would say something flippant, like, "I'm *glad* to get rid of this piece of junk," and toss an item into her box, and I'd look into the box and say, "But *I* like it," and she'd say, "Too late!"

Mom said we could each take "one small thing" to Portugal. This brought up a lot of questions, such as, how small was small, and among the small things, which one deserved to be the *thing*? Terry had taught me to knit, and I'd completed at least twenty rows of a neck scarf. Examining the scarf with a tenderness I hadn't felt before, I asked myself, *Is this the one small thing?* The rows weren't straight. The stitches were too tight (the yarn squeaked when the needle entered), and there was a hole in the center where I'd dropped a stitch. But it was my handiwork. I'd imagined wearing the scarf to school, and the other girls saying, *Cool scarf,* and me saying, *Thanks. I made it.* Now I tried to imagine wearing the scarf in Portugal and having a similar interchange with the girls there. *Cool cachecol . . . Obrigado. Fui eu que o fiz.* I threw the scarf into the box. I put my paint by number set, bead collection, and board games through the same interrogation. *Want to play Parcheesi?*, according to Dad's phrase book, was *Queres jogar um jogo de Parcheesi?* Nothing seemed to fit the precise criteria of *one small thing*, in which case I was briefly convinced I would bring nothing. And then my eyes fell on my troll. The troll had never had any practical purpose.

For a doll, it failed in the one way that mattered: it was not lifelike. Worse, it was ugly, with its bugged-out eyes and foolish grin, and orange, pointy-tipped hair. But trolls inhabited deep dark forests and brought good luck to the humans who caught them. Plus, they fit neatly into your hand, and could easily make a transcontinental journey.

"I'm bringing my troll," I said to Terry. Dancing the troll around in the air, I said, "Hurray! I'm going to Portugal!" in a high-pitched voice.

Terry rolled her eyes. "Good for you."

As a matter of honor, Michelle got first dibs on all my stuff, including my precious board games, of which I had about a dozen, and I crossed my fingers that she'd reject those so I could sell them for tons of cash. This was a pretty safe bet since Michelle wasn't a game player like I was, but a craftsperson. I was not surprised, then, that she eyed the booty carefully, picked out the dolls' clothes and furniture, and finally asked, "Where's your knitting needles and bag of yarn?" When Michelle had bagged up every crafty thing I owned, we sat together in silence. I don't know if she was thinking what I was thinking, but it suddenly hit me that knitting was no fun if you didn't have someone to knit with.

In the Womb, Dad hit a wall. He'd boxed up everything he could. The Purple Heart truck came and went, and he still had close to a ton of stuff—mostly books. "What are you going to do with all your books?" was one of the first questions Mom had asked when Portugal became a reality. "I'll take the good ones with me and leave the rest," had been his simple answer. It had taken Dad several days to separate the chaff from the wheat, and at the end he scratched his two-day beard.

"Mart!"

Mom entered the Womb and stared at the towering mess, her

fists plugged into her hips. "I thought you were going to make two piles."

"I did."

"I only see one."

"That's the second one over there." He pointed to three books: a medical dictionary; an economics textbook; and *The Environmental Atlas of Alaska*.

"You're taking . . . *everything*?"

"I don't know what else to do."

Mom picked a book from the good pile. "Do you have to keep"—she read the spine—"*The Catcher in the Rye*?"

"It's one of my favorites."

"But you've already read it."

"Yeah, but I read that one at least once a year."

Mom-the-Saver sympathized. "Well, all I can say is you'd better find a way to transport all these books."

Dad had two old trunks, and when he filled them they carried about a third of his library. He wasn't going to leave two thirds of his books behind, so he made a phone call to a shipping service and asked about shipping crates. The guy on the phone asked, "How much weight are we talking here?" Dad replied, "I'd say at least two thousand pounds." The man on the phone said he could build three large pine crates, deliver them to the house, and transport the crates to the shipyard "all for one low price." Dad was a sucker for the convenience and Mom was a sucker for the one low price. A week later the crates came, and they were roomy enough not only for the books but for the entire contents of the Womb, including his file cabinet, files, encyclopedia set, atlas, dictionaries, magazines, maps, posters, globe, pens, pencils, clock, ashtray, letter opener, battery-operated pencil sharpener, clock, and Underwood type-writer. And because Mom had discovered that suitcases can only carry so much, she added another thousand pounds to the crates, stuffing in clothes, shoes, canned food, dry goods, blankets, pillows, her Singer sewing machine, and several small appliances. Dad hammered nails into the crates, addressed them to the Porto de Lisboa, and soon a flatbed truck hauled them to the Port of San Francisco for transport.

INTERESTED BUYERS CAME to see our house. At first, Mom gave tours like a professional real estate agent. She took the phone calls, wrote down the appointments, hid the boxes and suitcases in the garage, stuffed the clutter into closets, arranged flowers on the kitchen table, and propped the pillows on the beds for the best *visual*. When the doorbell rang, she answered it smiling as she wiped her wet hands on her apron.

"Hi, I'm Martha Arnold. So nice of you to come. I'm sure you're going to love the house. We hate to sell it, but we're leaving the country."

She guided potential buyers from room to room, fanning her hand out like Carol Merrill on *Let's Make a Deal*. "And here's the master bath. As you can see, it is conveniently attached to the master bedroom and inaccessible from the hall."

But with our flight coming up in just a few weeks and so much still to do, she couldn't keep up the pace. Now when the doorbell rang she opened the door as she raced by with a suitcase in one hand and Jennifer clasped in the other, and didn't stop to see who it was, but yelled over her shoulder, "Come on in. Take a look around! Sorry about the mess!"

Dad, paint can in hand, asked potential buyers lots of questions, like where their ancestors were from and what they did for a living. If the person happened to be an immigrant, the conversation might take off. "The Declaration of Independence is a pretty dumb document," I heard Dad say to one house-hunter who was not American. "It says that the authority of government comes from the people—an idea that follows Locke, who was an ultra-modernist—and that the governed can abolish government. What happened when the South tried to do that? Lincoln massacred the governed in order to preserve the Union."

On the day of our garage sale, Terry painted a sign on a plank of plywood in her fanciest calligraphy and leaned it against the maple tree by the street:

LEAVING AMERICA!
for sale!
EVERYTHING!

Mom wore her clip-on sunglasses and sat in a lawn chair with a price tag dangling from it. We kids sat on blankets that displayed our stuff. Cars rolled slowly by, and faces peered through windows at the family that was leaving America and selling everything. The cars parked, and the people got out and walked over. Mom took the money and made change like a hot dog vendor at a ballgame, and people walked away with little parts of our life: our hand mixer, pressure cooker, cookie pans, casserole dishes, old jewelry, the kitchen clock, the wicker hamper, the ironing board, the bassinette, Vinny's plastic play tub, Jennifer's white quilted toy box, the rocking horse, the high chairs, booster chairs, bathmats, throw rugs, and Dad's Giminiani ten speed with the alpine gear that he rode to and from college.

When a girl my age asked how much all of my board games were, I was overcome by vertigo. "*All* of them?" I asked as if she were part of a buyout conspiracy. She nodded. I glanced at the games spread out on my blanket. I hadn't imagined them all going at once. I'd imagined a perfectly suited buyer for each one. A sole buyer for the entire collection was like net fishing. It was unsportsmanlike. One scoop caught it all. "Some of them have missing pieces," I said, trying to turn her off the idea. She shrugged, still waiting for the price. "The hat is gone from the Monopoly game. I had to replace it with a button." I wasn't getting anywhere. She had me. I sighed. I'd been to too many garage sales with Mom not to know the correct procedure. "Twenty-five cents a piece, or ten for two dollars." She handed me the two dollars, collected the ten games, and walked away, and I dropped onto my knees to stop the spins.

Dad opened the garage door to sell his speed bag and heavy bag. As he unbolted them, the buyer asked where we were moving off to, and Dad told him. "Isn't Portugal a dictatorship?" the man asked. "I wouldn't give up a liberal democracy for any country in the world." Dad put down the adjustable wrench he was using to unbolt the heavy bag, and his speechmaking voice rang out across the yard. "One of the biggest cons ever inflicted on mankind was the idea of modern democracy because it is based on the lie of equality. Equality doesn't exist in this world. Look around. In botany an orange tree is superior to the common weed. In biology the eagle is superior to the bat. Compare a Charlemagne to a Hun. How can you justify a democracy when it allows people with an IQ of seventy the same voting power as people with an IQ of a hundred and fifty? It's wrong to base a government on equality. Even our founding fathers knew it. They were all modernists, true, but they still had a modicum of common sense. The only real equality there is rests upon the fact that every human being has an immortal soul." The conversation lasted over an hour, and the man eventually walked away with a free speed bag and heavy bag (courtesy of Dad).

*   *   *

ON MY LAST day at St. Mary's, Miss Elliott threw a going-away party for me, which was a nice gesture considering that Mom had written scores of letters complaining about her short skirts and no bra. It may have been that Miss Elliott was glad to see me leave.

Over the chocolate sheet cake with *Bon Voyage Veronica* written in white icing, the students asked me a lot of questions.

"So *where* are you going to live?"

"In Portugal."

"Where's *Portugal*?"

"Nnnnnext to Spain."

"Why do you have to go *there*?"

Shrug.

"What are you going to *do* there?"

"I don't know."

"Do you have a *house* there?"

"Nnnnnot yet."

"Well, do you have friends there?"

"No."

"When are you coming back?"

"Never."

"Whoa."

Mom had insisted the St. Mary's kids would be jealous of me. Now they stared at me like I was a freak. Families that left America for no apparent reason and no plan to return were just plain *weird*. And kids were never jealous of weird people; they just pitied them. I could have given them a reason. But the reason was complicated. It didn't seem fair that I got to go somewhere safe while they all had to stay behind in America and be invaded by Communists and get blown up. That wasn't something you passed around.

At home, only days away from our final exodus, we were still not even close to being ready. Had Mom done *any* packing? Dad wanted to know. The bathroom was a treacherous zone of nonentry, the bathtub towering with books, photo albums, and 75 rpm records, the sink with prescription bottles, shampoos, and creams, the hamper with shoes. A kind of low-grade panic buzzed as Mom began to fling whatever her hands could grab into suitcases, and boxes, and the babies pulled them back out, and Dad tripped over everything in his path and yelled that it shouldn't have been put there, and Danny and Nick rolled around nonsensically punching each other, and Terry and I walked in circles, colliding, speaking little and avoiding each other's eyes. The question had come, and it remained: How do you end a life in a place? How do you give up a way of life? How do you stop being one thing and start being another?

5

halfway to nowhere

Excerpt from Dad's letter home:

11—13—72 Necessitas non habet legem. "Necessity has no law." As many of you can attest, our last day in Yankeeland was one of shrieking rush and whirling confusion. Marty and I left the biggest mess I've ever seen in my life, and ever hope to see, for our friends to make sense of and clean up. Mea culpa, mea culpa, mea culpa. And thank you all.

NIGHTS LIKE THIS live on. You might grow up and have experiences more harrying, but the night your family runs away from America will play and replay forever in the theater of your memory as a way of reminding you of who you are and where you come from and how come your heart still flutters with a *no—wait—stop* sensation whenever you board an airplane, and why you have a thing about your own bed.

It was sunset when we said our last tearful good-byes to the Pooles, piled into four taxis (two for luggage), and rolled away. In the back window, Myrtle Avenue dimmed colorless under the setting sun, and the neighbors, their hands raised in farewell, shrank and finally disappeared. Up ahead, Highway 101 unfurled into the darkening valley, skirting the low tide of the bay, a runway of glowing signs announcing the cities Dad had combed through in his search for a traditional church—Palo Alto, Redwood City, Menlo Park. In San Mateo, our convoy rolled to a stop in front of Grandma and Grandpa's trim gray house, and Grandma, plump in her pink-flowered muumuu and slippers, trotted heavily to the curb and hustled us inside, where we ate ham and cheese sandwiches as the pendulum of the grandfather clock swung its sad, iambic meter, *good-bye forever . . . good-bye forever . . . good-bye forever . . . good-bye*.

Leaving was a force that pushed from behind. A wind that drove at our backs with a strength steady and powerful enough to keep us moving, but not so hard as to make us fall. The force put me to sleep wearing my travel clothes, woke me up at midnight, lifted me onto my feet, tied my shoes, buttoned my coat, put a carry-on suitcase in my hand, guided me toward the door, and channeled me from Grandma's house. *Good-bye forever . . . good-bye forever . . . good-bye*.

Outside, the dark world swelled like cotton under a slow-falling mist. Grandpa's long brown Oldsmobile rested like a cargo ship in the vaporous glow of a streetlamp, its insides stuffed to the ceiling with suitcases, its roof balancing a dozen more. Dad labored with twine in the spot where Grandpa focused a foggy cone of light. Two yellow taxis, their trunks gorged with our suitcases, idled nearby, white clouds of exhaust ballooning from their tails. Mom was cajoling Nick, who was crying, to get into the front taxi.

Danny was already inside, his eyes glittering in the dark. Grandma, in her camel-hair coat, was holding Vinny's hand and singing a lullaby of encouragement in her crackly voice: "You're a lucky guy. What a lucky guy you are. You're having a big adventure. Yes, you are. Oh yes, you are!" Mom noticed me standing on the curb. "Oh good. Ronnie, you'll sit next to Nick," and I balked as if I'd just lost my balance on a tightrope. "But I want to ride in Grandpa's car," I said for want of an excuse, but Mom waved me toward the cab. "It's full of luggage, Honeybun. In you go." Powerless against this draft of destiny that pushed, I slid in beside Danny, and Nick crawled in unwillingly after me, sniffling and rubbing his nose. The car smelled of smoke from the taxi man's burning cigarette. The seat was cold under my thighs.

Doors slammed. *Good-bye! Good-bye!* Grandma waved her lipstick-stained tissue as we rolled away from her little gray house. In minutes our tires were hissing along the freeway. San Francisco glowed white through a drifting gauze. On the Bay Bridge dewy ghosts flew at us, swamped the car, and flew away. The driver used the windshield wipers to fling them off. Up ahead the Oldsmobile swayed under the weight of our luggage. A foghorn moaned a deep guttural pitch from beyond the edge of the world.

"Well, this is exciting," Mom said, even though her face was serious. The streetlights passed like flash cards across the surface of her glasses. She held Jennifer close.

At Oakland International Airport, Dad paid the cabbies and they drove away (I was sorry to see them go, as if they were another part of my life that was disappearing forever), and Dad and Grandpa unloaded the Oldsmobile. At the Servair ticket counter, a dough-faced man slapped a Sun Trips sticker onto each suitcase before it disappeared on the conveyor belt.

"Where are you headed to with all this luggage?" he asked.

"Portugal," Dad said without making eye contact.

"Portugal? People *leave* Portugal. No one *goes* there."

"All the more reason," Dad said.

The clerk's eyes wandered to us kids standing nearby in our good coats, and his mouth pinched down on a smile.

"Your flight departs at three-fifty a.m.," he said, handing Dad the boarding passes. "Gate Seventeen . . . Far end."

Dad pocketed the tickets and turned to Grandpa. Their eyes were full of the good-byes already given. Now they hugged silently, four hands patting. Grandpa passed out Tootsie Pops to us "from Grandma." The next minute his back was blending in with the night outside the glass, and we were alone in the gaping-wide, blinding-bright airport. *Alone*. It felt that way, even though there were eight of us.

Ahead was a wide, luminous, empty corridor that looked as long as Highway 101 and seemed to taper to infinity—although it supposedly went to Gate 17. Gazing down the corridor, Dad saw crowds I couldn't see.

"Kids, don't talk to anyone," he said. "Don't even look at anyone. If someone approaches you, don't give your name, age, or destination. Just walk away and find the nearest authority or police officer."

Dad had saved a ball of twine from the Oldsmobile, which he now tied from his belt loop to Vinny's belt loop. "I'm not taking a chance with you, Bean Bag," he said by way of an apology. "This is your lifeline. Got it? You just hang on."

"Hang on," Vinny said. "Hang on."

And we were off. With Dad in the lead, we clumped, shuffled, and lurched in single file under our carry-ons and sweaters and coats and purses and shoulder bags down, down, down that wide hall. On his tether, Vinny half-walked and half-slid across the smooth vinyl floors, like a clown skidding across a stage with the wind at his back. Watching the world file past, I said quiet good-byes to the last parts of America I would ever see. Good-bye cigarette machine—Marlboro, Winston, and Benson & Hedges. Good-bye blue post office box, standing upright and looking so friendly. Good-bye newsstand. Good-bye glowing Coors sign. Good-bye telephone booth. Good-bye restroom. Good-bye chairs.

Dad began whistling a no-particular-song, searching for a melody in his head and not finding one. "Imagine!" he said. "On this very night thousands of foreigners are crossing *into* America, fleeing Communist countries all across the globe, sneaking out of the Eastern bloc through cracks in the iron curtain into Western Europe, boarding planes and flying to the U.S. in hopes of political asylum, crawling off leaky boats from Vietnam and Cuba, risking their lives to live in a free country, where they can practice their faith without fear, and own a house and property without the Red Army stealing it from them for the benefit of the Communist Party."

I think of what this means when we pass a Mexican woman emptying ashtrays into a rolling garbage can. Did she come across the border on a night like this? What would she say to us if we told her what we were doing? That we had a nice house and plenty of money and food and two cars, but that we wanted to get rid of it all and live somewhere else. And that we had no idea where that place was, or what we'd do when we got there, but that we were putting our faith in God to help us figure it out. What would she say?

There was a crowd at Gate 17. People were standing and sitting, eating and smoking, sleeping on the floor and gazing emptily at the pages of magazines and books. One man was gently plucking at a guitar as two girls nodded and hummed. Most of the passengers looked college age, men wearing beards, women in miniskirts, men and women with long hair, some barefooted. Dad mumbled to Mom, "What do you know. It's a Che Guevara revolutionary rally," and Mom frowned. All the seats were taken, so we lowered our burdens into a pile on the floor and stood around it, wondering what to do. Dad hoisted Vinny onto his hip, and Vinny fell asleep sucking his thumb, the twine dangling from his belt loop.

I leaned my weight against a wall and slowly crumpled downward until I was sitting on the floor. Terry flopped beside me, and together we quietly scrutinized the hippies. They were a colorful lot, so dramatic-looking, almost like actors in a play. I didn't know what Dad was worried about, they didn't look one bit dangerous. Secretly, I admired their attention to color, so different from the bland, conservative Catholic attire I was used to. I loved the bold swirls on one man's bellbottoms, and a lady's neon pink jumpsuit with its electric orange belt, and the giant purple flowers on a plastic raincoat, over stark white boots. A woman in a transparent T-shirt yawned and stretched, exposing her large brown nipples through her thin white shirt. I thought about how ignorant she must be of the concept of mortal sin, and how that one act could land her in hell for eternity, and wondered why anyone would choose an eternity in hell just to show her big brown nipples that were not even nice, but really scary-looking.

Mom didn't like what she saw one bit and took out her beads and crossed herself and started to pray and as usual didn't attempt to hide it. I shot a glance around the room to see what people would make of this and caught sight of the guy with the guitar smiling and his two girlfriends nudging each other, and a few others looking up from their reading. I was ashamed for Mom. She always made me want to hide my religion. I checked my scapular to make sure it was tucked safely out of view inside my shirt.

Departure time crept up slowly, and by three-thirty I was asleep

again, with my head on Terry's shoulder. A shout woke me up. It
was the Servairman from the ticket counter talking loudly through
a microphone and causing feedback through the speakers:

*. . . boarding Sun Trips Flight 802 . . . Oakland International . . .
Luton Airport . . .*

It wasn't like an emergency fire drill; it was like the real thing.
People came alive, snatched up their coats and bags, and made a
lunge toward the doorway as if the plane were already moving and
they had to sprint down the runway and leap aboard. There was
excitement and panic in the air. Mom and Dad hastily scooped up
our things—so many things they seemed to have spread like spilled
paint all over the waiting room—and called out commands, "Boys!
Wake up! Time to go!" Jennifer started crying and dragged her
Snoopy Dog by the ear as she followed every step Mom took, and
Vinny wailed as Dad forced fallen jackets onto Danny and Nick,
whose faces were pink and sleep-soft, and reached under chairs to
pluck out G.I. Joe's and Matchbox cars. Terry and I scrambled to
keep up, holding things in a wide embrace as we caught the current
and moved along with the crowd toward the gangway. My heart
was pounding and my skin was cold and crawly, and I didn't know
why, but I was shoving up against the person in front of me as if I
needed to hurry as fast as I could to grab the very last seat, as I kept
one eye on Mom and Dad and the others, who seemed in danger of
being left behind.

*Getting onto the plane was like the commuter rush of a New York
subway. We all carried with us everything our individual maxi-
mum physical strength would allow, including the kids. I had to
tie Vincent to me, and I'll never in my life forget the screeching
the poor little guy made when boarding the airplane. "Don't go
Dad!"*

Sun Trips was a charter flight—the cheapest flight Dad could get to the Old World at $149 per ticket and no charge for extra baggage. There was only one problem. The closest Sun Trips Charters came to Portugal was England. But Dad wasn't worried about that. The distance between Luton, England, and Lisbon, Portugal, wasn't much more than the distance between San Jose, California, and Grants Pass, Oregon, and he could drive to Grants Pass in six hours if he kept the speedometer up around eighty.

So we flew to Luton, and it took a long time. I remember the sky turning blue, and our own big country going bright with the dawn below us, a vast spread of green and brown and gold squares laid out in perfect patterns like a country-style quilt, and me thinking what a wonderful place *America the Beautiful* was. Staring out across the expanse I comprehended, for the first time, the sheer size of the world. From that high, I saw it for what it was: a planet, within a solar system, within a universe. Its size raised big questions, the first being, how could Santa Claus cover all that land on Christmas night? How could he visit all those cities and towns, and not miss a single house? There didn't seem to be an easy answer to that. Although my imagination struggled over several possibilities, it was incapable of conjuring up a distinctly practical explanation. Instead, the problem of Santa Claus led to similarly unanswerable problems. Such as how did Our Lady of Fatima locate the three shepherds from the height of her throne in heaven, which was surely much higher than the airplane in which we were flying, and how did she travel to and from each location? And speaking of Our Lady of Fatima, how would she handle the Chastisement? How would she designate which areas had to be annihilated? Countries and states weren't like maps with lines that showed their borders. How would she know where to direct the asteroids? And what about God? How could He manage such a gigantic planet and keep track of its people spread far and wide on islands, mountains, and valleys? Even for God it seemed too big a job, especially considering how new souls were being born and new ones dying every second of every day, as I'd heard they did. Even one missed soul would mean God was not omnipotent.

The thought winded me. A flawed God would be a terrible thing. More terrible than anything I'd ever thought of. When it came to your eternal soul, you wanted to be able to trust that God knew what He was doing. The questions kept coming. Like where was limbo located, and did God ever think about those unbaptized souls and consider letting them out? And where was hell located, and did God worry about all that eternal suffering? And why was I born me? Ronnie Arnold in San Jose, with this brain and this body? What significance did I hold in relation to such hugeness? And might God accidentally forget about me in the constant loop of souls living and dying? Questions without answers lined up and I placed each one on hold, to be revisited when I answered the one after it. But when I reached about number twenty, I felt a rising sense of panic and decided I'd better stop asking questions or go insane. I didn't have to know everything. Knowing everything wouldn't change anything. Maybe it was better to just *be*—a little like a fish or a bird went about being a fish or a bird without making a big deal about the *why* part. So I tried that out for a while by focusing on the sky and watching it turn from blue to gray and then to pink and then slowly to invisible-black, and looking down to see the Atlantic Ocean follow it into obscurity as if a huge hand (God's?) had reached out and turned down the dimmer light, and I sighed sadly more than once because when you stop yourself from asking *why*, you feel kind of blank.

It didn't help that I couldn't move. For hours, Terry slept heavily on my leg, her glasses cutting into my thigh, as I stared emptily out at that death-black night, my ears filled with the droning acoustics of the plane, my eyeballs as dry as marshmallows, my right leg numb from the weight of Terry's head, my mind at a mulish halt in the center of a complicated junction of questions from which all roads led to dead ends. It was with a sense of gratitude that I was snapped out of my inertia by Danny throwing up into a white paper bag, which caused a stir among the flight attendants who crowded around him with wet cloths and offers of water and peppermint sticks, which awakened Jennifer from a tentative sleep, who got to crying so hard she barely paused to breathe, and by the plane descending and the interior lights coming on and people donning coats and hats and making another mad rush to disembark before the plane accidentally took off with them still inside.

Once out of Lutin [sic] we had to transfer, with all our thirty-two pieces, to Heathrow Airport. It was now about one o'clock AM, and the trip was made on a bus, and took close to two hours. And then the fun began.

On a warmly throbbing bus, we rolled through the rainy night. At Heathrow, Dad unloaded our luggage by increments into the luminous, empty terminal, and arranged it into an orderly mountain in the middle of the ticketing area. Mom's face was tired but forgiving. She'd had a glass of sherry on the plane and had started laughing at Luton and couldn't stop, and now she was all laughed out. I'd never heard a laugh like that, and could tell she thought Luton was anything but funny. Dad didn't laugh. In the bright terminal at Heathrow, he squatted down before us and explained that in the morning we'd have breakfast and feel better than we do now. And when the ticket office opened he'd arrange for another flight with a new airline, and we'd get on another plane. And that plane would take us to Portugal.

"And then we'll be all set. Things will fall into place. But right now we just have to be patient, and try to get some sleep. And if you can't sleep, say your rosary. We need the prayers."

Sitting on the cold waiting-room bench, I settled my stare on the mountain of our luggage and took out my rosary and wondered how many it would take to get us out of this place. I said the *Credo*, but the rest of the rosary wouldn't come. I'd just seen the world from above, and it had shocked me, like seeing Mom or Dad naked would shock me. I couldn't stop thinking about it. The earth was a *real planet*. A huge revolving ball suspended in space. Somehow the sight of it had changed me. I didn't know how or why, but I knew I was different, and that I would never return to the person I was before I saw it. The knowledge of being different made me miss the person I used to be. And suddenly I didn't want to board another plane to Portugal, or go to sleep, or say the rosary. I wanted to go home. To our house on Myrtle Avenue, with the juniper tree and the big, square lawn and my own bed with the fairy stickers across the headboard and my own soft pillow. It wasn't just that I missed home. It was that I craved it with a hunger that went through me full-bore, like an eviscerating machine, from my head to my heels, metallic and biting. The feeling was so large it required me to use every muscle of my body to hold it inside. I wasn't raised to bawl over hurt feelings. And I wasn't about to start bawling then, in full view of everyone. Tears were for sissies, and I was no sissy. I was tough enough to sit in perfect stillness as my throat cramped over boxed-in sobs, and my chest tugged at inner spasms, and my stomach wrung itself into a tighter and tighter twist, and I inhaled deeply and clamped over the feeling forcing it into a tighter space.

But somehow a single tear managed to squeeze out between my

eyelids and roll down my cheek, and just then an arm wrapped around me, and I felt myself pulled right into Mom's warm body. And as a haywire snaps off a hay bale, my chest released the pressure and the sobs spilled out. But now they had a place to go. Right into Mom. Holding me close, she spoke quietly into my ear. She said, "Offer it up to God and Our Lady and everything will be all right."

Resolved: I will never again: 1. Believe that such an ambitious move as the translocation of eight people, thirty-two pieces of luggage and three thousand pounds of crates halfway around the world; and the liquidation of two cars and a four bedroom home with all its furnishings can be cleverly accomplished in a month's time. 2. Book passage on a charter flight, ever, at any time, to any place. 3. Be overweight on baggage allowances. 4. Postulate that honorable intentions rule out incredible and unforeseen traveling perplexities. So help me God.

The night was long, cold, sad, and empty. Dad paced and prayed the rosary. Mom fell asleep sitting up. Danny, Nick, Jennifer, and Vincent sprawled on the floor. I lay my head on Terry's shoulder and she didn't push me off. Sighing over this small luxury, I closed my eyes.

When I opened them again it was morning, and an English woman's crisp voice was announcing delays and departures over a scratchy loudspeaker. People were everywhere, skirting around our mountain, their legs scissoring past as they raced off to different sections of the airport, to board planes, presumably, or meet passengers, or book flights. Many of them had to step over our mess to get where they were going. On their faces were looks of disapproval mixed with curiosity as they craned their necks, probably wondering who the family of Gypsies was, and why we looked so downtrodden.

At a counter, Dad was arguing with a BEA official, and I could see by his expression and the way he pounded his fist on the counter that he didn't like what the BEA man was telling him. Dad shouted, and the official crossed his arms, and Dad shouted more, and the official stood proudly. Finally, Dad marched back to our group, where he repeated the argument word for word to Mom. He'd booked our seats to Lisbon, and then he'd "un-booked us," because BEA was going to charge him for overweight baggage— "the shysters." We weren't getting on a plane after all.

"Stay patient," he said. "We'll get to Portugal if we have to swim there."

I didn't like that option, but he raced off. Our luggage was on the plane, and he had to ferret it out from thousands of other suitcases. So for the rest of the day we sat in a sloppy powwow as our luggage returned to us piece by piece until it grew into the size of a small mountain again, and continuous streams of people rushed around us like whitewater around boulders, sliding by and through, parting and rejoining, stepping on our sweaters and coats, hopping over our carry-ons, always trailing a look of curiosity behind them.

Staring widely at the flow, I found myself envying those people with their tickets and lightweight bags and real destinations to real places. They'd planned their getaways in advance, making all the necessary arrangements to and from, and weren't going to arrive in a country and sit on the airport floor, holding their rosaries, or arguing with airline employees. Their carry-ons were crammed with bathing suits and suntan lotion; not rice and dried pinto beans and spaghetti noodles. And their checked luggage didn't contain all their earthly belongings.

Things were not going as planned. And I sensed that from here on out, things would never go quite as planned. That even when we did make a new home, it would never be a real home because home wasn't something you could create at will. Once it was gone, the mold was broken. You had to make a new one from scratch. And homes made from scratch had flaws and irregularities that constantly reminded you that they were remakes. I also knew that I needed to find answers to all those questions I'd put on hold way up in the sky, or I'd end up carrying the questions around with me the rest of my life just like thirty-two pieces of luggage.

IT WAS SOMETHING like morning when Dad threw open the curtains of the Town House Bed and Breakfast, letting in a grayish light. "Wake up, snakes, and shake your rattles! We're in London. And when in London, you do what Londoners do. You be completely rude and uncompromising to someone truly in need. Just kidding. You get up and you have breakfast."

Outside, my windbreaker was instantly soaked by rain, becoming a soggy skin over my T-shirt. Terry's brown camel-hair coat drank a gallon straight out of the air; Mom's ratted, heart-shaped bob gained a pound of weight, sagged, and took on the shape of a popped basketball; and both of their glasses got misted up. The babies plodded spacily along sucking their thumbs, but stopped often to exclaim over the prevalently running water. Danny and Nick perked up like reconstituted mushrooms, and hippity-hopped on every surface, blinking into the wet spray, and digging their fingers into shadowy corners for whatever might be hiding there.

"Look around, kids," Dad said from ahead. "England used to be a great nation. Thanks to St. Augustine of Canterbury, who converted the Anglo-Saxon pagans to Catholicism in the sixth century, and then the Normans, who invaded the country in 1066 and reestablished Catholic rule. England has a fine, noble history. But England surrendered her greatness, threw it away with both hands. She could have led the world against the heresies of Luther, and Calvin, who were the founders of Protestantism in the sixteenth century. But she didn't. She went the opposite way. She spearheaded the Protestant Revolution, which was the first revolution that took place against the Church. She murdered her heroes and crowned her heretics. She embraced the ideals of the Renaissance: humanism, pride, and narcissism. Her goal was 'The devil's work, done by the devil's ministers.' Yep. England became what she deserved: the whore of Babylon."

"For goodness' sakes, Lyle. Don't spoil England for the kids," Mom said.

"I'm not spoiling England," Dad said. "England spoiled itself."

We were off the main road now, heading toward some shops that promised food. Dad pointed to a closet-sized enclosure with fogged windows and a sign with a fat king on it.

"Look, kids. The King Edward Chippy. You can't go wrong with a restaurant called the King Edward Chippy, now, can you? Let's go. I'm starved."

It always amazed me how Dad could travel back through centuries, and the next instant plop himself back into the present. I was still thinking of England as the whore of Babylon murdering her heroes, while Dad was peering through the glass, saying, "Yum, yum."

A bell tinkled as we entered. Inside, the air was close. People stopped chewing and stared. A teenage boy standing by a cigarette machine grinned at Terry and she flicked her hair at him, and then removed her glasses. At the counter, Dad peered through the steamed glass at the golden food inside, and exclaimed loudly on how good it all looked.

"Gosh, I feel like having one of everything," he said cheerfully.

The counter lady said, "Please?" which was a strange way to ask for an order, and Dad said, "Thank you," even though she hadn't done anything for him yet.

Then he ordered some strange food for himself: battered codfish, chips and vinegar, mushy peas, and a pickled egg. Mom ordered "shepherd's pie"—which she said was like a hamburger and fries all mashed together into a pie crust—for herself, and macaroni and cheese pies for us.

"And?" the counter lady asked, as if we'd forgotten the most important thing.

Dad said, "And . . . What's the damage?" and pulled out his wallet.

"Six pounds forty, please."

"I love it. *Pounds*. It's so nice to buy things with pounds. It doesn't feel like spending money at all. Just dropping weight."

At the table, Dad bowed his head and crossed himself, and the rest of us automatically bowed our heads and crossed ourselves. "In the name of the Father, and of the Son, and of the Holy Ghost." During Grace, I kept my head down, careful not to look to the right or left, or straight up at the lady behind the counter. I didn't want to see anyone staring at us. I didn't want to see their expressions. I was afraid of what their faces would reveal. Surprise. Humor. Curiosity. The same looks we got back in America. So I hunched close to the table, and prayed quietly and crossed myself at the end, and continued to keep my head down as I ate my food. It was good, and I soon forgot about Grace and my shame at being caught having a religion, but then Dad, who finished first, wiped his mouth on a napkin and said in a voice that carried, "Not bad for a country that betrayed the Catholic Church."

THE SKY IN England hangs so low that as hard as you stare at it there is no way of telling where it begins and where it ends. Rain whispers against the windows, rolling down the glass in rivulets, gathering on the ledge, and spilling onto the street. Below, black umbrellas bump and pass along Queen's Terrace Lane like great hooded termites along a shiny-wet road that moves like a river beneath them. Heavy-coated figures rush against the spray, hop over puddles, and hunch into cabs.

Staring out the window, I found it hard to believe such a wet place was the land of my ancestors, but Dad said indeed it was.

"Grandpa's great-great-great-grandfather, John Norwood, was a member of Parliament, in Kent, in the sixteenth century. He had a son called James Norwood, who emigrated to America and bought a farm in Louisiana. Then James had a son named William, and when the Civil War broke out, William and his son both joined the North Carolina militia and fought on the side of the Confederacy."

"Do you mean our ancestors fought the Yankees?" asked Terry, whose favorite book and film both happened to be *Gone With the Wind*. It was our second day in London, and Dad was tying his shoes, getting ready to go out to battle with the Brits over our transportation to Portugal.

"You bet they did. Your ancestors were Rebels to the core. No Yankee pansy blood on my side of the family—although I don't know about Mom's."

"Were your ancestors Yankee pansies?" I asked Mom.

"I don't know, and I don't want to know," Mom said, wisely I thought.

"The South losing the Civil War was one of the great tragedies of American history," Dad said. "Things would have been very different if the South had managed to secede from the Union—which it had every right to do, and don't ever forget that."

"Why did the South want to secede?" Terry asked.

"Different ideals from the North," Dad said. "The South was agricultural and traditional. The North was industrial and progressive. The two sides had very little in common. Just like the pre–Vatican II Church and the post–Vatican II Church. Different ideals, different goals, completely antithetical in nature. Think of how different things would be if it weren't for Vatican II."

He stood up and pulled on his raincoat, and it came to me that if it weren't for Vatican II we wouldn't be in this bed and breakfast in England, and how ironic it was that a pope who didn't even know we existed was the cause of us sitting in this cramped room waiting for passage to Portugal. It was shocking. To think of the invisible strands that grew from unseen events that took place between people I couldn't see and were now dead, and reached out their long tendrils that became entangled with my destiny. It wasn't fair. Simple as that.

"I thought the Civil War was about slaves," I said, although I wasn't very sure why I thought that.

"Slavery had very little to do with the Civil War. Everyone is all ga-ga over Abe Lincoln, but Abe didn't want to free the blacks—that was just his ruse. He wanted to ship the blacks back to Africa. When the Southerners tried to secede from a centralized government and rule themselves (which was their God-given right), Abe dragged the South into a war that killed six hundred thousand of his own people. He did it to preserve the Union of white people. He said it himself. 'My paramount objective is to save the Union. If I could save the Union without freeing any slave I would do it.'

Abe was a dictator operating on the Hobbesian idea that the first principle of human behavior is self-interest, and that self-interest translates to power, and Abe wanted absolute power in government. And he got it. And ever since then the U.S. government has followed Hobbes's philosophy. Power, power, power . . . No, the Civil War had nothing to do with slavery. It had to do with ideals. Ideals are what start most wars."

And Dad aimed his umbrella like a rifle, fired it at the wall, and walked out the door, singing:

> *Oh, I'm a good ol' Rebel soldier, now that's just what I am;*
> *For this "Fair Land of Freedom" I do not give a damn.*
> *I'm glad I fit against it, I only wish we'd won.*
> *And I don't want no pardon for anything I done.*

When the door closed, Terry threw herself into the chair and fanned herself with an invisible fan, and said in her Scarlett O'Hara voice, "If you say *war* just one more time, I'll shall go in the house and shut the door. I've never been so tired of any one word in my life as *war*, unless it's *secession*. Pa talks *war* morning, noon, and night and I get so bored I could scream!"

And we were faced with another full day of waiting for our lives to begin again. As Mom tried to keep the babies entertained in the adjoining room, Terry turned on a small black and white TV screen that had never heard of the NBC peacock and we spent the day absorbing grim images of a bleak world in which people politely suffer, such as *Cathy Come Home*, a program in which Cathy's husband loses his job, and Cathy and their two kids become poor and homeless, and as they get sadder and sadder and filthier and filthier and more and more hungry and cold and wretched, the people in the town politely complain to the police, and in the end the police approach Cathy in a London railway station and politely take her children from her as she sobs on the street. And I wasn't surprised that this would happen in a country that murders its heroes and crowns its heretics.

"See what happens when your dad quits his job?" Terry said teasingly. "You end up like them."

Danny said, "No way. Dad'll shoot those guys."

"No, he won't, dumb cluck," she said. "He didn't bring his gun."

And the day drifted by. And another day drifted by after that. And another. I didn't count them because they were not days, but gigantic blocks of wakeful boredom. Each day seemed churned out by a clock that had rusted inside, and struggled at a fraction of the regular speed, in a room that felt like a shoe two sizes too small. I would be surprised later to learn we didn't live there for a year, but under a week.

For six days I tried every imaginable approach to get the family to Lisbon: buying a car; renting a car; rail; ship. It took long hours to deal with each possibility. Just trying to ascertain rail prices for thirty-two pieces of luggage by rail freight took me two or three hours of phone calls. They'd never heard of such a thing, and it seemed nobody could find out how to accomplish it.

There was no way around it, we had to fly. But Dad refused to give a cent to a British airline. So he took his business to TAP, a Portuguese airline. At the gate they did body searches on each one of us—something no other airline did—because they were fighting communism, and had to take extra caution. Dad approved. Leave it to a Catholic country to understand the necessity of security. Two hours later, we were circling the red rooftops of Lisboa (which the stewardess pronounced *Leesh-boa*), with the sun-splashed Atlantic Ocean glittering to the west, and the yellow-garbed, green-spotted hills unfurling to the east, and a glorious sun bathing the endless gray-blue sky and whitewashed city with a waxy high-buff polish.

"There she is," Dad said, leaning into the window. "One of the greatest countries in the world. A land of great explorers . . . and great warriors, too. When the Mohammedan infidels invaded Portugal, the Portuguese warriors were outnumbered as much as a hundred to one. But they drove them out, aided by the Divine Saviour himself who appeared to Alfonso *to strengthen his heart in the conflict,* and lay the Catholic kingdom *on firm rock.*"

On the firm ground of Aeroporto de Leeshboa, a woman's voice spoke Portuguese over a loudspeaker: *Senhores e senhoras, bem vindos a Portugal.*

Bem vindos. Welcome.

Welcome to Our Lady's country. Welcome to the Catholic haven of the world. Welcome to the land of miracles, where grace is so prevalent it is part of the sunlight that touches your face and the oxygen that you breathe. Welcome to the place of everlasting and eternal faith, where the dogma of the Church will always remain intact. Welcome to your soul's salvation.

The air was warm, and the building just a little bit scarred and dilapidated, but in a friendly way, and the movements of the airport officials were relaxed and unhurried as if their work was a pleasure and not at all stressful and came with plenty of coffee and cigarette breaks and wine-on-demand and even a midday siesta. As we stood beside our mound of luggage waiting for Dad's mysterious Portuguese contact to appear like a heavenly ambassador and sweep us off to a prearranged hotel, I was sure I could feel a buzz in the atmosphere that had been touched by Our Lady's presence—a kind of spiritual energy that softened the anxiety of all our worldly concerns. I was hungry, but the buzz diffused that worry. We had no place to live, but the buzz gave us confidence in Our Lady's goodness. We had no Portuguese money and couldn't speak the language, but the buzz reassured us that those were petty logistics. Our Lady would oversee all necessities. The buzz was so pervasive that even after two hours of waiting in plain view for this English-speaking Portuguese friend-of-a-friend-of-a-friend, Dad didn't appear on the verge of putting someone in a headlock as he had back in London, but calmly wondered if he might have confused *terça-feira* (the third day of the week) with *quarta-feira* (the fourth day) by mistakenly counting from Monday instead of Sunday, and Mom, who'd been using the time to get in several rosaries, laughed at Dad's bumbleheadedness with foreign languages and said it was a mistake anyone could have made. The buzz remained when Dad got on the phone and with the help of his *Portuguêse-Inglês dicionário de bolso* attempted to find us a temporary residence on his own and came out unsuccessful, and it remained when a kindly stranger realized our situation and performed the merciful work of Our Lady by arranging room and board at an affordable *pensão* she knew about, and it remained when we loaded our tremendous pile of stuff into the trunks of four cabs and sped toward central Lisboa.

It was our first taste of life the Catholic way. We were in a Catholic country. The government was Catholic. The people were Catholic. Even the dogs were Catholic. Here they knew that nothing mattered beside your everlasting soul. Here the chaos of modernism would not penetrate the shield that Our Lady had placed around her chosen country. You could actually feel the relaxing effect of this knowledge, as if you'd swallowed a pain pill. I found myself taking long, deep breaths. People here would carry rosaries in their pockets, and pray in post offices and stores and cars, and say Grace in restaurants just like us. What a relief to know you were in a country where you could practice your religion openly and no one would think twice. For the first time since Dad announced his plans to bring us here, I felt an ounce of hope that maybe we were doing the right thing after all, and as we sped through *Leeshboa*, I said a secret prayer of thanks.

6

not quite paradise

Portugal is the cleanest country I've ever seen. Even their dirt is clean. One gets the notion of this everywhere: everything looks white-washed and scrubbed. Little men roam the city with little brooms and pans whisking away this or that rubbish. They wear these clean little uniforms that remind me of scenes out of Brave New World. *Remember the Delta Minus class?*

WE WERE IN Portugal. But we weren't *in Portugal* until we stepped through the peeling double doors of Pensão Casa de São Mamede, and Mom said, "Now *this . . .* is *Portugal*."

Portugal was not like California. In Portugal, a whiskered old lady clothed in long black skirts mashed a kiss on both your cheeks as if she were your long-lost grandma, handed you a cup of milky coffee even though you said *Não obrigada* at least twice, and then laughed at the look on your face when you tried to get a swallow down.

"Mom!" I whispered after the old lady cleared away the cup. "Do we have to drink coffee even if we don't like it?"

"Of course you do," Mom whispered back. "And you'll be polite and say *muito obrigada*."

"But I *hate* coffee!"

"Too bad."

In Portugal, you could be standing there minding your own business when suddenly a ghastly aroma might discharge from an open doorway like a belch and bowl you three steps over. Or you might be sitting on the toilet when a rusty pipe poking out of the ceiling right over your head might snort, giggle, and hiss with such ferocity you were forced to bolt and take cover, or risk your life. In Portugal, you never knew what surprising thing you might encounter when you walked around a corner: a legless man in a wheelbarrow; a kid your own age smoking a cigarette; a grown man peeing against a building; a barefooted child playing a concertina; a toothless fat lady in a leopardskin print dress. The problem with Portugal was not the surprises, however, but that everything was worth looking at, and that you had to look at it secretly or Mom would say, "Don't stare. It's not polite."

On our first walk, Dad filled his lungs with Portuguese air and said, "Aah! Can you smell that? Now *that's* what a city should smell like." Danny and I looked at each other and wrinkled our noses. In meat shops flies buzzed in and out like hurried customers, dogs too. Weeds sprouted between the roofing tiles. Pigeons flew in giant flocks and splattered their white paint on parked cars. Dog-piles hardened in the sun. Horse manure spread under the traffic. Pee stains garnished the white marble tile on buildings.

In California, buildings were as clean as hospitals, with freshly painted white walls, lots of neutral space to move around in, lights that illuminated, invisible speakers that played cheery music, and air that was either perfumed or odorless. In California, stairs did not creak, faucets did not drip brown water, hard-bodied worms did not occasionally drop from the ceiling joists and lay curled on the floor, the electricity did not go on the blink with such frequency that you never knew, from minute to minute, if you'd be sitting in pitch-black, and cigarette smoke did not ascend freely from dozens of abandoned ashtrays as if the place were the set for a horror movie. In California, doors and hallways were built for the potential passage of two adults, not one small child, and flushing the toilet did not require you to pull a chain like an American truck driver honking the horn of his sixteen-wheeler.

In California, the most delicious foods came from boxes or cans; people did not take things from raw nature and serve them on a plate. On our first night at the Pensão Casa de São Mamede, when I looked into my soup bowl, I was torn between the urge to laugh hysterically or to break down into loud, coughing sobs. Not prone to dramatics, I took a deep breath and shot an imploring look at Mom across the table.

"Mom," I whispered. "This soup has . . . *grass* in it."

"*And* it's delicious," Mom said, sipping at her spoon. "*And* you will eat every bite."

"But Mom . . . I *can't.*"

"You can. And you will."

"This is a . . . *fish*," Nick said, his eyes bugging at the giant sardine. "Look, it's got eyeballs and a tail."

"It's called *peixe*. And it's probably freshly caught. Maybe just a few hours ago."

"*Fresh?* I can't eat a *fresh* fish. It's full of *bones.*"

"Of course it's full of bones. How else could it swim? Just take them out."

"But there are *hundreds.*"

"Well then, you'd better get started."

"My soup has . . . *leaves* in it."

"And it's probably a centuries-old recipe, and you're probably the first person in Portugal to ever question the leaves."

"Why do we always have to drink coffee?" Danny asked. "Coffee is *disgusting*."

"All the children in Portugal drink coffee. You'll like it once you get used to it. Now be polite, and don't forget to say *obrigado*."

"That man just poured wine into his soup," Terry said.

"That's what they do here."

"Can I pour wine into my soup, too?"

"No, young lady, you may not."

All the residents of the Casa dined together at a long communal table, and by the way they talked excitedly through every course, working their way downward through the various bowls and plates without ever once running out of subject matter, I guessed they must have known each other all their lives. Of course, as the days passed and I began to notice certain people missing and new ones replacing them, I realized that they were all strangers who just happened to like each other right away. The conversation was almost always a loud stream of conflicting voices raised over full mouths, sometimes accompanied by a fork or elbow or thumb to make a point, and always seeming on the verge of turning violent. The oldest guests seemed to have the most to say and to require the highest volume to say it, and if they lost their false teeth in the middle of a sentence they just talked without them. The younger adults seemed to respect the older adults' authority on all topics, but that didn't stop them from yelling back with exasperated gestures of their own and pretending to disagree.

Dad seemed to feel right at home with the noisy debates—probably thinking their passion had something to do with Vatican II. Slurping his grass soup from a large spoon, guzzling the red wine, and popping the green olives into his mouth as fast as peanuts, he grinned with obvious delight as he sized up his new countrymen and found them exactly to his liking. By the look on his face I guessed what he was thinking: *Just as I expected! The Old World unchanged. And Catholic to the core!*

The Portuguese people in Portugal didn't speak the same language as the Portuguese person on Dad's Berlitz tapes. On the tapes, a woman gently articulated, "*Sente-se por favor* . . . Please sit down." The people here used a strange tongue made up mostly of *oozh* and *ão* sounds and sometimes *ewe* and *oy*—combinations that had a way of sticking together and then stretching apart like taffy between your teeth. Trying to understand meaning in all that stickiness, I grew quickly discouraged. Not only could I not make out a word, never in a million years would I be able to make my mouth do gymnastics like that.

"That man just said *magoei*," Danny said. "That's because this fish slime is so ma-*gooey*!"

"I don't want gooey fish," Jennifer sniffled, pink-faced and on the verge of tears.

"It's not gooey, for cryin' out loud," Mom said, as she forked the meat off the bones. "It's tender and flaky."

Danny wiggled in his chair to the Fig Newton tune. "Ooey-gooey, rich and chewy inside. Golden cakey, tender flakey outside. Wrap the inside in the outside. Is it good? Darn tootin'! It's the big *Peixe* Pukin'!"

Jennifer started crying.

"Now *that's enough*," Mom said to Danny. "You're not making things any easier for your sister."

"Ooey-gooey," Vinny grinned, twiddling his fingertips together. "Ooey-gooey, ooey-gooey, ooey-gooey."

"Man alive," Terry groaned, hiding her face behind her hand. "We are such freaks."

She was right. We were freaks. When I looked around at my family, I was struck by how our Americanness stood out like a billboard. Our jeans and T-shirts and tennis shoes said *American*. Mom's tall, ratted hair and cat-eye glasses said *American*. Dad's short-sleeved checkered shirt with the little spiral notebook and pen in his breast pocket said *American*. Vinny's thick glasses and rope tied to his belt loop said *American*. Terry's bright flowered purse and my blindingly blond hair said *Brady Bunch American*. We used words like "ooey-gooey." We picked the bones individually from the fish. We were on a search for the aura of Catholicism in a country that knew more about it than we did. Was this what the Portuguese meant when they called us *os americanos*?

The only people to exchange any dialogue with us were a retired British couple from Manchester who had been coming to the *pensão* every year of their married lives since their honeymoon. Thrilled to speak "the Queen's English" to native speakers, Dad told them about our reasons for coming. I remember the British people nodding and smiling politely, asking a few vague questions, and then going back to speaking with the Portuguese.

"Nice couple," Dad later said. "I may have gotten the English all wrong."

HARRY DOTEN'S CONTACT at General Electric couldn't fit us into his schedule, so he sent one of his air conditioner salesmen, a man named Sérgio Leandro, to the *pensão* to help us out. Sérgio was twenty-one, with a thick head of black hair, a pure white smile, and an acoustic guitar in the back of his tiny European car. Terry was impressed. "*Dang*, he's cute," she whispered so low that only I could hear. I looked at Terry, and then at Sérgio. Twenty-one-year-olds were *men*. And men were not *cute*. What did she see that I didn't? It was always like that. I was always scrambling to see something that wasn't there. "Yeah," I said. "He's really *cute*." Sérgio smiled a lot, and said, "Ees nowt a prowblem," a lot, and seemed glad to be getting the day off work to hang out with his new American friend. Dad liked him, too. "Did you know Sérgio fought the Communists in the Portuguese colonies of Mozambique?" he crowed to Mom. "He touched off a booby trap and was blown to bits. Spent the last few years in and out of hospitals." I looked closely at the man. For someone who'd been blown to bits, he sure looked healthy. Mom must have thought so too, considering the way she locked him in her biggest bear hug and shouted her appreciation at him. (Mom spoke loudly to foreigners to help get her English across.) Sérgio repeated his "nowt a prowblem" with a wide grin, and after a thrown-back espresso offered by the *pensão* hostess, packed Dad into the passenger seat of his little car, and the two sped off in the direction of Fatima to go house-hunting.

"Well!" Mom said, beaming. "With Sérgio's help, I'm sure your father will find a house soon. Come on, kids. Let's go shopping."

It was always different being with Mom than with Dad. Mom never talked about things you couldn't see, hear, and touch. Mom was someone who plugged in to what was happening right there in front of her and operated on efficient power. Walking from shop to shop, she picked items individually off shelves, studied their names, and converted the price from escudos and centavos into dollars and cents using a pencil and paper. Dad could talk all day about Portugal's Catholic history and how they had vanquished the Moors. Mom was going to make Portugal work for us.

"Apples. Four escudos a kilogram. That's only . . . let's see . . . about twenty cents a pound. Or wait. That can't be. Did I calculate that right?"

"Remember the name of this bread, kids. *Bola caseira*. Have you got that? According to my dictionary, it was baked in a firewood oven."

"*Bacalhau*. Salted cod. I'm going to have to find a recipe that neutralizes the salt."

The other difference about being with Mom was that she knew when to call it quits. When Jennifer began to fuss and rub her eyes, and Vinny was refusing to budge, and Danny and Nick were fighting in the aisles, Mom turned away from the shops, saying, "Time to go!" and made a beeline for the *pensão* where our milky coffees awaited us.

That evening, Dad broke the news to Mom.

"Rent prices in Fatima are way over our budget. Twice what they are outside the area."

"That must be because of the visions."

"That's my guess, too. We're going to look further out. Check out some of the towns nearby. Sérgio is going to make some phone calls. I'm sure we'll find something."

The next day Dad walked to the closest church to find out the Sunday mass schedule. When he returned he looked confused, as if he'd boarded the right train but ended up at the wrong destination.

"There's a Vatican II table on the altar," he told Mom. "I don't understand it."

Mom frowned, showing the dimple by her lower lip. "Maybe it's just there for looks, and they don't actually use it as an altar."

"Why put a table there if you don't intend to use it?"

"Maybe it's a *Novus Ordo* church."

"According to Sérgio, it's one of the oldest and most traditional Catholic churches in the city."

"Well, I wouldn't take his word for it. Look, Sérgio's a great guy, Lyle, but I don't think he knows what he's talking about. He's not even a practicing Catholic."

"He seemed to know exactly what he was talking about when he told me it was traditional. Anyway, I don't like the look of it one bit. If I spoke Portuguese I'd go right back there and talk to the priest."

I didn't want to admit it to Dad, but I secretly liked how the Catholic Church in Portugal seemed so connected to the sea. Churches everywhere seemed to be practically floating on blue tiles that depicted crashing waves. In their cobbled courtyards were mosaics of anchors sunk deep into sand and seaweed, and lapping waves rising onto the tiled foundation. Tiles on one church showed sailing ships, on another crabs and squids, on another clams and seashells. On an iron cross, a giant sea monster with gaping jaws and a thrashing tail replaced Jesus. I noticed, too, how the statues of Christopher Columbus and Vasco da Gama seemed at least as big as those of Jesus, Mary, and Joseph. I wondered what Dad would make of all this and decided not to bring it up. What mattered was that the traditional Tridentine Mass was intact, and surely there would be no surprises there.

That Sunday, I unrolled my one and only church dress from the darkest recesses of my carry-on suitcase where it had lived crumpled and unmissed, and I grimaced. The dress had cinched sleeves that pinched my upper arms and slid into my armpits and had to be tugged down, and a stupid black plastic belt that was cracked at the buckle hole, and a hem of fraying lace that tickled my knees. I deplored this dress more than anything else in the world. I deplored *all* dresses. Dresses were like hair shirts to me. But I knew I had to wear them if I was going to be part of the anti-revolutionary international. And I was determined to be a part of it.

"What if the mass turns out to be *Novus Ordo*?" I asked Terry, as we dressed on Sunday. "What'll we do then?"

Terry shrugged. "How do I know?"

"Well, *what if*?" I stared at her, wanting an answer.

Terry was working on her hair with her boar bristle hairbrush in case she saw some cute boys at mass. "Geez. Give me a break. I'm no fortune-teller."

I pondered the problem. Would Dad take on the Lisbon diocese like he'd taken on the San Jose diocese? Would he write letters, storm their offices, and lecture to the priests and bishops about Fabian tactics? Would he go on a parish hunt all over Portugal looking for the aura of Catholicism? Would he stand at the far back, and withhold his donation from the basket at collection? Worse, would he stop playing the harmonica and lie on his bed with his eyes covered by his dark gray T-shirt?

That Sunday we left the *pensão* and walked to Igreja de São Roque, a church that was ten times the size of St. Mary's and a hundred times more beautiful. Once inside, I sighed with relief. No one, not even Dad, could help but be inspired by this place. It was like a palace. Such a high ceiling, such enormous paintings of the Stations of the Cross, such giant candleholders! Statues seemed to grow out of the walls; light sprang from the marble floor as if originating there; stone arches welcomed you to enter prayer rooms with smaller altars where your thoughts and prayers had privacy. But most magnificent of all was the main altar. Instead of a large crucifix hanging over it, this one had a golden throne where Our Lady stood holding the infant Jesus. Above that hung a painting of the Crucifixion, and above that hung a painting of God Himself. This Igreja de São Roque made St. Mary's Church seem like a poor church. Everywhere you looked gold laid upon gold, angel upon angel. It seemed that in Portugal, all the riches must be inside the churches, and not in the government buildings like in the States, and as miffed as you were about modernity that was something you could appreciate. Every minute that passed, I grew more heartened by what I saw, and more hopeful that the short table standing in front of the main altar wasn't an actual *table* for breaking Protestant-style bread, but a decoration. *Please God,* I said in my head. *Let this be the real thing.*

The church bells stopped ringing, and Mom took a missal from the pew and opened the pages, and I saw from the dimple that sank deep and by the way she shot Dad a glance that there was a problem. Picking up a missal, I looked inside. One language. I read the words:

> *Que Deus e o Espírito Santo*
> *estejam contigo.*

The liturgy was not in Latin but in Portuguese. The vernacular! I looked at Dad. His missal was closed on his lap. His face was set—disappointment written all over it.

The bells behind the altar tinkled and the priest entered, and what happened next came as no shock, considering the liturgy. He walked to the table and faced the people and began to pray in Portuguese and not Latin, and instead of the somber air required for the unbloody sacrifice, he had the glint of a smile on his face, and a casual way of addressing the congregation even while he was supposedly performing the ceremony. Dad lasted about three minutes. As the mass got underway, he stood up, and glanced at the rest of us. We stood up too, and as a group, marched out of the church.

Released to the outside, Nick and Danny instantly skipped off to look for lost treasures. Jennifer said, "Go bye-bye?" Vinny put out his tongue to taste the morning sunlight. Dad was red-faced, holding back his fury. Mom looked helpless. No one spoke. Walking back to the *pensão* I felt heavy, as if a boulder had settled in my belly. If such a beautiful church as the Igreja de São Roque had given in to Vatican II, wouldn't all the churches? Had Portugal failed to remain true to the dogma of the faith? Was Portugal helping to bring on the Chastisement?

Mom's reasoning was this: "Lisbon is a big city. Big cities are always more modern than anywhere else. You go outside the big cities, into the villages, where things are slower and more stable, and no way will you find the Vatican II table and the *Novus Ordo* mass. The country has an *entirely* different way of life."

Dad seemed to consider Mom's reasoning. And the more he considered it, the more he liked it, so that by the time we were climbing the steps of the *pensão* he was almost cheerful. "You know, Mart, I think you may be right," he said. "We're in a big cosmopolitan city. Lisbon is no different from London or Paris or *New York*, for cryin' out loud. Of course the Tridentine Mass isn't here. The Vatican keeps close tabs on major cities. Where *we'll* be living the people probably won't have even *heard* of Vatican II. I'm really glad you mentioned it. For a second there, I was really worried."

DAD AND SÉRGIO didn't have much luck finding a house anywhere near Fatima. Even the nearby towns seemed to be cashing in on the religious fame. So after a week of searching, Dad became fed up and took Sérgio up on his offer to find a house around his own town, Oeiras, which was about fifty miles south of Fatima.

We'd spent so many days lounging around the *pensão* waiting for our lives to change that it was a shock when Dad suddenly swung open our bedroom door wearing a big smile. "Kids! Get up off the floor," he said, looking at us sprawled out. "Pack your things. We'll be catching the first four taxis we see tomorrow morning. We're going home."

The next morning the old innkeeper kissed us all on both cheeks, and rubbed her eyes with chubby palms as if she were saying good-bye to her own grandchildren, and we piled into four taxis along with our thirty-two pieces of luggage and drove away.

In Portugal, there were practically no cars on the freeway. And no cops to pull over the few cars that were there—all of them speeding. Trash blew alongside the road and got caught on your windshield, and if you listened carefully the roadside cicadas chirped louder than the car engine.

"Carnaxide . . . Laranjeiras . . . Porto Salvo . . . Arneiro." Terry read each sign with a perfect accent. She was getting Portuguese down faster than any of us. "*Desvio emergência.*"

The hilly countryside glinted in the sun, and disordered clumps of houses in white, periwinkle, goldenrod, and salmon colors clung to the hills like mollusks to a rocky shore. Once outside of the greater Lisbon area, the cities shrunk to villages. In Sassoeiros, our taxis slowed to a crawl as the drivers skirted the roundabouts and sink holes, their tires rumbling on rough cobblestones, and finally pulled up at a friendly green and white house standing tall with its back to the village and its front facing an undulant lake of green grasses.

It was a mansion. Or it seemed that way, after the weeks we'd spent cramped up in small guesthouses.

"Wow," I breathed. "If only the Pooles could see this."

We leaped out of the taxis and some of us jumped up and down out of excitement as the drivers unloaded our bags, slammed the doors, pocketed the wad of paper and coins counted out carefully by Dad, and drove off in a cloud of dust.

And we were alone. For a moment, an odd silence hovered over us. I could hear in the distance the bleating of sheep, along with the wind hissing through the long grasses, roosters crowing, and dogs barking, but otherwise the place was silent. I looked up and down the street. There were houses and a few parked cars but I didn't see any people around. It was midafternoon, so maybe they were having a siesta? I had a sense that they were spying on us between the slats of their shutters, staring in surprise at the strange family of clowns that just sprang from the city cabs in their colorful, wrinkled clothes with their heaps of luggage and bright blond hair. After a moment, something caught my eye, and I spotted her: a solitary woman wearing a black dress, a black head scarf, black stockings, and black shoes standing in a yard, camouflaged by the shadows, frozen in the act of hanging her laundry, staring at us. I smiled and she didn't smile back.

Dad stood quietly, too. Looking at each of us in slow succession and then at the house, he seemed to be evaluating the place and our role in it now that his vision had materialized. Our gluttonous baggage, some of it damaged and held together by adhesive and twine, leaned against the black wrought iron fence like a wounded beast leaking its innards. Jennifer, who was gripping her stuffed Snoopy by a neck worn to the circumference of a pencil, sat on the sidewalk to suck her thumb, her hair tied into a "tree" on top of her head and her face still tear-stained from the last *peixe* episode. Vinny stared through Coke bottle lenses toward the fields, the sky, the ethereal beyond, listening to what no one else could hear. Mom watched Dad watching us.

Eventually she broke the spell.

"Well!" she said, clapping her hands once, and rubbing them together. "Isn't this great? We're finally home. What do you say, everyone? Should we take in the luggage?"

Each of us grabbed a suitcase and dragged it toward the house, and as Dad fiddled with the key to the front door, I turned and looked back at the old woman, who had finished hanging her laundry. She turned away, entered her house, and closed the door behind her.

Inside our house, the space was roomy and cool, with comfortable mix-and-match furniture, wooden floors with plenty of throw rugs, windows that opened up to the fields, and even a television set. It felt so normal, almost as if this had been our real home all along and we were returning from a long vacation to Myrtle Avenue. A sense of being home-at-last injected us with giddiness and sparked our legs into frenetic action, and as soon as Mom was preoccupied with putting the babies down for a nap and tackling the luggage, we slipped outside to introduce ourselves to our new world.

TERRY TOOK THE lead, her long legs stretching, her hair swinging confidently, her eyes squinting slightly without their glasses. Danny and Nick hopped and fluttered in multiple directions like opportunistic blue jays. I stuck close to Terry, my stance defiant. I was sure I could hear the gossip catching fire from house to house. *Americanos* were here. Strange and foolish-looking *americanos*. The gossip flew faster than we could walk. Kids came out of their homes, barefoot, shirtless, smiling, some of them smoking, and all of them staring. In an open area beside some old apartments, we suddenly found ourselves surrounded by them. Our presence there seemed to them such a wonderful joke. But as the energetic group crowded us, they all sang and laughed together, *Ingleses! Ingleses!*

Terry frowned. "They think we're English."

"Let them!" I said, feeling somehow more superior as an English girl. "They won't know the difference."

"No way!" she said. "I refuse to be thought of as English. Hey, you guys. We're not *ingleses*. We're *americanos*. *Nós somos america-nos!* What dimwits!"

The kids stopped singing and looked at one another. Then they continued singing, *Americanos! Americanos!* A boy wearing a hat made out of cardboard shouted louder than anyone else. "*Vai para o teu país.*" That made everyone sing louder. "*Americanos! America-nos! Vai para o teu país!*"

"They said go back to your country." Terry said. She pushed her fist defiantly into her hip. She was chewing gum. "You should hit that kid with the weird hat," she said to Danny. "You could easily take him down."

The merest suggestion of a fight to Danny came off like a red cape to a bull. At St. Mary's, he was famous for his playground battles—so famous that Dad had signed him up for boxing practice with the Police Athletic League, but then subsequently pulled him out because of his temper. Danny fought blindly. It was his weakness. Now he turned to the dark-haired boy and charged, driving him off his feet, and the two rolled in the dirt, their fists swinging, and Danny went blind just like he always did at St. Mary's, and the kids cheered on the fight like the St. Mary's kids, only these kids kicked at Danny as they cheered, and dogs came running from all around and nipped at both boys and tried to get in on the action, and soon the dust had risen so thick that it was difficult to see who was winning. A cluster of old men smoking at a table nearby watched with amusement. An old lady sweeping a porch glanced with indifference. Finally, I could hear Danny crying: "Get off of me, you Portuguese pig!"

The kid rolled off him, and Danny stood up, his nose dripping blood, which he smeared with his sleeve—dragging a path of red from nose to ear. Leaning on his elbow in the dirt, the other boy laughed up at Danny. His laugh sounded like an insult, so Danny took a step forward and kicked the boy in the thigh with all his strength. The boy grabbed his leg and howled, and now all the kids rushed as one and we fled up the street, our legs and arms pumping, our hair streaming, the dogs barking alongside us, and the kids jeering and pelting us with pebbles as they all sang the same chant, *Americanos! Americanos! Vai para o teu país!* Close on our heels, they could catch us simply by reaching out, but they didn't reach out, and as we closed in on our house—which seemed to have moved a mile further down the road—the kids and dogs magically reined back, and by the time we were inside our gate they had disappeared entirely.

Breathing heavily, we sat on the doorstep and took quiet stock of the situation. To me, it couldn't have gone better. We'd made a pretty respectable entrance into town, and been given a decent reception in return. The kids were lawless and game, and the adults were hands-off. And we'd gotten to know the most important fact of all: That we were *americanos* and willing to fight for who we were. With that fact firmly established, we could go about a normal relationship with our Portuguese friends.

"You had that gutless wretch," Terry told Danny.

Danny smiled. "I'll get him good next time."

7

secondhand smoke

I HAD TO find a substitute for Michelle, so I quickly bagged a new best friend: a skinny girl in a short dress with china-doll hair and scared-kitten eyes who I spotted hanging clothes on a wire attached to a stick. Her looks fit the bill perfectly, but I soon found out that Rosário was no Michelle. For one thing, she didn't speak English, and she only whispered Portuguese. She didn't paint rainbows, or spy, or take dares, or do macramé, and she didn't snort when she laughed. Like her name, she was humble, religious, and saintly, spending all her time outside of school hours caring for her grandmother and doing boring housework. From the start I knew I wasn't going to have much fun being Rosário's best friend. The penalty was too high. From day one, my job was to sit quietly in a chair while she scrubbed the kitchen floor and did other tasks, and there was no TV or radio to help me pass the time. What there was was her grandmother. From her chair across the room the old woman's eyes stuck to me, following my every move, which scared me into making no moves at all. It was like that every day. As

Rosário washed dishes, cooked, scrubbed the laundry, swept the floor, dusted, and performed all the household chores, I sat perfectly still on my chair while her grandmother kept me in her scope like a short-range sniper holding position on a target. I was convinced that old lady knew my thoughts before I did and could head me off so far in advance that she'd drop me even before I took a step.

Perhaps this was guilt taking over, because in fact a plot was developing in my head, and the plot was against *her*, the grandmother. I wanted to emancipate Rosário from her life of enslavement to that disagreeable old woman. I had it all planned out: first I'd teach Rosário English (it was a much easier language than Portuguese), and then I'd explain some things to her in English: such as how dresses were only good for sitting and standing, and how much fun she was missing out on, like catching lizards, climbing trees, spying on the boys, having sleepovers, eating chocolate chip cookie dough, and watching TV (*Laurel and Hardy* aired in English every Thursday night), and how she was wasting her whole life working for no reason at all. One job a day was one thing. Ten jobs a day was something else. At least she should be paid an allowance so she could go out and buy candy. The girl had to stand up for herself. It was up to her to change the rules, because Grandma certainly wasn't going to. And the clincher to my plan was this: If Rosário couldn't manage to fix her life, I'd get Mom and Dad to adopt her. She could become my sister. Pure and simple. Then her problems would be over.

Mom argued ferociously against my plan. According to her, I shouldn't try to change Rosário but the opposite. "You should let Rosário be an example to *you*," she said. "In Catholic countries, girls don't run around in the streets like tomboys. They know their place is in the home helping their families. They learn to cook and sew and prepare themselves for motherhood." I huffed at that ridiculous notion. Stay at home and cook and sew? What kind of pathetic bull manure was that? But I didn't argue with her. I knew that Mom knew nothing was more ridiculous. Protest as she liked, I'd already figured Mom out. I knew she secretly believed in a healthy dose of female empowerment. Still, I wasn't about to test her on it.

Terry had also scooped up a new best friend: an older girl named Francisca, who was fourteen, had long straight hair, and spoke English. The biggest mark against Francisca was her lack of a boyfriend. Like Rosário, Francisca never came outdoors where the action was. While her mother worked full time in an office, Francisca stayed home and did all the housework, and when she finished the housework she did schoolwork, and when she finished that she got a jump on the next day's tasks. Francisca wasn't even remotely interested in boys. Terry gave that girl a week, and then gave up on her. I was more patient with Rosário, but eventually I admitted defeat, too.

Danny and Nick had made a slew of friends in the very first week—the same kids who had chased us on the first day—and Terry and I adopted them by default. Being that they were boys, and Portuguese, we didn't bother to learn their names, but labeled them by their identifying features: Cardboard Hat, Glasses, Hurt Foot, Big Nose, Sixteen Year Old, Long Hair, Birthmark, and Twenty-one Year Old. Only Mário Joãon had a name, which he stamped on our minds by pointing to his chest and repeating it whenever we were near. *Mário Joãon. Eh! Mário Joãon!* Mário Joãon had light brown hair and green eyes and a shy, devilish smile. At eleven, he smoked cigarettes and drank beer after school and jumped onto the back of the bus with Danny and Nick for free rides to Carcavelos where the stores offered more choices of candy to steal. My crush on Mário Joãon was instantaneous, and

I decided that when the time came, he would be my boyfriend. It would be years yet (boys still verged on gross), but when the time was right he'd be the one. The only obstacle would be language, but naturally he'd learn English. Otherwise, it wouldn't work. One incommunicado friend was enough for one person.

So we are getting something of a settled feeling now. We've rented a completely furnished home with large garden and fenced yard for about $185 (5,000 Escudos) a month. Mart is about two minutes walk from neighborhood shops where she goes daily to buy supplies. We are conveniently close to the mass transportation system (I have no desire whatsoever to drive yet: the people here drive like nitwits!), and medical help is also close. Soon we will begin tutoring lessons for the whole family, and then the children will be put in a Portuguese school. Already they have made numerous friends; the Portuguese are so easy to become friends with! The national police still haven't given us clearance to stay—which certainly makes one aware of his foreign status, though I'm actually not worried. I've had to generalize this sketch a lot, but it will give you a simulacrum next time. Later!

In Jesu et Maria.

Lyle and family

Dad finished writing his letter, and took it and the four carbon copies to the post office in Carcavelos to mail them off to America. Then he took the train to Cascais to register for Portuguese classes. He wanted to get reasonably fluent before Harry came to help set him up in business. In the meantime Mom stocked the kitchen with staples from the small corner shop, and then hit the open-air market in Carcavelos for the rest. At the market, the six of us trailed behind her, keeping close as she moved from vendor to vendor. The open market was not like American shopping centers, where you had your shopping cart, and took food in cellophane packaging out of glass refrigerators. Here, thousands of eyeballs stared at the sky; flabby pink tentacles lolled in steaming heaps; chrome-colored fish with toothy grins wove like ribbons over mountains of ice; and the ground beneath your feet—the runoff of melting ice that glittered with scales—slithered with rainbow-tinted fish oil as it trickled between the cobblestones. Over the open market an unbreathable cloud that no one seemed to notice hung silent and lethal at head-level as so many women touched, eyed, squeezed, and weighed the goods, and then bartered furiously over the value of some small piece of flesh before succumbing to a price. And in the center, bagging up the most repulsive specimens she could find, was Mom, Jennifer on one hip, her pencil and pad in hand.

"*Quanto custa?*" she asked, and scribbled a quick conversion.

"That's it," Terry murmured on our first trip there. "We've lost her."

Early one morning we took the train to Fatima to visit the spot where Our Lady had appeared. Mom and Dad seemed moved, but to me Fatima was a disappointment. I'd expected the place to be just like the scene from the holy cards, but it was nothing like it. The bush was gone. The pasture was gone. The whole area had been leveled by tractors and built over with concrete and stone. Instead of grazing sheep there was a sprawling esplanade, a chapel, and a gigantic basilica. People prayed at the Stations of the Cross—countless numbers of them, some of them walking on their knees over the rough cobblestones, others brushing right by, one eye behind a camera, one eye in a guidebook.

Now that I'd seen Fatima, I was glad we lived in Sassoeiros.

*   *   *

IT WAS OUR first Sunday morning since settling in, and excitement was in the air. Dad was up early to grab the bathroom before everyone else could get it. His shower lasted a long time. Then he ran his electric shaver, brushed his teeth, and pumiced his feet in the bidet even though he knew it was a *butt bath* and not for soaking his corns. Dad always took forever in the bathroom when he wanted to look his best, and today he wanted to look prepared for a Marine Corps inspection. As Terry stood in the hall waiting to brush her hair in front of a mirror, and Danny and Nick hopped up and down holding their pee, Mom shouted from downstairs, *Lyle, the kids need the bathroom!* but Dad didn't answer. He couldn't hear her over the running water and the blasting of church music in his head. He was finally going to be treated to the Tridentine Mass. No heretical modern stuff here. The altar would face the crucifix as altars should. There would be no handshaking for peace, no parishioner participation like an audience on *Let's Make a Deal*. Just the priest performing the unbloody sacrifice the way Christ ordained at the Last Supper in the traditional language of Latin.

"Finally!" Terry shouted, as Dad threw open the door and a hair-gel-shaving-cream-cologne-soap cloud billowed into the hallway. Dad's wavy black hair was slick and shiny and mirrored the light. His face was pink and baby-smooth. His sky-blue eyes were joyful, expectant. "It's all yours!" he said, marching down the hall with a towel around his waist on buoyant, bare feet.

In my room I solemnly removed my one dress that still resided at the back of my carry-on bag. Holding it between my thumb and forefinger, I carried it downstairs to Mom, who was ironing the boys' shirts, and handed it to her with a look that said, *I will wear it for church, but only for church. Otherwise, don't expect to see it on my body at any other time, or in any other place. I don't even want to hear it mentioned.*

Mom glanced at me and frowned. "Oh, stop being so dramatic and put it on the pile," she said. "It's only a *dress*, for Pete's sake."

I sighed loudly, wanting sympathy, but a million sighs wouldn't have moved Mom, who felt that whatever you disliked in this world should be seen as an opportunity for you to offer it up for a soul in Purgatory.

As usual, we didn't eat breakfast but each drank one glass of water to prepare our stomachs for the Holy Eucharist. When we were all ready, clothes ironed, faces scrubbed, nails clipped, and hair combed, Dad closed up the house (he was a fanatic about locking up and double-checking from the outside) and we all filed out the gate. In his corduroy jacket, white shirt, and tie, Dad took the lead. From his years at San Quentin Dad still sauntered like a prison guard, and I admired the exactly balanced performance between the heel-to-toe stride of his rolling legs and the pendulum swing of an invisible nightstick. It was a beautiful walk, lazy but upright, that promised order and harmony in an old-fashioned kind of way. It was the walk of a man who was convinced that he was right about God, about politics, about everything. Danny and Nick, in their white Oxford shirts and blue school pants, danced close on his heels, skipping, pirouetting, exchanging punches, falling back, and racing ahead. Terry, in a tight yellow sweater with her party balloon breasts bouncing ahead of her, walked in isolation like a fashion model enjoying the spotlight on a catwalk. I followed behind her in my flowered suit of armor, scratching my arms and knees where the lace tickled and pulling at the elastic bands pinching my arms. Mom, looking as smart and classy as a foreign diplomat in her bright red polyester dress, took up the rear, holding Vinny's hand and carrying Jennifer on her hip like a duffle bag.

It was a twenty-minute walk up our street to the village church (named São José like our own California town), and because there wasn't the least bit of traffic we took up the whole road. To our right, a tall stone wall stood high before fields that waved gently under the breeze. To our left, the village was awakening and making a commotion. Clotheslines laced along the alleyways like spiderwebs with their catches of bright white insects fluttering in the tunneled breezes. Pockets of odors drifted and collided and fused together: dirt, barbecued sardines, coffee, sheep dung, fresh bread, car exhaust, dog doo, rotting animal corpses. An old car blared its horn and belched out a nose-singeing gallon of black smoke as it rocked by on its way toward Carcavelos.

In the apartment complex where Rosário lived, people rolled up their metal shutters, yelled to each other from their windows, and didn't quiet their babies' crying. Collarless dogs raced out from hidden places and trotted alongside as if they were part of our troop, stopping frequently to chew their tails and scratch their ears and sniff at the sun-baked leftovers from other dogs. Children raced out too, in their underpants or pajamas, and skipped beside us, just for the sake of it, and then split off like satellites to answer their mothers' calls.

Cardboard Hat appeared from around a bend, leaned against a wall, and smirked at Terry, tilting his weird, homemade hat to the side. "*Bom dia, menina bonita . . .*"

Mom looked at Terry. "And who might that young man be?"

Terry looked the other way. "I have a policy of ignoring anyone who thinks a cardboard hat is stylish."

Other boys, Big Nose and Hurt Foot among them, were up ahead, leaning against each other's shoulders and grinning as we marched by. "*Onde vão, americanos?*" they sang out softly. Danny picked up a rock. Mom, whose peripheral vision saw all, said, "Danny, put the rock down. You don't want to start something with these shady characters." Danny pretended to drop the rock, but secretly pocketed it. They were his friends, but there was always room for mischief.

From the distant hill I could hear the church bell clanging its one note, like a buoy bell sounding in the fog, guiding the lost ships to harbor. It was a friendly sound, but as we headed toward it I began to sense something wasn't right. Nobody in the village seemed to be going to mass. Everyone was dressed in casual clothes, hanging out in doorways, smoking and chatting as if it were a Saturday. The old women were sweeping their porches and standing around in housecoats, and the old men were lounging in the shade under olive trees, napping or playing checkers. And then there were the omnipresent boys gathered in their usual clusters, their hands in their pockets, staring at us as we walked by. Though the church bell summoned, nobody paid it the smallest mind.

Catching up to Dad, I thought I should announce the obvious. "Hey, Dad! No one's going to church."

Dad didn't seem concerned, but it was hard to tell. "There are two masses every Sunday," he said patly. "Some people prefer to go in the afternoon."

Up ahead stood the Igreja de São José, a simple, whitewashed structure with clear windows and a short belltower. Shuffling in through the open front door, we stood in a bunch looking for the holy water font to bless ourselves. There was no font, so we blessed ourselves with dry fingers. Mom, Terry, and I placed our mantillas on our heads and we filed into the nave.

My first impression on entering was that we were early. Maybe by hours. Chatter and laughter came from some people who were moving around the room. There were no burning candles. No one was kneeling at the communion rail to say the rosary. No last-minute confessions were being heard. The atmosphere was open, airy, and well lit, like a meeting hall. Tall banners decorated with white doves and the words *Aleluia*, *Paz*, and *Alegria* hung from open beams. Halleluiah? Peace? Joy? Those were Protestant sentiments. My second impression on entering was that this must be a Protestant church. *Did anyone check the sign out front?* The altar was a plain-looking table with a plain white tablecloth and nothing else standing near the center of the room. The cross hung alone in the chancel, almost forgotten. It was tall, smooth, and wooden, and there was no Christ crucified on it. Like a Protestant cross, it was as clean and vacant as a brand-new piece of Scandinavian furniture. My eyes darted to the right and left. I saw that there were no votive candles, no Stations of the Cross, no communion rail. The walls bore acoustic panels. The floor was covered with linoleum. There was no balcony, no baptismal font, no shrines. The hanging lights were fluorescent. There were potted plants instead of cut flowers. This was what Dad called a "worship space." It was not a church. I looked at Terry. Her face said, *Uh-oh*.

Several city-style people milled about and talked. It was easy to recognize them for what they were: game-show Catholics. Many of the women wore pants, and none wore head scarves. The men looked dressed for a picnic, in sandals, jeans, and casual shirts. There were few old people, and what old people there were didn't wear black, they wore yellow, beige, orange, lime-green, and pink. Everyone glanced at us with welcoming smiles and mild curiosity. And they continued to talk as if there were no particular reason to observe a reverent silence in the church.

My thoughts stumbled on clubbed feet. *This doesn't seem like the kind of church where the traditional Tridentine Mass unchanged for five hundred years is celebrated*. I looked to Dad for his take on it, but Dad was looking at Mom, and Mom was ogling the banners. I looked at Terry, who side-glanced me, her jaw askew, as if paused midway through chewing a piece of gum, and then I looked at Danny and Nick, who stood awkwardly, only their eyes moving. So it wasn't just me. It was everyone.

As if a timer went off, Mom stopped ogling the banners and turned to Dad, but now Dad couldn't bear to meet her expressive eyes and looked away. He seemed to not want to consult with Mom right now, as if there were no time for discussion or argument. He seemed to want to sit down and figure out exactly what was going on, and give the matter some careful thought. So he walked to a polished pew and sat. And one by one we all slid into the pew after him, and faced the table and the abandoned cross in the distance.

I could see Dad was confounded beyond belief, and Mom, too, and in fact I was too, although in a strange way I wanted to accept what was, and even get into the spirit of this boldly progressive church. I wanted to say to Dad, *Hey! It's a matter of taste. People out here in the countryside probably like air conditioning and fluorescent lighting. Maybe it means less upkeep. And why should Jesus care if his dead body isn't hanging right there on the Cross? We all know he was crucified and buried and rose again. And who cares if there are banners? Banners have helpful messages of hope. People need that kind of thing. Uplifting messages are cool.* The feelings welled up, and I wanted to believe in them, but the speech dammed up behind my tonsils. I knew I couldn't fight for this church. The Igreja de São José was a bomb. A catastrophe. The Igreja de São José was Vatican II. There was no way to defend it. We weren't going to last two minutes here.

A man in an oversized sweater walked in carrying a guitar and everyone hailed him and he hailed everyone back and sat down and started to tune his guitar, but Mom and Dad didn't get up and leave. They stared blankly at the man and his guitar, as if he were a man in a dream they'd once had. Again the feelings welled up, and

I wanted to say, *Hey, it's just a guitar. Guitars can play the same notes as pipe organs, can't they?* But I didn't. Then a lady sat beside the musician, and warmed up her voice with a song that had *amor* in it. I didn't know any Catholic songs with *amor* in them, but I wanted to point out that love could be worth singing about. Couldn't it?

As we all watched the guitarist, the priest—or what seemed to be the priest—entered breezily from a side door. He was dressed in a light blue gown with flowing sleeves and greeted all the churchcomers with a caring smile and a soft brown hand. *Bom dia. Bom dia. Bom dia. Como é você?* Everyone said aloud that they were doing fine, and the priest said he was doing fine, too, and told a funny story about something that had happened to him *esta manhã*, making everyone laugh, and then he surveyed the room and spotted us in the back pew: *os americanos*. The foreigners. The freaks. The smile stayed locked on his face. What did he think? We wore scarves. We were conservatively dressed. Did he nail us for traditionalists? Did he know about the anti-revolutionary international?

The priest walked toward us with his teeth gleaming and his hand outstretched. Almost protectively I wanted to warn the priest that we didn't give handshakes in church. We waited until the mass was over and gave them outside. But the priest was quick. His hand whipped out of his sleeve and clasped ours quicker than a lasso. I took his grip and smiled and said *Bom dia* as he made the rounds. When he got to Dad, I held my breath. To my surprise, Dad lifted his hand and offered it to the priest. Mom did, too. And both of them said *Bom dia* just as they were supposed to. I was relieved. For a second I'd envisioned Dad getting him into an armlock and giving him the *Miranda* rights. But Dad just seemed confused. As the priest moved around the room making witty comments and humming to the song with *amor* in it, Dad's shoulders started to slump and his face began to sag. The baby-pink freshness left his face. Mom's dimple cut deep. Taking her rosary from her purse, she began to pray.

When all the socializing was done and the guitar was tuned up and the people had settled into their pews, the priest walked straight to the table, stood facing the congregation with his back to the bare cross, opened a thick white book, spread his hands outward, and began to pray in Portuguese into the open air over our heads.

And the mass had begun—or seemed to have begun, but it was hard to tell. In this mass—if it was a mass—the prayers were chatty-sounding and upbeat, and there was plenty of eye contact between the priest and the people as if to mutually reassure each other that things were going well. In this mass, the priest did everything himself without the help of altar boys. Not that there was much to do. There were no thuribles to swing, no silver bells to ring, no towels and fingerbowls for washing hands. Only some singsongy prayers and blessings, with nothing complicated thrown in to make you think. It was like a poor reproduction of a good play: I recognized the storyline, but many of the details were missing. And with every lost detail, the mass seemed whittled down into a kind of billboard announcement of the performance.

Dad seemed to be holding out. Minutes ticked by. I chanced a peek at him. He looked like a block of wood, not breathing, blinking, or praying. His face was stiff and pale, his eyes rounded and hypnotized. I grew fearful of what was building up inside him. Or dying inside him. Mom was holding out, too. She too was rock-still, staring with fixed, lidless eyes at the empty cross, a stone facing a piece of wood. Heat and vibration generated through my body. Dread, fear, regret, mortification stepping over each other to be on top. What now? Dad looked as if his joy had been doused forever. Would he be like that—a fixed, hardened, pulse-dead statue—from now on? I looked at Terry. Only her eyes moved, and their rounding arch told me her thoughts on the matter. *What a disaster!*

When it came time for the consecration, Dad suddenly woke out of his reverie. With a jolt, he stood up. His lips were pressed together and rimmed in white. His temples were veined and his eyes were glittering. He looked like he was about ready to cry, or kill someone, or both. The priest paused and looked up. Some of the people turned to look. Dad stood shaking for a minute. Mom put her hand on his forearm. It was like the moment in one of our favorite films, *High Noon*, when Grace Kelly says, "Don't try to be a hero," and Gary Cooper says, "I'm not trying to be a hero. If you think I like this, you're crazy." Dad looked up Main Street and turned away. Then Mom picked up Jennifer, took Vinny's hand, and we all followed him out of the church.

Outside, the world was behaving as usual. The sun was shining, dogs were barking, children were playing. But the world seemed different. It had changed when we weren't looking. Or maybe we had changed when the world wasn't looking. Or maybe we'd been looking so hard at the world we couldn't see what was right in front of our noses. It was hard to tell. All I knew was that we had believed in something that had turned out not to exist. We'd come all this way for a mass that wasn't here. It was strange to be wrong about something that had seemed so right. And how wrong we'd been! We couldn't have been *more* wrong. There was something decidedly unnerving about being *that* wrong.

I could feel shock waves of distress generating through Mom and Dad as we followed them back home. There could be no doubt about the size of this tragedy. No one spoke. I had the feeling no one would speak for a long time. Maybe ever again. I wanted to speak. I had a lot of questions. Like, what did this mean for us? And what would we do now? Would we go on a parish hunt? Would we stop going to mass altogether? Would we go back to the States? Back to St. Mary's? Compared to this church, St. Mary's wasn't so modern after all.

After several minutes Dad did speak. He said, "The Catholic Church is dead."

His voice had the weight of sand, and Mom had only two hands to catch it when what she needed was a bucket. "Now, just a minute," she said. "Don't be so drastic. There are other churches. Other parishes. We just have to look elsewhere. Sérgio told me about a conservative church in Carcavelos: the Igreja de Nossa Senhora dos Remédios . . . We should go check it out. We should see for ourselves if . . ." Her voice trailed off and the sand slipped through.

Dad shook his head. "I will never step foot in a Catholic church again."

Walking home, I pondered this declaration of Dad's and it brought up more questions. Did that mean we were no longer Catholics? Did that mean we were apostates? Would we be excommunicated? There was an unexpected boon to this. If we never entered another church, that meant no more dresses. When we got home I could take off this horrendous garment and stuff it into my carry-on suitcase, and then remove my nylon slip with its scratchy seams and my church shoes with their slippery half-inch heels and stuff those in with it. Then I could shove the suitcase deep under my bed all the way to the back and forget it was there, and if Mom told me I had to wear a dress for something I would be able to say, *I don't have a dress*, and it would be true. From this day forth I could dress in jeans and T-shirts. I could take deep breaths of air and expand my rib cage without restriction and run with my legs and arms outstretched and do cartwheels without baring my underpants. I was sorry for Mom and Dad, but at the same time I wanted to skip and swing my arms and let the joy of liberation lift me off the ground.

Reaching the house, we coagulated on the porch while Dad searched every pocket for his key and unlocked the front door. Inside, he took off his suit jacket and hung it on the coat tree with such a look of finality it seemed as if he too had no more use for such a formal piece of clothing, walked heavily up the stairs into his room, closed the shutters, and lay on his bed. The rest of us scattered like quail to different parts of the house, instinctively putting space between ourselves and potential firepower.

The only movement in the house came from Mom, who went straight to the washboard and began to scrub the heaping pile of dirty clothes, wet sheets, and diapers. Although Sunday was a day of rest, on this Sunday there seemed to be an awful lot of work to be done. When she finished scrubbing the laundry, she filled the kitchen sink with bubbly water and scrubbed the dishes. Then she scrubbed the kitchen floor, the countertop, the stovetop, and the tabletop, and then hauled the area rugs out to the porch and beat them each with the grass broom, and swept the wooden floors and stairway with the same grass broom. Then she scoured the bathroom with the Ajax cleanser she brought from America and wiped down the shutters with ammonia water, and polished the windows, and swept the front porch. And never once did she complain that Dad was lying in bed with a dark T-shirt over his eyes, not even noticing we had the cleanest house in Sassoeiros.

8

fields and dreams

THE WIND IS bulldozing off the sea. Shaking the metal shutters, lifting layers of dust off the road, and powdering the face of the sun. The high grasses of the fields are bowing like dancers to a whistling audience. They exhale as they bend, a million strands in concert, and inhale again as they stand upright. Then they sway together softly, side to side, whip into a crest, and flatten down again in their swan lake dance.

Demons are howling through the open windows, their voices a deep, threatening *aaaaaaah* sound. It is the sound of doom, the sound of the end of the world. Jennifer is rocking on her hands and knees, banging her forehead against the headboard of her crib. *Wham, Mississippi, wham, Mississippi*. Vinny is sitting at the bottom of the stairs with his tongue pointed far out, hoping for a taste of a grape- or a lemon-flavored demon as it flies by. His eyes sparkle with anticipation, a kind of religious ecstasy. Danny and Nick are out on the road whooping and hollering as they throw lemongrass into the air and watch the wind ferry it into space.

I am pacing the house. Portugal betrayed Our Lady of Fatima. It was supposed to stay true to the dogma of faith and didn't. And now Portugal is the first to get it. And this is how it starts: with a giant wind. Soon the cobblestones will loosen and roll like dice, and the boulders in the dikes will pop out and catapult like asteroids through the air smashing into windows, cars, and people. The houses will uproot and tumble roof over floor, flinging furniture and appliances out their doors and windows. The sheep farm will split like a watermelon and the sheep will be sucked out of their barn straight into the sky and dropped far out at sea. The barn's moldy roof tiles will blow away like confetti in all directions, and the pebbles, brick, and mortar will spray like shrapnel into the horses, wagons, haystacks, and beyond, across the endless miles of fields.

Mom and Dad are in their bedroom with the door closed. Dad is talking so loud he isn't aware that demons are slamming the shutters against the house and *aaaaaahing* up the stairwell, and filling every corner and crevice like a swarm of bees about to fly the house away. I go upstairs to tell him he can stop yelling at Mom because the Chastisement has started, but when I get to the door, I pause. The pitch of Dad's voice is like the muscular whine from an engine with a loose generator belt as it strains on a slow uphill climb. He is talking about the Church, of course. Dad seems to think that if he explains Vatican II to Mom one more time, it'll all make sense, or maybe he thinks Mom will fix what's wrong since Mom is so good at fixing things—*and when Archbishop Bugnini rewrote the Mass, he created a tank of destruction and pulled off the most significant professional crime in history next to the Crucifixion.* Mom is making her usual *M-hmmm, I know* sound, but Dad doesn't hear it. He talks over her, putting all his horsepower into his hill. *So wouldn't you think Paul VI would rescind the* Novus Ordo *and reverse his heretical position? On the contrary. He's reinforcing it. And what are the neo-Catholics doing about it? Not a bloody dang thing. It's incomprehensible!* I hate to interrupt Dad when he's on a train of thought and working so hard to explain to Mom what she needs to know, but I also worry that if he doesn't shut off and cool down the pistons will seize, and so I tap gently on the glass.

"Dad?"

In a moment Mom opens the door, and her face is flushed pink, making her freckles dark. "Not now, Ronnie. Your father and I are talking."

"But, Mom . . ."

"Not *now*." She closes the door.

I know better than to knock again, so I clamber downstairs two steps at a time and part the lace curtains in the front window to watch the world fall apart. Danny and Nick have taken shelter in the house under construction. I can see them hiding behind the stack of bricks and throwing dirt clods at the wind. That's when Terry strolls up and stands beside me.

"Wow," she says, parting the old lace. "It sure is windy today. Want to go into the fields?"

I stare at her, bug-eyed and blinking.

"What? You were thinking it's the Chastisement, weren't you?" She huffs like Morris the Cat on the 9 Lives commercial who wishes his owner weren't so idiotic.

"No."

"Liar."

"I *wasn't*."

I let the curtains fall closed, feeling a little ashamed but mainly disappointed. A minute ago Portugal was the first to get hit by the Holy Chastisement, with the winds giving way to torrential rains and earthquakes and asteroids, and it would have been exciting and dangerous at the same time and Dad would have been able to stop griping about the Church and be thankful that soon Our Lady's Immaculate Heart would triumph. But one word from Terry and the *aaaaaah* sound isn't a pack of demons. It's just a hard wind squeezing through a dozen small spaces around the house. Soon it will die down and the old ladies will come out of their houses and sweep away the leaves and dirt and shake the dust out of their laundry.

"So are you coming? Or are you chicken?"

"I'm coming. I'm coming."

Upstairs, Mom has left the bedroom to stop Jennifer from her head-banging and Dad is back to tapping on the Underwood, so I pull on my blue stocking cap and hunch into the wind as we head through the fields at a slow trot. Ahead of me, Terry is a blur of whipping hair and fluttering skirts and flapping shawls and I believe that if she only gathers her yards together she can catch the wind and fly into the sky like a kite, and with this in mind I stay close on her heels in case I have to grab hold of a tassel from her shawl. Terry knows these fields better than I do. And she knows the surrounding fields, and the little villages beyond them. She's told me about horse corrals where the horses do tricks, and a house being built by dwarves, and wells that you can walk down inside, and castles that are still inhabitable. It is always an adventure being with Terry, and as much as I hate her I also admire her. Bookish Terry. Artistic Terry. Terry the cook, the storyteller, the actress, the beauty. She is running with the wind and taking me somewhere I've never been.

You can run for miles along the fields without stopping and end up at the sea. That could be her plan. If the fields are whipping and whirling and lashing like this, what will the sea be doing? It will be white with peaks and vales like spirited whipping cream. It might stir up a sunken ship from its depths and spit it onto the shore. "There are hundreds of sunken pirate ships off the coast of Portugal," Terry said once. "And occasionally they wash up. And if you're the first person to discover it, you get to keep all the treasures." I can picture the handfuls of pearls and silver goblets we'll find, and the swords and shields and helmets and chain mail. I set my heart on this pirate ship. If anyone can find it, Terry can, and when she does we'll be rich.

Miles down the narrow dirt path we come to a wall and the worn-away carcass of a castle. For weeks we've stared at the silhouette of this castle from our front window and imagined the queen who once lived there. Terry said it was a black queen who performed black masses in her castle and was feared by everyone in Portugal. The queen had lived well past a hundred and had died alone in her castle and nobody came to bury her except the crows, and the crows covered her in grass, and she rotted and sunk into the earth. And when the castle roof decayed and caved in on top of her, it was the only gravestone she had, and there she lies to this day in her own castle-grave that nobody goes near. Where Terry got all her information I don't know and don't care because here is the whole structure standing before us, a giant, crusty hulk of twelfth-century decay, and it's as gruesome and haunted as I'd expected. As we stand before it, panting hard, our hearts beating, our mouths open, the winds wail through the gaps between the stones and I imagine all the dark evil that is churning around inside the grassy center of this open-topped shell.

"Come on!" Terry turns away from the castle, swims through the taller-than-us grass toward the center of the field, and lies down, spread-eagle, her hair, blouse, and skirt fanning out around her. I follow her and lie down beside her, my arms and legs outstretched.

We lie there a long time looking up at the mile-tall grasses waving their tips against the bright blue cloudless sky. After a while, Terry closes her eyes and I do too. I must behave exactly like her if I want to experience whatever magic she is conjuring up.

"Stop copying me."

"I'm not copying you."

"Yes you are."

"Am not."

"What-*ever*."

The air down here is warm and pungent with the smell of wet earth and crushed vegetation, and the grasses are violently hissing walls of green. I'd like to stay here on the moist ground and talk about the black queen and her crows and the dark evil that is churning away in the castle, but Terry says, "Let's make a pattern that can be visible from the sky. You go that way and I'll go this way." And she begins to roll over the grass, leaving a trampled trail behind her, and I roll the opposite direction, creating a swath of flat green. Then we come back together and roll again, making an *X*.

"Let's climb to the top of the castle and see it from above," Terry says, and heads toward the crumbling behemoth.

I hesitate. Not because the castle is actively collapsing before our eyes, with dust and small pebbles blowing off and clattering down the rough surface. But because of the dark evil. This is not like the castle at Miniature Golfland on Blossom Hill Road back in San Jose, which is made of hard plastic and looks like a fairy-tale castle. This is the real thing. This castle contains the birth, death, pain, murder, dreams, marriages, love, hatred, curses, and blessings of many, many dead people. It isn't a structure you tap a golf ball into when the bridge lowers over the moat. It is a living thing, with likes and dislikes, and I don't imagine it will take kindly to us climbing it at this moment when it is rapidly diminishing under the bulldozing wind.

"What's wrong? Scared?"

"Are you kidding? *No*."

Terry is halfway up and I'm about to miss out on the point of our adventure. So I begin a careful ascent, but it's a difficult climb: the boulders shift under my weight, and my leather-soled school shoes are as slick as glass slippers on ice. Sandy pebbles drop from every surface. The wind drags at my back and I have to pull my body close, like the lightning lizards that grip sideways to the stone walls, or I'll be lassoed by the wind and chucked off. Terry is already at the top, and I'm ashamed by this. Terry is heavier all around and shouldn't even be up there.

"Come on, slowpoke!" she shouts down to me. "What's taking you so long? You may be tetherball champion at St. Mary's, but you sure are a rotten climber."

When I reach the top I can't bear to look down, and I settle onto a flat portion of the top like a horse rider. Laughing at me, Terry reaches over and yanks off my hat and throws it in the air, and it takes a whirly-bird flight to the next field. *Oh man!* I shout. I can't stand not having my hat. My hair swirls in my face, blinding me, and I feel lightweight and vulnerable. *Now go get it*, I say. She says, *Get it yourself*. But I don't move because I don't want to slither down that vertical surface and take my chances with the wind, so I sit where I am and shield my eyes in the crook of my arm as my hair lashes wildly in the wind.

That's when Terry begins to show signs of insanity. Standing up, she teeters under the force of the wind and shouts loudly into it as if she were on a stage in the middle of a Greek production. "I'm the Black Queen of the Castle and I've returned from the Underworld to have my revenge on the world!"

I grip the wall with my knees as the wind wraps around my waist and pulls with all its might, trying to fling me into outer space. I feel slightly sick when I look down, so instead I squint out at the wide-open fields with their lashing grasses and feel like we are as high as the moon and wonder how we'll ever get down.

Terry points to the giant X we made in the field. "There is my signal. Let the world know that I am back and boy am I *mad!*"

I think that if this is Terry's idea of an adventure, then she's crazy and I was duped, and now I want to go home. Besides, the way she is standing in the wind with her skirts and hair flapping, I'm afraid she's going to become airborne and meet her death somewhere in the next parish, and I don't want to be the one to have to explain it to Mom.

I shout, "I'm taking off my shoes and going down."

That's when I lean over to pull off my shoes, and the stone under my right hand gives way after seven centuries of holding fast, and my hand follows it into space, and my body dives after my hand, and my legs trail behind my body. And now I am looking upward, not at the sky but at the ground, which is lumpy with boulders big and small and blowing dust and weeds. And I zoom through space, watching the earth come fast, and the trip takes a strangely long time but comes to an abrupt end when my face smashes into a boulder, and then my chest, and then my legs. And my body deflates like a popped ball and I can hear my voice leaking out of me, little by little, until it is less than a squeak. And I don't inhale. I am solid. Airless. Dying. My brain seizes on that word. *Dying.* Incredible. *Death.* My thoughts reach for instructions, but are confined to the amazement of this moment, the tragedy of it, the fleeting end so quickly approaching.

Above me Terry is screaming.

"Help! Help! Heeeeeeeeelp! SOS! *Somebody!*"

I can't breathe and I am dying on my face. A dimming light in my brain darkens to gray and then to black. I am asleep, or maybe I am dead, but then I am neither. The black lifts to gray, and now to bright white, and I am floating in soft, pillowy arms with the glare of the sun in my face, and Terry is jabbering from the direction of my feet as I glide through the air across the fields, the furious wind swirling outside the fortress of my saviour.

"I *told* her not to do it, but she wouldn't listen," Terry is saying. "My sister is so dumb, I swear. This is *so typical*."

A head fills the sky like a moon eclipsing the sun. A woman's voice vibrates through my bones, thrums in my marrow. *Calma. Calma.* The warm flesh blocks the onslaught of the wind. Can this be a dream? Has the Virgin Mary come to carry me to heaven?

She knocks at the door of our house. Mom opens the door and sees me and says, "Oh, no. What happened?"

The lady says, *"Ela está gravemente ferida."*

Mom takes me in her muscular arms and speaks the few polite words she knows in Portuguese to the Virgin in Black—*"Obrigada, Senhora. Muito obrigada"*—and carries me up and up, not to heaven but to my own bedroom, where she lays me onto my bed.

Now Terry is jabbering to Mom—"but she wouldn't listen. She's *so dumb*. She fell from the *very top*."

I'm taking tiny mouse breaths and I can't feel my face. I'm lying on my bed, and I can't breathe enough to speak. There is a cluster of eyes staring at me. Danny and Nick are trying to get close to my face, hoping to see an exposed bone. Mom is dabbing cotton balls on my flat rib cage. The cotton balls are scarlet. Dad walks in and sucks his head back like a turtle.

"Holy mackerel! What happened to Ronnie? Did she break her nose?"

As a boxer, Dad knows all about broken noses.

A tear trembles at the corner of each eye, but I can't take a deep enough breath to sigh or let out a choke or tell him I almost died and it's only by a miracle that I'm here.

Mom calls the doctor and he comes and puts his cold stethoscope on my bare chest and listens. He says "breathe" in English, and I try, but my white, nearly transparent skin and pale pink nipples hardly rise over my tiny mouse breath. The doctor frowns. His eyes trail around my fleabites and I detect the smallest of smiles.

He talks to Mom and Dad in warped English.

"I'm now shoor how bad eet ees weethowt . . . how do you say . . . *os raios* . . ."

"X ray?"

"Yes . . . But I think one or two—reebs . . . they are fractured. And da nose, ees broken. But ees okay. There's nowthing for to feex such theengs. Your dowter must stay een bed. Don move around too much. For da pain. You know."

"How long do fractured ribs take to heal?" Mom asks.

"Ees hard to say. She weel know. The pain weel let her know, I am shoor. Just tell her, *stay cool*—like you say een America."

Then the doctor is gone, and now that I'm not dying anymore things go back to normal.

"I believe you have some prayers of thanks to say," Mom says, handing me my rosary, but somehow I don't feel like praying. I look up at Terry, who stands over my bed looking down on me.

"Wanna see your face?" she asks. I nod, and she goes to the bathroom and returns with a hand mirror and steadies it for my gaze. "I really hope, for your sake, it isn't permanent . . . But it doesn't look good."

I fall silent with shock. It isn't the two black donuts with slits for eyeholes and the baboon-pink nose that bothers me. It's the bright

rainbow of purples, greens, and yellows that rim my eyes like the
rings around Saturn. I finally locate my voice.

"Gross." My voice is hardly a whisper.

"Puke city, huh?"

"I'm gonna puke my *guts* out."

"I feel like spewing right now."

"Look at my *face*."

"Thoroughly horrific to an extraordinary degree."

"Intensely putrefying."

"You are a ghastly sight of exceptional proportions."

"I can't stand myself."

"I can't stand to be your sister."

"Take the mirror."

"Happily."

Terry takes the mirror and returns it to the bathroom.

Even if my two black eyes aren't permanent, it'll be ages before
I can leave the house. For weeks I'll lie flat in bed, unable to yawn,
laugh, cough, sneeze, take a deep breath, or sit up. Outside, life
will go on without me. The sheep will commute past the house
every morning, their white backs bouncing against the green, their
dainty hooves ballet-stepping along the cobblestones as the sheepman shouts and Tracy the dog yips. Cardboard Hat will whistle
through his fingers from the covered bus stop, signaling that a
game of marbles is about to start. Mário Joãon and Hurt Foot will
loiter on the street with cigarettes hanging from their lips waiting
for Danny to sprint out the door with a stolen handful of Mom's
chocolate chip cookies, and Sixteen Year Old and Long Hair will
walk slowly by the house hoping Terry will notice how good-
looking they are.

Every hour in bed feels like an hour lost. I don't know what is worse, the deprivation of movement or the lack of company. Everyone is busy doing something, and no one seems to remember that I'm lying flat on my back with nothing to do but scratch my fleabites and take tiny mouse breaths and listen to the activities of the house. Downstairs Mom moves here, there, and everywhere, making a racket wherever she goes because cleaning a house is a noisy business, and I wish she would come and sit next to me and smile that sad-loving smile that says, *If it isn't one thing with you it's another.* Down the hall Jennifer bangs her head in perfect rhythm against her crib. Danny and Nick seem to be in every room at once, running, bouncing, skidding, leaping, and—when they cross paths—fighting, while Mom yells at them from different parts of the house, *Now you boys stop your horsing around right this minute and go outside and play!* Terry is always quiet: I never know if she is reading in some hidden place in the house or off on one of her mysterious adventures beyond the fields. Dad is in his bedroom tapping away on his Underwood. He is writing a book about his philosophy, and by the sounds of it it's going to be a tiresome book.

"What do ya think of this, Mart?" he says, and follows her around narrating his latest chapter. I catch morsels through the noise of housework and siblings:

Reflection . . . Most people are oblivious to the need for reflection . . . Why should they care about reflection? The modern world provides something better. It gives them pictures on the tube and speeded up music and amusement parks with dizzying rides, and sensationalized stories in the daily news. And on Sunday, the same, because of the new mass. Loudness. Loud noises from priests standing behind tables deliberately shouting like Bible thumping Protestant preachers. Loud conversations right inside the church both before and after the new loud mass, making individual prayer and reflection impossible. Then, on Monday, back to work pumped up with hyper-tripe instead of reflection. When the Church took on the ways of the world at Vatican II to eliminate reflection, the ending can only be what Fatima predicted.

"Not bad," Mom says. "But I'm not the literary type. You should ask Terry what she thinks."

At night, Dad turns on the television and watches the news. When the din of gunfire and protest marches blasts out from behind the drone of the Portuguese commentators, I know the news is about America. Dad watches the pictures and relays to Mom what seems to be going on.

"It's about the Hanoi bombings. Violence is breaking out all over the place. Fires, flag burnings, arrests. The pope denounced the bombing. He should pair up with Jane Fonda. They'd make a good couple."

"Looks like the peace accord is a go. Peace with honor, Nixon says. What d'ya think, Mart? Have we lost to the commies with honor?"

"LBJ is dead. Heart failure."

"The first POWs touched down."

"Six point five earthquake in Nicaragua destroyed Managua and killed about ten thousand people. And that's nothing compared to what's coming. The world had better sit up and take notice."

"The Supreme Court made abortion legal. Of all the sins mankind commits, killing babies is one that cries out to heaven for vengeance."

My only visitor is Vinny, who gets up from his nap and wanders into my room, puffy-faced from sleep, and stands by my bed looking at me from behind thick glasses with his green eyes bouncing left and right.

"Hi, Bean Bag," I say with my gentlest voice so he knows it's me behind my monster mask, and I wonder if from his point of view I'm the one who is bouncing.

Vinny's frown is serious and sympathetic. He blinks slowly and refocuses his bouncing eyes. Because of his mental disability his face is different from everyone's in the family, which always makes me stare at him longer, and with loving fascination. Finally he says with his stopped-up voice that seems to lack air, "You hab a hurt?" His lips are so thick and his teeth are so small he can't make the V sound.

"A little one. But I'm getting better."

He is silent as he thinks, and doesn't put out his tongue to taste the problem. He doesn't like injuries. He doesn't like anyone feeling pain. It makes him frown and blink slowly, contemplating. I give him a smile to reassure him that I'm okay, and he studies my smile, wanting it to be true.

"Give me five," I say. And he does.

AFTER TWO WEEKS, when my eyes are the yellow and brown colors of an overripe banana, Mom tells us to lay out clean clothes for the next day.

"Why?"

"Lessons start tomorrow."

"But Mom! I can't go out looking like this!" I say.

"Oh don't be silly, you look just fine. No one will notice a thing. Anyway, the doctor says it's time for you to get up and move around."

"But Mom, I *can't*."

"You can and you will. Mrs. Mendoza is expecting you."

With my stocking cap pulled to my eyebrows, my hair combed close around my face, and my hands in my pockets, I ignore Terry's snickers as we all board the bus to Oeiras the next morning. On a street named after a Marxist, Avenida Salvador Allende (Dad called the name a slap in the face of Catholics), we knock at the door of a house and a distinguished-looking older woman wearing an apron answers the door.

Her eyes land on me. "Poor child!" she says. "You have a frightening face. Please come inside."

"Ha!" Terry says. "Frightening is an understatement."

"Why don't you put on your *glasses*, four-eyes?"

Our teacher leads us to a room with lace curtains and a ticking clock, and gestures for us to sit where pencils and paper have been prepared for us on a table. Taking a seat, Terry instantly starts sketching a galloping horse and Danny makes the preliminary folds for a paper airplane.

"Children! The paper is for *work*, not *play*."

The discipline of schoolwork seems slightly ridiculous and irrelevant, but silence settles over us as we wait for instructions, which are slow in coming. First we are given coffee and plates of cookies and told to enjoy them. When we are finished, Mrs. Mendoza sits at the head of the table and looks at each of us with regal quietude.

"Repeat after me: *O meu tio, a minha tia*. My uncle, my aunt."

"*O meu tio, a minha tia*. My uncle, my aunt."

As if yanked by an invisible hand, Danny falls on the floor and the chair falls on top of him and Nick and I snicker. "What a dumbhead you are," I say. Danny says, "Oh yeah? Well, you're even dumber." I say, "At least I don't fall out of my chair." Mrs. Mendoza quietly waits for Danny to return to his seat and the arguing to stop before she continues.

"Repeat after me: *O meu sobrinho, a minha sobrinha*. My nephew, my niece."

"*O meu sobrinho, a minha sobrinha*. My nephew, my niece."

Danny falls off his chair again, taking the pencil and paper with him, and Mrs. Mendoza again waits for him to reestablish order. When he's seated, she says, "Young man. We must sit *still* during our lessons."

Danny folds his hands on the table in front of him. "Sorry," he says.

Terry says, "You are *such* an imbecile."

"Repeat after me: *O meu marido, a minha mulher*. My husband, my wife."

"*O meu marido, a minha mulher*. My husband, my wife."

"Now let us write down what we have learned."

Danny picks up his pencil with the intention to write, but breaks his pencil tip and snatches Nick's pencil from him. Nick says, *Hey*! and grabs for it, and they both fall on the floor. As Mrs. Mendoza is sharpening a new pencil, Danny knocks a small plant off its stand. Mrs. Mendoza swings on him, now, frowning. "I must warn you," she says, showing the first signs of temper. "I spank."

Danny's eyes bug with horror. Terry glares at him. "Can you be any *more* obnoxious?"

Mrs. Mendoza tolerates us for five straight hours, and then sends us home, and I don't know who is the more relieved to part ways. But she's been paid in advance for the month, and so the tutoring continues. We rarely do our memorization. We never do our written exercises. Some days we show up hours late. Some days we come barefooted with beach sand between our toes. Some days we don't come at all. No one tattles. Not even Mrs. Mendoza. She seems to understand.

There is simply no room in our lives for tutoring.

There is barely enough room to eat and sleep.

Life is a current. It moves with you and around you. You have to go with it or drown. It takes strength. Talent. Ingenuity, even. It takes learning how to swim without gills (that's like flying without wings), which means operating without the proper equipment. Such as words. In Portugal, you are deaf and dumb in a world that speaks and hears. You are like an animal behaving like a human. Animals rely on instinct to survive. They have a sixth sense for danger. They read the signs. You have to read the signs too. Your friends are not always your friends. Sometimes they're your predators. It helps to know the difference. When you hear *merda* or *cabrão* or *caralho*, you have to know the chase is on and zip through the tall grasses like a flea through a dog's coat.

When you're in the current, you've got to keep your head up and your eyes and ears open. That means knowing the exact length of the chain that stops the lone ram in the field by the farm from mauling you. Miscalculate by an inch and you'll be rammed and hoofed into bloody burger meat. It means being stealthier and smarter than the evil white dog that guards the farm, to circle the outside, ignore the sharkish fangs snapping in a feverish fury, and always, *always* have something to tempt him with—even something fake, like a rock—which you should throw in the opposite direction. Keeping your head up requires that you have excellent equilibrium when walking above the bullpen, and no fear of falling in. That's trickier than it sounds. Look down at the bull and you *will* fall in, and there's no getting out of it, you *must* look down at the bull. You must also have a hawkish radar that detects all incoming stray dogs. The big black ones are the nastiest, but even the small ones can rip you to pieces.

In the current you get to know the smell of lanolin—kind of a cross between candlewax, vegetable shortening, and a hamper full of dirty sheets. You also get to know the taste of sheep's milk straight out of the teat, and how it feels when it's shot in your eye. Fresh sheep's dung has the luscious texture of butter, and the trapped air of fifty sheep in a barn is probably flammable. Fleas own the surface they land on. Twenty-eight have claimed my legs—countless more the rest of me. Fleabites can put you into a frenzy of scratching. The best antidote to a fleabite is a stiff hairbrush. Rub the bristles hard over the bite in a circular motion until the bite bleeds. Then spray the area with Final Net hairspray. When the stinging stops, rinse with cold water. Pat dry.

In the current you never stagnate. There are no routines, duties, schedules, or expectations. There is no Mrs. Mendoza (she quit the day she earned out the month). There is no church, no sacraments, no penance, no rosary, no school, no homework, no grades. In the current there are only sensations, colors, light, shadows, joy.

My parents don't swim with the current. They cling to what doesn't move, hanging on for dear life. They don't feel the bubbly rapids of joy beneath them. They don't see the light. They see things in black and white. They sit at the dining-room table after we've all gone to bed and stare at numbers on a page. Dad blames Mom for the unsatisfactory numbers. "Don't be ridiculous," Mom says. "We can't get a car. We're paying five thousand escudos a month in rent." Dad does a quick calculation. "That's a hundred and eighty-five dollars. We can't afford that much." Mom says, "Short of moving to a smaller house, we have no choice." Dad says, "If we don't shave our bills in half, we'll be out of money in two months." Mom blames Dad. "I've already cut the bills in half. The only thing left to cut is wine and cigarettes." Dad says, "Well, you might as well cut off my head. I can't live without wine and cigarettes." Mom says, "Well then, what are we going to do?" Dad shouts: "I don't know! Harry has gone AWOL on me. He was supposed to *fund* this adventure! I'm at my wits' end."

In a black and white world, black spells betrayal on the white clean surface. The betrayal by the Vatican of the Catholic Church. The betrayal by Portugal of Our Lady. And now the betrayal by Harry Doten of Dad. He was supposed to come in the first month. We've been here for five. Dad has called, left messages, written. Nothing. Not a word.

Mom says, "Well, we can't just sit here and run out of money. We've got to do *something*."

And Dad says, "My book is coming along nicely. With luck, I can sell it. If it doesn't make us rich at least it should keep us afloat for a while."

Mom doesn't reply. She's taken out her rosary.

9

utopia lost

A BLACK MERCEDES leaned in front of our house, one wheel in the weeds, one in a pothole. Coming in from the fields, Nick, Danny, and I put our hands on the hood. It was warm, the engine ticking as it cooled.

"The *Americans*," I said. Our eyes simultaneously darted to the house. I removed my hand. The word still had the power to set off a string of buzzes in my body.

"The *Dotens*." Danny said.

So they'd finally come. You could feel their presence in the air. You could hear it in the pitch of Mom's seal laugh as it barked through the French doors, and in the clink of glasses and ice cubes. You could sense the importance of it in the way the wind shushed its warning through the grasses and the Mercedes ticked like a time bomb. Tracy, our mutt companion, sniffed the circumference of the car. Her usually active tail was tucked low, her ears cocked, her eyes worried-looking.

There was something cockeyed about Americans showing up

in Portugal—in *Sassoeiros*. Something screwy. Like wearing shoes on the wrong feet. Or playing a broken instrument. Or using a hammer when pliers were needed. Americans didn't fit in here. They were off. Cumbersome. The fact that *we* were Americans didn't apply. We outdated the term *"americanos."* In the last six months we'd all grown at least an inch; darkened a shade or two; grown out of our clothes (although we still wore them); learned to worship gods Americans didn't know about—gods we could see, smell, and touch; ate food Americans would wince at. What was America to us? What were we to America?

Our curiosity was excruciating. We had to see what America looked like. But we didn't want America to catch us looking, so our investigation had to be a stealthy matter of eavesdropping. *Sshh*, I whispered. I pointed to the lemongrass. "Camouflage." Pulling up handfuls of lemongrass, we bent low and, with our heads sprouting green stems and yellow flowers, moved quietly through the gate and garden and edged up to the front window. I was the first to feast my eyes on the spectacle. There were five of them, two couples and a baby. They were . . . kind of *big*. Like characters on a billboard. And they looked . . . *clean*. Like soap opera stars. And they were dressed like . . . *Jolly Ranchers*. Their clothes made your mouth water: blueberry slacks, lemon-lime blouse, cotton candy scarf, peppermint pumps, vanilla and orange checkered cap, licorice and lemon cravat, sour green apple skirt, tart cherry handbag. I wondered how they smelled. I had to know. I waved my brothers forward, and we skirted round the house, snuck in through the back door, and peeked around the stairs.

The smells didn't correspond with the candy-wrapper exteriors. Instead of sweet, tart, tangy, and sour, they promised a pharmaceutical cleanliness. *Listerine, Old Spice, Certs, Dippity-Doo, Dentyne, Hai Karate: Be careful how you use it. Dial, Dristan, Bromo-Seltzer,*

Noxema, Pepsodent. Formula 44, Vicks Vaporub, Kool cigarettes.

The novelty had a catalytic effect. In our bottled-up state, Danny snorted and shoved Nick, I shoved Danny, and we all fell into the room.

Harry Doten popped like a cork from the couch. "Well! Would'ya look at what the cat dragged in! Lyle, you didn't tell me you were running an *orphanage* here in Portugal. Ha! Ha! Where are your *kids?*"

"Gosh, I don't know!" Dad said. "Mart, where *are* our kids?"

Harry laughed continuously. He snatched the hat off my head and hooted. He put Danny into an armlock and howled. He pulled Nick's nose off his face, bit his thumb, and guffawed. His laughter was catching. Gail and the other Dotens laughed with him. Mom laughed. Dad and Terry laughed. Danny, Nick, and I gave in to a few chuckles. And then I got tired of all the mirth and stopped laughing.

"Oh, look at the dears," said Gail. "So *wild*, and . . . *wooly.*"

Mom agreed. "Yes . . . well. The kids have certainly . . . *adapted.*"

Mom poured more drinks, and Dad smoked a cigar. They both seemed flushed, optimistic, hopeful, and giddy. Now that the Dotens were here, it looked like things were going to be okay. Harry would write a check and deposit it in our bank account. Dad would get to work and make a living. Mom would buy groceries, pay the rent. The numbers would start to make sense.

That night, Mom cooked her fanciest meal: cow tongue, mashed potatoes with a whole stick of butter, green peas, leafy salad, garlic bread, wine. The Dotens toasted.

"To us," Harry said.

Everyone held up their glasses. "To us."

"To Europe."

"To Europe."

"To a damn good time."

"To a . . . damn good time." Mom and Dad looked at each other.

"Surprise!" Harry said. "I've got it all planned out. Wait till ya hear. First we'll do Portugal, of course. And then Spain . . . France . . . and Germany. My treat. We're gonna do Europe like Europe ought to be done. See the sights. Eat the best food. Drink the best wine. Really live it up. Leave the world behind. What d'ya say, ladies and gents? Is it time to kick some European butt, or what?"

Mom and Dad packed their suitcases.

"And don't forget to buy milk," Mom told Terry. "And bread. And propane. The money is in my top drawer. And make sure you count the change. And keep Vinny off the stairs. I don't like him on the stairs . . . I've asked a neighbor lady to check in at night. She doesn't speak English, but the phrase book helps. And if there's an emergency, call Sérgio. And if you can't get ahold of Sérgio just stand outside and yell *socorro* which means 'help.'"

"Don't worry, Mom," Terry said. "I've got it covered. Have a good time. Really."

Mom and Dad kissed us good-bye and crammed into the Mercedes with the Dotens and were gone. And we were alone. At first Terry put on a pretty good Mom act, enforcing baths and clean teeth and bedtime with a loud voice. "All right, you guys. Bedtime. And I don't want to hear a single peep out of any of you. It's lights out and that's final." But after a day or two, she reverted back to being twelve. "Is this movie boring or what?" she'd say when midnight came around. "I think it must be time for bed." (Most of us were asleep on the floor already.) In the morning she made breakfast. "Hey! Guys, wake up! I made oatmeal! And not the regular kind. I made cookies which is just like oatmeal except sweeter, and baked instead of boiled." The second time she made oatmeal she skipped the baking part and handed us a bowl of batter and five spoons.

She'd always liked cooking, and now she rifled through Mom's stash of supplies and found the good stuff. Grandma and Grandpa had been faithfully mailing Mom boxes of American products that she couldn't live without: peanut butter, Rice Krispies, chocolate chips, brown sugar, marshmallows, Jell-O, powdered sugar, Cream of Wheat. Terry followed the recipes on the boxes and made fudge. And rice pudding. And waffles with maple syrup. Pancakes. French toast. Rice Krispie Squares. Sometimes what she made came out great. Sometimes we had to scrape the top half off the burnt bottom half.

Eventually, though, she ran out of ideas. "I think tonight I'll just make this steak," she said, extracting a thin slab of meat from the not-very-cold refrigerator. She couldn't get the oven going, so she fried it in a pan with lots of salt and pepper and A.1. Sauce. The meat looked a little green and smelled kind of funny, and she made quizzical faces at it, and leaned close to give it a sniff. "Does this look green to you?" she asked each of us. The more she stared at it the greener it seemed, so even though we were lined up with our plates she pushed the greasy pan to the back of the stove and covered it and said, "I think I'll make macaroni and cheese instead." But I wanted steak—it looked so good sitting in its bed of shiny grease—and when Terry wasn't looking I put the slab on a plate, gave it a good coating of salt to help with the taste, and gnawed my way through several forkfuls. Then I went back into the living room, where everyone was passing the time watching a Portuguese soap opera, and flopped into the easy chair.

In a few minutes (or was it hours?) I began noticing that the people on the screen were mixing with each other and leaking colors from their skin. I grew frightened. I started to cry.

"What's wrong with *you*?" Danny asked.

"The TV is icky."

"No, it isn't. You're just weird."

"I don't like this show."

"Too bad. There's nothing else on."

"But I can't stand it!"

"So leave."

"I don't want to leave! I want you to change the channel!"

"There nothing else on. Don't you get it? Geez, what a cry-baby!"

Terry said, "If you guys don't shut up I'm going to say it's bedtime."

I continued to cry. My face was hotter than beach sand at noon. My throat was parched. I felt like vomiting. My body hurt. Finally, I couldn't cry anymore. I lay there panting. Terry put her hand on my forehead. "Dang, man. You're hot. Have you got a fever or something?"

The neighbor lady came with her two teenage sons, one of whom spoke a little English. He lifted me up and carried me up the stairs to bed. I remember noticing he smelled like fish and thinking I should be mortified at being touched by him, but not caring. The world mixed and bled colors. Terry flipped the pages of the phrase book and got tripped by the *eus*, *aos*, and *ois*. The neighbor lady spoke in Portuguese to her son, who mumbled back. I wanted them to go away. I wanted Mom.

Sleep took me down, and I went deep. I don't remember Sérgio picking me up and packing me into his little car. There was no car ride to Oeiras, or passage up two flights of stairs to his apartment where Maria made a bed out of blankets for me and laid me on the floor beside baby Pipa's bed. The doctor didn't come—although they would later tell me he did—and I didn't vomit blood on the carpet. The baby didn't cry, although Maria later apologized for all the screaming ("I'm so sorry. She had a tooth coming in"), or throw her bottle which bounced off my head. I vaguely remember the cold bath. Maria squeezed water from a sponge over my head as I sat naked and convulsing. I remember thinking, "Am I naked?" and being shocked by the fact but not knowing how to correct it. I know that Maria woke me up every two hours to give me water and pills for a "bad infection" because she later told me that she did. What I didn't tell her was that each time I looked into her face, I thought she was the Virgin Mary. She spoke gently. She hovered. But then she retreated and didn't take me with her. Sadness filled my being. Somehow I'd always known I would be left behind. I was alone. Around me the horizon was a dark, flat, and featureless stretch of place. The Virgin Mary was gone and I had nowhere to go. I cried in my head without tears, and thought, *I'm not going to heaven.*

When at last I awoke, I had no idea where I was or what time it was or how long I'd been asleep or even whether I was alive or dead. All I knew was that I was lying on the floor of a baby's room beside an empty crib. Sunlight eked through the shutters. I didn't recognize the feel of my body. My rib cage creaked sorely as I breathed, as if I were a centuries-old antique. Sitting up was difficult. Standing up was almost impossible. Only when I opened the door and stepped out into the hall and saw Maria standing in the kitchen did I know for sure I was alive, and that the Virgin Mary had been Maria. She rushed toward me and embraced me.

"You have been so sick!" she exclaimed. "I was so worried!" Pipa squealed from her high chair.

"How long?" I said.

"Oh not so long . . . Three days."

Three days! I sat down. Three days of life going on without me! I looked at the shimmer of sunlight on the windowpane. It was so beautiful it brought tears to my eyes. Maria made me some broth. I sipped it from the cup with a spoon. It was the most delicious thing I'd ever tasted. It, too, brought tears to my eyes. When I finished I was exhausted and wobbled down the hall to my makeshift bed, lowered myself on the blankets, and lay down to sleep. Maria soon appeared and sat down beside me. In the half-light I saw how I'd mistaken her for the Virgin Mary.

"Can I go home?" I asked.

"Tomorrow," she said. "I want to make sure you're okay."

I said, "I'm okay."

She said, "You were very sick . . ."

"Honestly. I'm okay." I didn't have the strength to explain to her that God didn't take souls before their time, so it clearly wasn't my time.

After a nap, Maria brought me a pad of paper and some colored pencils. "Would you like to draw?" she asked. "No, thank you," I said. Maria smiled, and left the materials on the floor, and I soon picked them up. I had it in my mind to write Mom and Dad a letter and ask Maria to post it to them. But then I drew a picture instead. It was of the road home: at one end, a tall apartment building labeled *Oeiras*, and at the other a green and white two-storied house and the grasses of Sassoeiros.

The next day, Sérgio drove me back home. Everyone gathered around me as I sat on the couch. "You look ghoulish," Terry said. "Are you sure you're not contagious?" Danny asked, "Did you puke?" "What color was it?" Nick asked. "Did you get ice cream? Candy? Soda?" Everyone wanted information, but all I could think about was how little any of that mattered. *I'm not going to heaven.* "So? What happened?" I said, "They put me in a cold bath to bring my fever down." They looked at each other. "Is that all?"

The next day, a taxi pulled up honking in front. As everyone raced madly through the house and burst through the front door, I stayed back, taking in the sight of Mom and Dad—pulling their suitcases from the trunk and paying the driver—from a distance. I remember the scene was a happy one, yet I was filled with inexplicable sadness. The thought kept repeating, *They didn't know.*

Everyone came toward the house. "What's wrong, Ronnie?" Mom asked as she hauled her suitcase up the steps.

"I . . ."

"Ronnie was *really* sick," Terry said. "She almost died."

"Oh, come now. I'm sure it wasn't anything the doctor couldn't handle."

"She had to go stay with Sérgio and Maria for three days. She threw up blood. She had a hundred and six temperature. The doctor came. They had to put her in a cold bath. She was delirious."

Mom put her arms around me and squeezed. "Well, you look fine now. Come on in the house. We have so much to tell you."

MOM DID ALL the telling (Dad didn't seem in the mood to tell), and painted a picture of thrilling extravagance. According to her, the Dotens had treated them to a whirlwind European holiday, complete with fine dining, four-star hotels, personal tour guides, and plenty of giftshop purchases. They'd visited castles and museums and cathedrals and a concert theater. They'd ridden on trains and airplanes and talked and laughed and toasted until they were all partied out. Then, exhausted by their two weeks of luxury, they'd ended their tour in Lisbon with lots of hugs and kisses and promises to keep in touch.

I couldn't have hoped for a better half of the story. The other half of the story—the half Mom left out and wouldn't talk about until we were "old enough to understand"—was not so wonderful. It went like this: In their two weeks of intimate togetherness, Harry never once spoke about his proposed business enterprise, and Dad didn't speak about it either. Dad waited for Harry to bring it up, and Harry probably waited for Dad to bring it up. At any rate, neither brought it up. And the more Dad waited, the more he felt embarrassed over his desperate situation. He didn't like being in the position of asking. And he didn't want Harry to know he was in the position of asking. And so he refrained from revealing the smallest hint that he was in such a position. He pretended to have nothing on his mind but a good time, when really he was having an absolutely miserable time. Every night in their hotel room Mom pushed him. "You've got to force his hand," she said. "You've got to corner him. Lay it on the line and get him to commit." Dad balked. "I can't do it. It was his idea. He should be the one. I'm not going to beg." Mom pushed harder. "You've got to. We don't have any flexibility. You've got to forget about niceties, Lyle. We're in the red. We already have to borrow next month's rent from your parents." Dad blew up. "Don't push me, Mart! You're always pushing me!" So the hidden half of the story was that Mom and Dad had spent their outrageously expensive tour of Europe in a state of anxious confusion and argumentation and social play-acting and growing resentment, only to see the Dotens pack up their money, laughter, colors, and smells, and leave us rotting in Portugal.

At the time, I didn't know the truth about the Dotens, but I sensed the truth about us. The thrill of living in Portugal was gone. After the Dotens left, a gloom settled over our house much darker than the one before they'd arrived. Dad stopped writing his book. He acquired a migraine and it wasn't going away, and now instead of writing he spent most of his time lying in bed with a dark T-shirt over his eyes. A quiet Dad was more alarming than a speechmaking Dad. A quiet Dad was an unpredictable Dad—a Dad who made rash moves. Mom was mostly quiet too, but then suddenly she'd blow up over something small. Mom couldn't fake a good mood for very long. When she carried around a problem you could see it in the way she pressed her lips close together, and in the dimple that was connected by a string to her heart, and in her bursts of outrage. She used to offer up the discomforts and sufferings in life for the souls in Purgatory. Now all her focus was the cost of something.

When she shut off the space heater and we complained about it, she snapped at us. "If you're cold, dress warmer. It costs nothing to put on a sweater." She dug into the backs of the cupboards and ignored the sell-by dates, and when we whined about moths, she said, "It costs less to pick out a moth than to buy a whole new package." She refused to bake cookies unless she could piggyback them onto a casserole. "No cookies until I make the tuna casserole on Saturday. It costs the same amount in propane to bake twice as much." Her funky Depression-era recipes came out of the little tin recipe box: slumgullion, succotash, and Hungarian goulash. These were meals she made when depression over the cost of food got the best of her. They filled you up with beans, starch, lard, vegetables, cheap cuts of meat that she'd tenderize with a mallet, and lots of potato—triple the called-for amounts. "Why so many potatoes?" "Because potatoes cost an eighth of the price of meat and are twice as nutritious and filling. That's why." ("But it tastes plain!") "Add salt. It's cheap."

Outside was an all-around better place to be than inside. At the farm, the sheepman might stick his arm right inside a sheep, while grinning at me with his grisly brown teeth, pull out a lamb, and leave it lying there, wet, slick, and steaming in the chill. He might yank a rabbit out of a cage, and with three quick, efficient moves, snap the head, hang the rabbit by its hind legs, and decapitate it; then, after the blood had drained out, skin it, gut it, and throw the innards to the savage white dog. Some days I'd get up early, along with Danny and Nick, and we'd trot the half-mile through the biting spring chill, plunge into the warm, moist atmosphere of the barn, grab a stool and bucket, nudge up to a tight pink udder, and begin pulling on a teat. Milking a sheep was like climbing up a warm rope but not going anywhere. You pull and pull, but remain firmly on your stool. With fifty sheep, the sheepman needed all the help he could get (even ours) and didn't mind a little mess and horseplay. If he didn't scoop up a handful of sheep's dung and throw it at us with a high-pitched giggle, we'd do it to him.

One night, as I lay awake in bed listening to the dogs barking and the TV blaring Portuguese, Terry turned to me and said, "This house is a real bummer. Want to get out of here?" I was wearing my feet pajamas, shawl, and stocking cap, and was curled up under four blankets because of the cold, but I threw off the blankets and dressed quickly in my farm-filthy clothes. If Terry was up for something, I was up for something. If she wanted to jump on a train to Barcelona, I was going to be on that train with her. She yawned. "All right then. Open the shutters and let's climb out the window and see what's going on outside."

Nothing much happened in the way of excitement that night, but the way in which the excitement *didn't* happen was so enticing and mysterious that it left no room for doubt that *next time* would be different. Wandering up and down unlit streets you saw and heard things that were not apparent in the daytime—the scurry of a rat, the gleaming eyes of a cat, or the dive and swoosh of a bat. A peal of laughter sounded sinister when it came solo through the dark, especially if Terry said, "My God, did you *hear* that?" A hammering knock took on life-or-death connotations. The old drunk who slept in the half-built house across our street seemed to be everywhere at the same time, swaying and coming after us on stumbling feet. Our terror was exhilarating. By the time we'd worked our way around the village, we were both covered in a cold sweat and happy to climb up the terrace to our open window.

The next night was the same except that as we circled back toward home we saw the light. It came from a basement pool hall window. Sneaking up to it, we looked inside. Everyone was there: Cardboard Hat, Glasses, Big Nose, Birthmark, Hurt Foot, Sixteen Year Old, Mário Joãon, Long Hair, and Twenty-one Year Old. Music played from a portable stereo. I remember "Popcorn" was playing, and that it made my heart jump and fall, just like the real thing. So this was where all the guys hung out.

"What d'ya think?" Terry asked. "Should we?" An opportunity like this—to see the boys up close, at night, without our brothers around—was rare. "I guess so. If *you* want to." She took off her glasses, found the door, entered, and leaned coolly against the wall. I came in second. There was a pause, several looks exchanged, a couple of shoves, and some smiles. And then the pool game continued. No one spoke to us for at least an hour. And then Sixteen Year Old stood by Terry, his eyes dreamy, his black hair hanging in soft springs. "You . . . uhm"—he gestured to the table—"would like . . . to play?"

"Not particularly." A long moment passed.

"You . . . are . . . uhm. *Desculpe*. How many years?"

"Thirteen."

I glanced at her. "What a liar you are."

"Well, I'll be thirteen next month."

"Yeah, *next month*."

Sixteen Year Old asked a lot more questions. What school did we go to? Where were we from? Was San Jose near Hollywood?

Did all Americans drive around in Cadillacs? He leaned close, and Terry was looking into his eyes, and I was getting nervous. Seeing a boy up close was one thing. Exchanging the same air was another. I held my breath on Terry's behalf. Sixteen Year Old's lips were only a few inches away. I could never tolerate Mário Joãon so close. "We should go," I said loudly. "Before we get caught." Terry rolled her eyes at me. "My sister thinks we should leave," she said. Sixteen Year Old smiled at me. "Ees late for yowr seester?" "Yeah, it's pretty late for . . . you know who." Terry looked in his eyes again. And before Sixteen Year Old could lay his lips on her, we were sprinting home, laughing the whole way. "Whew! That was close!" Terry said.

The next night, sometime around eleven o'clock, a quiet but insistent whistle came from the street. "Hey," Terry whispered. "Someone's sending us a signal." Four times the whistle came. The same soft lilt. She was right. It was undoubtedly a message. It said, *Come out and play*. Terry rolled up the shutters and opened the window, and we climbed down the terrace. Sixteen Year Old and Long Hair stood waiting on the street.

"Uhm . . . Yow like for leesten music?"

ON THE DAY Dad kicked his migraine, he got on the phone with Grandpa. The connection must have been bad because Dad had to shout. "Yeah, yeah, Dad. Great . . . Okay . . . Right. Well, I'll check with the bank tomorrow to make sure it came through. Thanks a heck-of-a lot . . . What's that? Well, I don't know yet. I'll figure out the car situation when I get there . . . No, just me. Mart and the kids are gonna stay put for a week or two. Right. I'll call you with the flight details. No. I learned my lesson on that. I'm getting a direct flight this time . . . Sure thing. Okay, Dad. Yeah, I'll tell her you said so. And give my love to Mom, too."

As if someone had thrown open the curtains, Dad's face filled with light. "America, here we come," he said. "For better or for worse!"

I stood stock-still. A variety of emotions seemed to come from every different direction and converge in the center of my heart, creating heat and light, and warming my skin until it tingled. I didn't know what to do—stand there, fall on the floor, run out the door, laugh hysterically, weep foolishly, go to bed and sleep off the shock, explode? But then Dad started singing one of his silly songs, "It Was a Tennessee Ghost," about a ghost that fiddles and picks, sounding like a thousand men or more, and Danny started doing the chicken dance, and then Mom did too.

Eventually, I got to laughing and couldn't stop. Danny's version of the chicken dance was more goose than chicken with his honking and long-necked strutting, and Mom's version was more like the Charleston, and when Dad joined in with his elbows flapping and his knees jutting, we all ended up in a breathless dogpile on the furniture. Maybe Dad was right. For better or worse, we belonged in America. I didn't think about the farm or fields, or about our friends. We were going to America. *America!*

Dad explained over dinner how it was all going to work. Once he got back to the States, he'd drive up to Sacramento, meet with the Zone commander, and get reinstated in the CHP. Then he'd take out a loan, buy a car, and put a down payment on a house on Myrtle Avenue—or close to it. When he had a place, he'd send for Mom and us. We could attend St. Mary's for the time being, but we'd soon go to a traditional Catholic school and church. (Harry said they were popping up all over the place.) Everything would be like it used to be, only better. "Think of our time in Portugal as a nice long vacation," he said. "When a vacation is over, you get back to work."

A taxi came and drove Dad off to the airport, and when he was gone, Mom got on the phone with Noreen and shouted louder than Dad had done.

"Me? I'm in high heaven. The kids? Well, a little shell-shocked, I think, but excited . . . Yeah, that's true. But they'll catch up. What's a year of school when you're young? St. Mary's, but only temporarily . . . Oh yeah? *Half off?* Well, *that's* a deal. No, garage sales aren't big here . . . No, they really aren't . . . I know, I couldn't believe it either. What's that? They *tore it down?* Well, what kind of a dumb thing to do was that? Of course. And probably *twice the price* . . . Good grief . . . Well, anyway . . . Okay! Put out the word. Yep! Can't wait to see you, too!"

When she hung up with Noreen, she took a deep breath and I think I must have too, because I could sense the amount of work ahead of her—and us. To pack all over again, and clean, and organize, and ship the crates, and say good-bye to people and places *forever* . . . it seemed like something you should only have to do once in a lifetime—not twice. I sighed several times over this, but Mom, who was not prone to sighing, clapped her hands loudly to dispel anyone's tendency toward premature exhaustion. "All right kids. Hop to! Let's get those suitcases out of the basement and packed. Come on now. I need some cooperation here. Get those feet marching! On the double! One-two-one-two!" And we all trudged into the basement, dusted off the suitcases, and transferred them to the house two at a time. Within hours, the cupboards and drawers were open, and their contents flooding the environment.

This time around leaving left no room for contemplation. This time everything we owned was coming with us—old, worn out, stained, it didn't matter. We had no money to replace it, so it was coming. The suitcases filled up first. What items we couldn't cram into suitcases—coffee, condiments, spices, toothbrushes, half a roll of toilet paper, shampoo, conditioner—went into coat pockets and purses. No space was left unfilled. Rice, noodles, and beans went into our carry-ons along with pajamas, socks, and underwear. We did well, Mom said. There was only one last dilemma: the sponge mop and broom.

"Can't we just leave them?" Terry begged.

"Nonsense. They've got a lot use left in them," Mom said. "I'll just bring them as carry-ons."

And she did. When the taxis came, she handed them to the driver, who shrugged and jammed their handles in between the suitcases in the trunk. Later, she carried them on board the plane, stowing them in the pilot's coat closet.

"If you can earn points in heaven for saving three dollars on a mop and broom, Mom must have the highest score," Terry mumbled.

As we pulled away from our house on the Avenida Gonçalves Zarco, I closed my eyes. Portugal was about to disappear, and I didn't want to see it happen. I knew the protocol. You drove away and a place disappeared. It had happened to Myrtle Avenue, and now it was going to happen to this place. No more two-storied green and white house. No more billowing fields of grass stretching for miles toward the castle. No more stone walls crawling with lightning lizards. No more grinning sheepman. No more herd of woolly sheep bumbling down the road. No more huddled groups of boys exclaiming over a game of marbles. Closing your eyes, I believed then and still believe, was the only surefire way to trap a place with all its brightness and beauty forever—at least in your imagination.

10

strangers at home

AT OAKLAND INTERNATIONAL, Dad lunged toward us like a linebacker, arms outstretched, and hugged us two at a time before he plucked our belongings straight from our hands and tossed them onto a baggage cart. "Welcome back to Yankeeland!" he said. Mom handed him the mop and broom. "I've never been so glad to be anywhere in my life. Take me home."

Hearing the word "home," I felt a familiar clench down my center—that torque of the bolt that holds the frame together. Home was a place you came back to after being away for a short time. It was where all your stuff was lying around just the way you left it. Home had a messy garage, and a hamper full of laundry, and crumbs on the table, and leftovers in the fridge. We weren't going *home*, so why use that word? House, apartment, hotel, motel, trailer—those words were more accurate. We should use them.

Dad's mood was high. At the baggage carousel he rolled up his sleeves and grappled with the sprawling swag of our belongings as they bumped and stumbled along on the conveyor belt, all the while talking over his shoulder to Mom. "You'll be surprised when I tell you about the backlash that's been happening against the progressives," he said, his voice riding over the noise of the airport. "There's a whole anti–Vatican II campaign coming together. Wait till I tell you. You're not going to believe what's going on."

"Of course there's a backlash," Mom said matter-of-factly. "Our Lady would never abandon her faithful."

"Is that blue one ours?"

"No, the other one . . . with the duct tape."

Seizing it with both hands, he hoisted it high, and plunked it into the heap. "Turns out—Harry's got some great connections. He's all fired up. He wants to lead the counter-revolution. He wants *us* to lead it. We're going to set up a—"

"And that one there, with the broken handle."

"—preliminary meeting and get the ball rolling. Gather the remnants of what's left of the Catholic Church and galvanize them. Build an army for Our Lady and act as her sword in the coming Chastisement."

Checking tags, stacking luggage, and corralling carts, Dad was like a man split in two: one half physically engaged in the material world, the other half bodilessly cavorting with the spiritual.

"We've got a plan on how to expose the conspiracy between the Communists and the Vatican, and publicize the ways in which the Vatican has been supporting the leftist movement."

Dad wasn't exactly paying attention to bag placement on the carts, and as the luggage tilted like a Dr. Seuss structure he dove toward it, body-blocked the shifting mass, and pushed it back into shape. Meanwhile the mess on the carpet was spreading—rice, broken bits of macaroni, dried oatmeal—creeping outward like a tide, and Mom, who never tolerated a mess, dug out a whiskbroom from a suitcase and began sweeping it into her hand.

"South America is really heating up. Militant Catholic groups are springing up all over the place down there, marching in the streets against Allende's Stalinist tactics and demanding he return the land to the landowners. Mark my words: It's a new era for Catholics. An era of combative resistance. A twentieth-century Crusade. The Catholics in Chile are poised to do what Catholics in Cuba didn't do: take their country back from Marxist infiltrators and return it to Christendom. They're an example to us here in the U.S., and to the rest of the world."

Dad paused, panting, his face beaming with battle-readiness, his eyes searching Mom's face for a hint of the exhilaration he was feeling. We all looked at Mom. She was still sweeping the airport floor and dumping the crumbs into an ashtray, one eye on Jennifer, one on Vinny, her ears on the rest of us.

Dad huffed impatiently. "This is important, Marty."

I looked into Dad's face, and then back to Mom. What did Dad want from her? What words did he want her to say? Was he waiting for a burst of applause? Did he think Mom had been dreaming of Allende being finished in Chile, and could now celebrate? Maybe he expected her to march straight up to the ticket counter and order eight tickets to Brazil, where we could join a militant Catholic group in their fight for Christendom.

Mom's reaction came off as a fizzle—a dud in the pack of sparklers. "It's good news, Lyle," she said. "Really. Very good news."

"You don't look excited."

"I'm excited."

"But you don't *look* excited."

The fizzle went black. "Lyle, I'm *excited*."

I wished at that moment Dad would leave Mom alone. Mom just wanted to go *home*, wherever home was, and put a meat loaf in the oven, and call Noreen Poole, and make plans to go to Sea Cliff. I knew this because that was *my* wish for *her*. And wishes were like the perfect gift you would give a person for her birthday.

"I get it," Dad said. "You don't have to explain. You're tired. You just got off a long flight. It's okay, Marty. This can all wait until later. I just thought you'd want to know right away."

"You're right," she said. "It can wait. I need a good night's sleep."

Satisfied, Dad's mood caught an updraft. "Hup we go, big boy!" he said, lifting Vinny on his shoulders and spearheading our rumpled clan out of customs, a parade of bulky vehicles leaving a trail of rice, oats, and broken pasta behind us, despite Mom's housekeeping efforts.

From the lobby I could see the big front doors and right outside those doors—just a few paces away—*America the Beautiful*, mirrored bright against the glass. The proximity of the United States of America—no longer a faraway place, but a country with color and substance and texture, and a flag with stars and stripes, and fast food, and colored TVs that ran cartoons in English, and anti-war demonstrations, and drive-in movie theaters—sparked a small inferno of anticipation in all of us that practically catapulted us into the sunshine, to stand blinking and squinting at the burnished world like blind people blessed with sight.

Outside, double-parked at the Arrivals curb, a Doten son loaded our luggage into a Ford pickup truck with two rifles displayed in the back window, then guided us into the cool interior of a sleek Mercedes sedan, and soon we were all speeding down I-880.

The Doten son drove in one lane and never honked at drivers or flashed them with his headlights. He flicked his cigarette butt out the window because the ashtray was too full to accommodate another one, and turned on the radio. On 810 KGO a voice chatted away in a wonderfully comprehensive way that made you feel as if the two of you were related. When the traffic report came on, a guy in a helicopter actually told you what he was seeing from above you in a lilting tone (*Nnnnnorth-bound 17 comin' in from the sssssummit watch out for a ladder in the lllllleft-hand portion of the roadway, CHP is reporting an officer headed there now . . . and further on some sssssslow-and-go traffic around Bascom Avenue comin' up into Los Gatos*), and the outlook on the weather was equally cheerful (*Friday and Saturday lookin' a liittle bit warmer with the weather cooooling off by Sunday afternoon, and some low clouds movin' in but no rainfall showin' for the week ahead*) making you feel reassured that the temperature was right where it needed to be and that the California authorities would keep you informed of any changes. In fact, everything about California seemed designed to make sense to its residents in a comfortable, non-threatening way, from the callboxes placed every half-mile in readiness to offer help should you have a breakdown to the relaxed way people drove, swimming along in one lane without any particular reason to pass.

California was not like Portugal. In California, the freeways were crowded with cars. As "Guantanamera" played on the radio, a hippie bus with flowered curtains announced the driver's left-wing opinions in a collage of bumper stickers. I drew in a quick breath at the sight of all those subversive colors and politics. Hippies were egalitarians that wanted everyone to be the same, which was just like post–Vatican II Catholics who, Dad said, were *pathetic saps that craved fellowship, handholding, and saccharine speeches in a cotton-candy atmosphere of demented utopianism.* Up ahead, Dad was probably saying, "*Save the whales.* Right. He's probably so high on weed he couldn't spot a whale if it swam across the freeway."

We passed a low-rider discharging a beat so loud from behind his purple-shaded windows that it shook the walls of the Mercedes. Low-riders, in my opinion, had terrific style and class, but Dad disapproved of low-and-slows with their pointless fanaticism over cars, and ticketed them if their frame dropped below the bottom portion of the wheel rim. I was sorry he did that. Growing up in San Jose, you knew that if the chollo couldn't drop the bomb low, the bomb couldn't scrape the pavement and spark up a rooster tail. And what fun was that? We passed other cars, and I knew they were probably filled with people Dad would disapprove of, like pukes, fruiters, deuces, and lillywavers, and even if they weren't filled with them, they'd be filled with egalitarians of all kinds. They certainly weren't filled with counter-revolutionary Catholics.

Later we inched up on a small procession of Hell's Angels, their knees pointed high and their legs spread wide as if giving birth to their machines. Passing a cop on the right hard shoulder writing a mickey to a motorist, the Angels raised their middle fingers high into the air. I thought the Hell's Angels were creepy lowlifes, but Dad liked them because they showed up at peace rallies to defend the vets and shout down Mario Savio's wimpy peaceniks, and anybody who did that was okay in Dad's book. Dad even called Sonny Barger, the leader of the Oakland chapter, a friend because of all they'd *been through together*. I'd heard Dad speak approvingly of how Sonny had pulled a gun on Keith Richards of the Rolling Stones at a concert that the Angels had worked as bodyguards. If he didn't exactly say, "Sonny should'a shot him while he had the chance," I'm pretty certain he felt that way under his skin.

In the distance, Mount Hamilton's foothills bulged softly under a spring-green blanket. Turkey vultures cut circles in the sunshine with bladed wings, and peregrine falcons stood like statues on the fence studs strung with barbed wire. Budding trees in military straight rows splayed out like spokes across the flat terrain. A handpainted sign advertised Bing cherries, apricots, and plums at the next exit, and another advertised fresh corn, and another

almonds, and another homemade jams and jellies. The Southern
Pacific rattled slowly alongside the freeway, an endless chain of
graffiti on rectangular metal boxes trailing a mile back. And high,
high above, the pale gray sky—a vast, indifferent sky—stretched
out like the inside of a tight balloon, the bright hazy sun flaring
out of the center with the seeming power of ten suns, so unlike the
soft, rich Sassoeiros sky, with its traveling gray clouds against a
lavender backdrop and low-watt sun.

America was teeming with harsh beauty, a term I couldn't
fathom but sensed along my spine. There was so much to see and
admire, but no soft place to land. The biggest comfort came from
all the English words, in the form of signs and billboards, that told
you where to go and what to buy. It was delightful to be able to
draw my lips into elastic shapes and do a rubbery dance over the
English vowels and consonants and know I was pronouncing them
correctly. *San Lorenzo. Dairy Queen. Union City. Coppertone Suntan
Products. Industrial Parkway. Winston tastes good. Auto-Mall Parkway. Fremont. McDonald's: 1 million served. Milpitas. Olympia: It's
the Water. The Montague Expressway. Gas, Food, Lodging: Next
Exit.* The words felt both foreign and familiar in my mouth, like
baby words I'd spoken long ago but forgotten after I'd acquired
adult speech. The Ford pulled off on the Berryessa Road exit.

"Berryessa Road," I said.

The Mercedes followed the pickup off the exit and sailed
smoothly toward the San Jose foothills as if programmed to go
there, and soon we were rising toward the sky as the streets steep-
ened and coiled around giant homes with expensive cars, tall
fences, and iron gates. When the Mercedes came to a halt, we
were facing a large whitewashed adobe palace with a terra-cotta
roof, and giant arched windows, surrounded by grassy grounds
with stone pathways that led off to a gazebo, patio nooks, and a

swimming pool shaped like a D. Parked in front were a Jaguar and another Mercedes, and there in the driveway, standing on cinder blocks, was the Ford truck's cab-over camper.

"At last!" Mom said. "Home sweet home!"

I looked at the camper, with its little screw-out windows opened to air away the fluttering cobwebs, and realized the home Mom was referring to. Harry and Gail stood in the driveway with their arms open wide as if they'd been expecting us for weeks.

"Welcome!" they said, sharing wrestling hugs with Mom. Turning to us, Harry surveyed our faces and clothes with rascally humor. "Hello, kids!" he said, showing his silver-edged teeth. "My, my. What a motley crew!"

He looked at my sweatshirt. "What's new, pussycat?" he said, reading what was printed there. Then, suddenly and without warning, he snatched the blue beanie off my head. My greasy, staticky hair exploded like popcorn. I inhaled sharply. Danny squawked with glee and pointed at me, and everyone laughed. I stared at Harry. Nobody was allowed to snatch off my hat. It was against the rules. Danny had tried it once and gotten his finger bent backwards. Nick had tried it and gotten pinched. Did I need to instruct Harry in the area of hat comportment?

"That's my hat," I said, trying to conceal my hurt behind a cavalier voice.

"This hat?" Harry held it out, initiating a game of now-you-see-it-now-you-don't as I snatched at it like a kitten. "Oops! It's gone. Where is it? Oh! There it is."

Mom stepped in, but covered for Harry. "Oh, honestly Ronnie, let Mr. Doten have the hat. You don't need it anymore. It's practically summer."

Harry said, "She's right, kiddo. You're back in civilization." And he pocketed the hat deep into his polyester slacks.

I took a controlled breath. I felt naked without my hat. And cold, as if someone had just opened a big window. And vulnerable, as if something might climb through that window to get me. And light, as if a gust of wind could carry me out that window. How could I live without my hat?

Mom must have noticed the emergency clampdown of my face, because she put her arm around my shoulder and gave a squeeze, and her words were tinged with sympathy.

"Come on," she said. "Never mind. Let's go unpack."

In her tour of the tiny camper Mom made many exclamations of approval, and then we all migrated toward the house, descended a long flight of wooden stairs, past floor beams and foundation footings, to the basement. And there, under a low panel of light, surrounded by boxes bulging with household items—old picture frames, cans of paint, broken kitchen appliances, and outdated stereo equipment—we came to four military cots lined up in perfect order on the linoleum floors.

Mom was saying, "For cryin' out loud, Gail. This is *more* than sufficient—"

And Mrs. Doten was saying, "I didn't have the chance to . . . Lyle called . . . It all happened so suddenly—"

And Mom said, "Don't be silly the kids will be *completely* comfortable . . . I'm just sorry we—"

"Oh for goodness' sake, Marty, don't you *dare* apologize to *me*—"

"But I want you to know how *much* we appreciate—"

"You stay as long as you like, Marty. There's really no pressure at all—"

"We shouldn't be here long, Gail . . . a week or two at most—"

"I don't care if it's a year . . . I'm just happy we can—"

And it was an ambiguous new beginning that marked an ambiguous new future. Every night Mom and Dad disappeared with the babies into the Dotens' cab-over camper, and Terry, Danny, Nick, and I went below ground to the basement, where we lay flat on the military cots that Dad had purchased at the army surplus store. The cots were made of an oily-textured green canvas stretched stiffly across a pinewood frame that stood on three pairs of scissor-crossed legs, and long—long enough to support a tall man—but so narrow you were forced to sleep sir-yes-sir straight—flat on your back, arms to your side—and so ungiving as to rule out any chance of a comfortable sleep. As the house grew quiet, my eyes would trace the myriad shadows and shapes that seemed on the verge of coming to life, and my ears would follow the echoes, reverberations, and muffled conversations that filtered down through the floorboards above our heads. When someone upstairs flushed a toilet, a rush of water gurgled above our heads on its route to the city sewer. The Dotens' noises were large and carried weight. The slam of a door, the drone of a washing machine, the whine of a vacuum—a sneeze, a shout, a bout of laughter—all seemed to avalanche into the basement, filling our little space with the continuous soundtrack of other people's lives. Our own noises, in comparison, seemed trapped in an air pocket under a thick layer of mud.

Upstairs, the Dotens entertained a constant flow of guests, including Mom and Dad, who'd leave the babies sleeping in the camper, or with us. Downstairs, we kids entertained ourselves as best we could, Danny, Nick, and I building forts with our cots, making paper airplanes, playing a game of Boggle borrowed from the cupboard, and Terry usually reading. Upstairs, a small army of maids wearing rubber galoshes scrubbed the floors with brushes and brooms and swiped the windows with squeegees. Downstairs,

Mom rolled up our sleeping bags and kept our luggage packed. Upstairs, a Spanish-speaking cook named Flauvia prepared meals and served the family on porcelain plates with real silver utensils. Downstairs, Mom boiled hot dogs on a portable gas stove and handed them to us through the camper door on paper plates, which we balanced on our laps as we sat eating on lawn chairs in the driveway. In the evening, the four youngest Doten children snuggled under white down comforters in their four-poster beds. We zipped up our flannel sleeping bags and teetered on our rickety canvas cots that collapsed if you moved too suddenly. In the morning, Flauvia cooked waffles and eggs and served them to the Doten kids in their breakfast nook. Mom boiled oatmeal on the tiny gas stove and Dad shaved over the tiny kitchen camper sink six inches from the flame. After breakfast we crowded over the same sink to brush our teeth as Mom hosed down the dishes in the garden.

The happiest place to be was inside the Dotens' swimming pool, and that is where the kids from both families gathered much of the time. In the pool there were no extremes of wealth and poverty, power and dependence. In the pool the Doten kids and the Arnold kids were equals, and we liked it that way. The only competition between us had to do with who could hold their breath underwater the longest, and we all fought fiercely for that honor, and in the meantime developed a solid friendship that would last long after what was to follow.

That month, Dad received a letter from Sacramento telling him that he was being transferred to Los Angeles. Dad conferred with Harry. There might be a vigorous traditionalist movement down there, he said. It might be worth checking out. Harry disagreed. Don't go to L.A., he said. Let's create a counter-revolutionary think tank right here at The Fun Spot. You can be the lead man. We'll set up a traditionalist parish, with a church and school and everything. We'll track down some good priests, and get some traditionalist teachers on board. L.A. is la-la land. Nothing's going on down there. Anyway, policework is a waste of time.

Dad told Mom what Harry had said. It was a drizzly evening and we were all in the camper eating meat loaf sandwiches around the small veneer table. Mom stood in Jolly Green Giant stance, arms akimbo, feet spread. The fluorescent panel lit up her glasses, giving her eyes a menacing look.

"Harry sure is full of ideas," she said. "What about money?"

"He said he's gonna get something going for me."

"He's said that before," Mom said.

"This time it'll be different."

"How do you know?"

"I just know."

"What about policework? If you don't take the job, there might not be another window. You're not getting any younger, you know."

Dad looked at Mom squarely. "The truth is, my heart isn't in policework anymore. It's in the counter-revolutionary movement. I've made up my mind. I really want to make a go of this."

Mom's shoulders dropped. The words "my heart isn't in policework" had disarmed her. It was either a bare-knuckle fight or surrender. She laid out two slices of bread.

"Who wants another meat loaf sandwich?"

THE "SOMETHING" THAT Harry got going for Dad was a truck driver's job with the Hamm's Beer Company, through friends in the Teamsters' Union. Now, instead of the tan shirt, royal blue tie, and gold badge, Dad wore a gray shirt with red pinstripes that showed a cartoon bear on the breast pocket, and a name tag that read, *Hello! I'm Lyle*. Now, instead of busting drunk drivers on

Highway 17, Dad delivered beer "from the land of sky blue waters" to bars and liquor stores across the wide Santa Clara Valley. To supplement the paycheck he made driving, Dad worked a booth at The Fun Spot, selling guns and knives.

Dad called his booth Cut 'n Shoot, and every weekend, wearing a short-sleeved cotton shirt, Levi's, and standard-issue military dress shoes, he sat on a stool under a corrugated aluminum roof and cleaned and polished guns in between serving customers. While Mom was out looking for bargains, Danny and Nick took turns walking around the carnival with Vincent tied to their belts with a yard of twine. Terry and I helped work the booth. Dad taught us how to open the cabinet and take out the boxes of cartridges, and operate the cash register. For payment, he gave us weapons. At twelve, I got my first real hunting knife, with a folding, lock-back 3 3/4-inch blade, a wooden handle, and a black leather sheath, which I wore on my belt everywhere. I also got a honing stone and some honing oil, and a lesson on how to sharpen a blade correctly. After one particularly heavy weekend, Dad gave me a wrist rocket, which was a little like a slingshot, only more powerful. Testing it out on a garbage can with a rock, I practically put a hole through it. "You can kill a cat with that," Dad said, winking. (Stray cats were plentiful around there.)

I liked working at The Fun Spot because it was almost as good as watching late night TV. People there were in their most natural state, uncensored, relaxed, loose, and free, doing strange, unpredictable things that sometimes bordered on comedy. In often one hundred degrees of heat, hordes of men, women, and children of all shapes and sizes paraded endlessly by our booth under the glaring sun. Tattooed women wearing frayed, crotch-biting cutoffs, their low-slung breasts swinging in elastic tube tops, pushed strollers as they smoked cigarettes and cussed at their babies. Bearded men wearing cowboy hats and butt-crack jeans spit dookie-smelling tobacco wads onto the ground and left them steaming there. Hippy chicks in long, gauzy skirts, haltertops, and floppy hats practically floated by, holding hands, and spinning around in whirling-dervish dances. Bikers, their sweat-stained tank tops stretched over bulging beer bellies, their legs bowed from riding motorcycles for so many years, walked with their girlfriends in neck locks. Couples in matching outfits and sun visors made loud comments to each other on everything they saw ("Look at this, Honey! What do you think?" "Hey! That would go nicely in the den!"). Delinquents skulked near garbage cans and looked inside. Packs of moms used their combined lung power to holler for kids that had wandered out of sight. And in any available cleft of space, bare-chested urchins darted like thieves, clutching cotton candy, popcorn bags, and prizes from the ring toss booth, their faces smeared with dirt, chocolate, and ice cream.

Our booth was popular with men. Almost every male who passed Cut 'n Shoot stopped to look at our stuff. And each one had a comment about what he could do with one weapon or another. He leaned against the counter, his eyes taking in the rifles, the crossbows, the guns, and the knives, his tongue licking his lips and his eyes glittering, and somehow ended up getting into a long conversation with Dad on topics like caliber, recoil, action, and rest-to-fire ratios. Some men preferred revolvers, others swore by semi-automatics. Some were Glock men, others Ruger men, and still others S&W men. Some were strictly rifle men, barely glancing at the pistols, and others were all about knives—their edge, groove, length, width, purpose, and size. But *all* of the men were .44 Magnum men. "Let's take a look at the Harry gun," they said. When Dad handed it over, they weighed it in their palms, slid a fingertip along the barrel, cocked it and uncocked it (dry-firing might damage the firing pin), then lifted the gun to eye-level, aimed it one-handed at the Merry-Go-Round, and said in a raspy voice, "I know what you're thinkin'. Did he fire six shots or only five? Well, to tell you the truth, in all this excitement I kinda lost track myself." Dad usually smiled when they did that, since *Dirty Harry* was one of his favorite movies of all time, and sometimes, to test the Harry fan, he'd say, "That man had rights, you know." And if the guy knew his Harry, he'd say, "Well, I'm all broken up over that man's rights."

While Terry and I sold cartridges, buckshot, holsters, knife sheaths, target arrows, and other accessories, Dad demoed the firearms, and you could see he enjoyed himself. When he had an appreciative customer, it didn't matter who the customer was: he could be a Yankee, a Protestant, a Communist, a hippy, or a post–Vatican II Catholic. All boundaries disappeared when it came to the common love of guns. "Ain't that a beaut?" Dad would say. "Sure the hell is," a customer would say. And Dad would say, "Look at the action on this baby," and with a jerk of his wrist he'd flip the cylinder out and back in, and the guy would say, "Sweet cherry pie." And Dad would say, "It's got one purpose only, and it ain't for huntin' squirrels." And the customer would say, "You got that right, brother." And Dad would say, "A guaranteed one-shot stop." And the customer would say, "Ace in the hole." And they'd both chuckle and the customer would tilt it to the right and left to allow the sunlight to glint off the barrel, and they would both nod approvingly when it happened, and it would occur to me that maybe Dad didn't agree with the modernists about very much but he could sure do business with them.

Cut 'n Shoot helped Dad buy a car. To get the best deal, he went to a man he called "Snuffy Smith" but was really named Brady (who, Dad half-suspected, sold hot cars), and told Brady that as a former cop he couldn't buy a car if he *knew* it was stolen, and Brady told Dad there was no problem there, it had an unknown history, and threw in a rough-up job for twenty bucks if Dad should ever need revenge, and Dad said, *You got a deal.*

Pulling up in the Dotens' driveway between the Jag and the Mercedes, Dad honked the horn and we all ran out, stopped abruptly, and stared, our faces scrunching in various places where a muscle lost control.

Mom said, "Oh, heavens. What is it?"

Dad hopped out and slammed the door, which made a steel-against-steel *thrack*. "It's a Cross Country Rambler," he said, as if naming the vehicle would somehow alter its looks. "It's a classic."

"Ew," I said.

The car, to put it mildly, was not what I'd had in mind. It was hick. It had a mangled passenger door. Did the door open? Looking through the window, I saw it had been roped from the inside handle to the opposite door's handle with a yellow plastic rope, right across the middle of the car. How was a person supposed to sit on the backseat? To make matters worse the windshield was cracked, and a window wing was missing—replaced by cardboard held on with duct tape.

"It looks like it might need some work," Mom said.

"The flaws are cosmetic," Dad said. "Trust me. It runs great."

"Well . . . At least it'll get you to work. And the kids to school."

And with her Good Housekeeping seal of approval, Mom left the scene. But when I glanced at Terry and saw her eyes were bugged out, her jaw cocked, and her arms clamped crossways, I knew the hideous truth. We'd sunk low. Lower than low. We'd entered the territory of extreme grossness. Cars were like clothes. They were an outward manifestation of your identity. They reflected your aesthetic, your soul, your self-worth, and your power—or lack thereof.

"That's it," Terry said. "Now we're the Clampetts."

"Tell Dad *no way*," I pleaded. "This *can't* be our car."

"*You* tell him no way."

"I can't."

"Well, neither can I."

No one could tell Dad no way, and it wasn't for lack of nerve. Dad was helping Harry lead the counter-revolutionary international. Telling Dad no way was like saying that cars were more important than heroism. Before you did that, you had to ask yourself one question. When the Chastisement came, did it matter which car you drove?

SINCE DAD REFUSED to set foot in a Catholic church, instead, the Catholic Church came to us. Every Sunday, Harry backed the cars out of his garage, Mom and Mrs. Doten swept the floor, set up five rows of aluminum chairs, clipped some flowers from the garden and put them in vases on the workbench. Soon after, Father Truitt, a tall, thin priest with a sharp nose and long fingers, arrived in his yellow Ford Pinto, and carried an extra-large suitcase into the garage. The suitcase contained all the things necessary for the Tridentine Mass. Father Truitt opened the suitcase, spread out the three altar cloths on the workbench, and then began to arrange the rest of the items in their proper places: the crucifix, the tabernacle, the golden chalice, the candles, the missal, the bell, the patens, the pall, the water and wine cruets, the finger basin, and the towel. With everything laid out, the workbench looked exactly like an altar. If you didn't let your eyes wander to the open cupboard full of chlorine products, or to the boxes overhead labeled *Christmas Tree Lights*, *Camping Equipment*, and *Baby Clothes*, or to the washing machine sloshing away behind the accordion door, you could almost imagine you were in a real church.

As Father Truitt dressed himself in his white and gold vestments, Dad lit the candles. Then, when Father Truitt gave Dad the signal, Dad hit the automatic garage door button. The door lowered and bumped to a stop, and Harry turned on the fluorescent lights. We women and girls put on our lace scarves. All of us opened our missals. When Father Truitt rang the bell, we stood. Mass had begun.

It was one thing to attend mass with Mr. Doten's own private priest in a two-car garage and know you were following in the noble footsteps of the early Christians who were murdered for their faith and celebrated mass on wooden altars in their homes and on the stone tombs of the martyrs in the catacombs until Constantine gave them liberty to build churches. It was another thing to watch Dad and Harry Doten being altar boys and think of them as products of this history. It wasn't just that they didn't make a convincing case. It was that they packed iron while they served mass, both of them wearing shoulder holsters on the outsides of their jackets, with Model 29 Smith & Wesson .44 Magnums poking out. The sight of those big guns gave you some big ideas. Like what kind of violent incident were they half-expecting to happen? Was the Vatican spying on our little garage-style church? Were the Communists? Were they surrounding the house at this very minute? Was the Latin mass against the law? Was it possible a masked SWAT team was outside right now, crouched in the bushes, ready to throw their grenades at the first sign of a gun-toting traditionalist? And if the SWAT team busted down the garage door, would Dad and Harry start a shoot-out with them? What if one of the guns went off and accidentally shot the priest?

Once, while we were in the camper eating dinner, I asked Dad why he carried a weapon to mass. He didn't pause over his mashed potatoes, but explained his thinking in easy terms.

"There's a war on. That's why."

"Like . . . a *real* war?"

"Of course."

"Like the French Revolution?"

"Worse. The Church and State should never have separated. A correct society is a combination of the two, with a monarchy overseeing it. Firearms represent the struggle to bring back the monarchy."

That made sense and eased my mind. But every Sunday, from my place in the congregation, as I knelt on my sweater to protect my knees from the concrete, and prayed the English words in my head while Father Truitt spoke the Latin, I found it hard to concentrate on the unbloody sacrifice. I couldn't stop wondering what Jesus thought about his altar boys carrying guns.

DAD FOUND A rental house eight blocks from Myrtle Avenue, and in midsummer we moved in. His heart was in the right place, but Jeffrey Street had crabby neighbors and weedy lawns and mean dogs and eight blocks that separated us from the Pooles, which proved too many to walk on a whim. We did, however, car-pool with the Pooles to St. Mary's, but only for a few months since they were planning (despite our desperate pleas) to relocate to Washington State, where Mrs. Poole had family.

Having skipped the fifth grade, I entered the sixth with trepidation. I was bound to be behind in everything. Mostly, I just felt distant, like an extra layer of space had opened up between my school friends and me. I'd spent too much time in my own company to remember how to behave around other girls. And too much time in the fields to find comfort in a routine. I didn't feel driven to prove my dominance at tetherball. I didn't have the confidence to strut my stuff on the kickball court. I sat out of volleyball and only played a little dodgeball. Usually, I ate my lunch alone. My friends Carol and Julie and Mimi were standoffish. It wasn't their fault. We couldn't pick up where we'd left off, so it was easier just to drop it altogether. The boy I used to have a crush on, Jovan, flipped me the bird while we were standing in line saying the Pledge of Allegiance. I was really hurt by that. In the fourth grade we'd written *I love you* on our palms and flashed the message to each other. Now his message was *fuck you*. But I didn't blame him. He was right. I'd changed.

We weren't at St. Mary's to stay, anyway, and perhaps that was the reason I felt so distant. St. Mary's people were *Novus Ordo* and I was Trad, and we were on different teams. I still didn't know what my team looked like, but I knew Dad was working hard to find a traditionalist school so he could pull us out of St. Mary's.

And that year, he found it. Holy Innocents School was located in Walnut Creek, about an hour north of San Jose—admittedly a little far for a daily commute, he said, but worth the effort. "It's unaffiliated with any organizations," he said vaguely. "Kind of a mixed bag of disgruntled traditionalists that have rented a little building behind a Presbyterian church. Kind of a depressing place, but the people seem nice enough."

Terry looked skeptical. "Weren't the holy innocents all those babies Herod killed in Bethlehem when he was trying to get rid of Jesus?"

Dad laughed hard at that, and I suspected he was laughing at the irony of our situation, and maybe because he'd read the Rules and Regulations sheet and secretly felt pity for us.

*The self-disciplined student will use his time wisely. The stu-
dents are taught that a self-disciplined person is one who enters
the classroom, takes out his textbook, opens to the correct page,
and is ready to learn before the class bell rings.*

It was 1975. Terry was in ninth grade; I was in the seventh;
Danny in the sixth; Nick in the fifth; Jennifer in the first (Vinny
went to a special needs school). Travis Doten, Harry's youngest
son, was in the tenth. Travis had just gotten his driver's license and
a fast new car ("1970 Buick GSX, with a 455 cubic inch engine,
hood scoop, Apollo White body, leather seats, and a kick ass stereo
with four built-in six and half inch speakers") and was elected by
his father to be our chauffeur.

Travis wanted to be a cop, and the reason he wanted to be a cop
was because cops got to drive fast. And Travis drove fast. With fifty
miles of Highway 680 aimed like two slings in his mirrored sunglasses, Travis drove at top speed at all times, but he wasn't truly
happy until he got the speedometer dial up to 100 mph. That was
the magic number for Travis. Keeping the Buick's three mirrors
tuned at precise angles to pick up the slightest hint of a black and
white, he'd cut through traffic impatiently, waiting for that clear
shot. When he found it, he'd punch the accelerator, say, "Come on,
baby. Take me to a hundred!" and cry out like a Comanche on the
warpath as the tires' rubber squealed and dug their teeth in and the
G-force threw us back against the seat cushions. From my corner
in the back, I watched Travis's evasion techniques breathlessly. I
thought Travis would make an excellent cop. I also thought that
with Travis going to Holy Innocents, maybe the school would be
a blast after all.

*   *   *

HOLY INNOCENTS WAS not a blast. What was it? In religious terms, it was neither heaven nor hell nor even Purgatory. It was more like limbo. You were *there*, in that rented cinder-block room behind the Presbyterian Church of God, but you didn't know where *there* was, or where you'd go from *there*. In the war between the revolution and the counter-revolution, the Holy Innocents people had forgotten to stab their colored pin onto the map. They didn't march to a tune, hold a banner, shout a motto, or pull out their sawed-off shotguns and slam them on the table. They just *existed*. A group of good-hearted people that didn't suffer, or yearn, or ache, or celebrate too much. Yes, they disagreed with Vatican II, but Holy Innocents people bore no vitriol against the Church. They were friendly dissenters who had created their own school in affable defiance of the local diocese, and, not to be under-sold, cheerfully endowed their K through 12 establishment with all the trimmings: team mascot (the Bulldogs), school newspaper (the *Innocent Bystander*), student body council, school play, senior ball, yearbook, graduation ceremonies (when Terry graduated, the only senior, she would be valedictorian by default and stand alone as the rest of the high school sang "Beautiful Dreamer"), and library with at least one hundred books. The paradox put you in a stupor. You were marginalized from everything, but how could you object when school spirit was so high?

The other two seventh graders, Mary Anne and Susie, wel-comed me with handshakes. They looked clean. Smart. Gifted. Superior. Totally indifferent to the fact that they were in quaran-tine from the rest of the world. Eighth graders Helen and Alison took me under their wings, and Anne-Marie, a prankster who wasn't above belching in class, showed me the importance of tak-ing life in stride. I wanted to be like them. Indifferent to the world. I decided to work really hard toward it. I would be cool and cheeky and self-confident; above caring what the public school kids down the street were doing; a cut above in intelligence.

But there was a problem. It was hard to be a cut above when your grades never rose above C's and D's. In a school that hired the parents to be teachers, the learning had a way of pooling at the top end of the room where the camaraderie was strong, and only spilling small amounts over the edge that may or may not form a rivulet large enough to trickle to the bottom of the class where I sat. If it wasn't for the one non-parent teacher, Mrs. Weyandt, a disciplinary hellcat who taught English and typing, I don't think I would have come away with much usable knowledge. Operating on the principle that if I remained quiet and appeared attentive I would be allowed to let my mind wander free, I was an obedient underachiever, spending a good portion of school time entertaining myself with the one alternative I had to a formal education: creative writing.

Physics Class. March 15, 1975

Father Kathrein walks slowly into class, dragging dirt, pebbles, leaves, and dandelion seeds under the hem of his long faded cassock. Standing in front of the class, his purple-tinted lips open, he begins to speak, the words drifting forth in a cloud of dust. "Please take out a piece of paper and write a ten page essay . . . on the principles of thermometry." Slight drool seeps from the corner of his cadaver-like mouth. "I do not (cough) . . . accept (cough) . . . late (cough) . . . papers (cough) . . . for any reason (cough) . . . whatsoever." His right leg begins to tremble, and then to convulse. He bounces his foot up and down like a fiddle player keeping time. His eyes never leave the students' faces as he reaches down and calms his spasmodic appendage with a death grip of bony white fingers, and then, after a violent blood speck-

led cough that lands on the foreheads and glasses of the front row
honor students, he lowers himself into his large wooden chair,
rests a physics book the size of a small car onto his broomstick
thighs (probably to force down any more tremors), and with a
voice that scratches the air like a dog's claws scratch at a wooden
door, he whispers, "You may . . . (cough . . . tooth falls onto open
book) begin."

I had to accept that Holy Innocents was a trade-off. It wasn't
as good as going to a public school, but it was better than being
home-schooled (always an unspoken threat). And with Travis at
the wheel of his Buick, did it really matter what school we went
to? It was enough just to be in that car, driving fast, arm-wrestling
with Danny in the back while Travis placed bets on the winner,
raising the bets incrementally to increase our incentive, sometimes
all the way up to five dollars—such a large amount of money that
neither Danny nor I would give up, and ended up straining against
each other for sometimes half the trip, our hands cramping and
our eyes tearing in mutual refusal to concede. It was enough to
get to smoke some of Travis's cherry cigar (it actually *tasted* like
cherry), and steer the Buick from the passenger seat. It was enough
to know that sometimes, although not very often, we might accidentally get lost somewhere between San Jose and Walnut Creek
and miss the morning rosary, getting to school right around recess
when the Bulldogs were starting a basketball game in the Church
of God parking lot, and be guaranteed that we hadn't missed anything important.

11

in search of a lost god

"FATIMA IS MY *Weltanschauung*," Dad once said.

Weltanschauung means "world outlook" in German, but so much more. When Dad said "*Weltanschauung*," he clenched his fist around the word and pulled it to his chest, and I knew what he was talking about.

Your *Weltanschauung* is the bone structure of your body of knowledge. It is the frame that carries the muscle, meat, and blood of your inner wisdom. It is the vessel that contains your essential being. Without a *Weltanschauung*, what are you? A vegetable with reflexes. You might as well sell your soul.

Fatima is what gave Dad the *Weltanschauung* on which to base his decision to quit his job. And leave America. And come back. It is what prompted him to trade a career in law enforcement for a nebulous role in the counter-revolution. It is why he continued to exchange long, typewritten letters with Principal O'Brien at St. Mary's School, debating canon law and the legality of the New Order, and why he refused to set foot in a Catholic church. It is why he was soul-sickened by everything he read in *Triumph* magazine, and why he was sinking into ever-increasing periods of malaise, his baby-blue eyes staring off at the angle of a broken tree branch.

The temptation to walk out on the Church was strong. Every day Dad said something along the lines of, "Well, that's it. It's over," or, "I just don't see the point." But I saw the point. It was his *Weltanschauung*. It wouldn't let him give up on the Catholic Church. Fatima wouldn't let him.

That was the problem with *Weltanschauungs*. They could be overpowering. And Dad's was like that. A growing thing, like the Blob, taking over the family, weighing us down, suffocating us, pulling us along with it wherever it went.

I wouldn't have minded so much if it hadn't made us poor. But it had. If it weren't for Dad's *Weltanschauung*, we wouldn't be living in a run-down rental house in a weedy, outback neighborhood, wearing old-fashioned, worn-out clothes scrounged from the racks of Goodwill, and driving a rusty old Cross Country Rambler station wagon with torn seats and no radio and a broken door that was roped to the car from the inside. If it weren't for Dad's *Weltanschauung*, everything would be different. We'd still have our dog Chema, and Mom would still play Johnny Mathis records instead of boring old Mozart. We'd still be going to the Capitol Drive-in and Sea Cliff Beach with the Pooles. And we wouldn't be getting up before dawn on this cold, wintry Sunday to go to church somewhere in a derelict section of San Jose where a "guerrilla" priest and a group of "schismatics" were celebrating mass in a rented building.

"Why do we have to go to church at all?" I ask from my seat by the broken door. At twelve going on thirteen, I want answers but I don't want them to be the wrong answers. "Can't we skip mass, like we did in Portugal? Can't we stay home and say the rosary instead? Who are these people, anyway?"

"People like us," Dad says cryptically.

"That can't be. *Like us?* How is that even possible?"

Could there be other families with *Weltanschauungs* that torture them and make them miserable? Could there be other families that don't know where they belong? That move from country to country and church to church and house to house in search of an aura that no longer exists?

If I had the courage, I'd launch a loud complaint right now. I'd tell Dad that I think our house stinks and I hate the dresses Mom buys me and all I want to do is stop worrying about Vatican II and live like normal people. But I can't say these things to Dad. I feel sorry for him, and I love him too much to hurt him. So I do what I always do. I gripe mildly and then cooperate.

"What does 'like us' mean, anyway?"

"*Real* Catholics," says Mom, the promoter of positive feelings. Mom doesn't get through to me like she used to. Now her words sound pat and uninformed, and when I hear them I cringe a little. Dad's anguish I can take. Mom's breezy compliance grates.

"The Society of St. Pope Pius X," Dad says.

"Yeah, I know, but what's so great about them?"

Terry groans quietly at my shoulder to remind me that when you ask Dad a question you get a Jacob's ladder answer: connected blocks of information that unfold from invisible hinges and extend toward infinity with no possible end.

"Good question," Dad says, flipping down his aviator shades against the early morning light. "Think of SSPX as the last remnant of the Roman Catholic Church, because that's essentially what it is. The last dying breath of the once vibrant Bride of Christ."

We're rolling at a wearisome pace down Hillsdale Avenue.

Danny and Nick are wrestling in the far back, Jennifer is asleep on the floor with one fist strangling her Snoopy Dog, Vinny is sucking his thumb, loose in the seat beside Mom (who is pregnant with number eight), and Dad is driving under the speed limit, which is what he does when his mind isn't on the road. I'm leaning back against the nylon rope that is keeping the car door on, and it's cutting into my back.

Mom says, "Pick it up, Lyle. At this rate, it'll take us an hour to get there."

Dad steps on the gas, bringing the Rambler up to the speed limit, but the more his thoughts focus on the Church, the more his foot relaxes on the pedal, until pretty soon we're back to a crawl.

"It was started by a French archbishop named Marcel Lefebvre who was actually a member of the commission that advised Vatican II—until he realized he was in a trap that had been set by the progressives."

Watching his face reflected in the rearview mirror, I can almost see his thoughts bubbling away in his brain like stew on the boil. He clears his throat, as he always does when he has something important to say, and looks at me in the mirror.

"Lefebvre saw through Vatican II like the judges saw through the SS at the Nuremberg Trials. He knew Vatican II was a backed-up toilet, and he couldn't ignore the stink. Whenever the other members of the council tried to push their liberal propositions, Lefebvre argued against them—argued them point for point. He knew John XXIII had an agenda and he wasn't going to let him get away with it . . ."

Terry's eyes are two glassy blue orbs staring into space. I wonder what she thinks about. Or if she thinks at all. Maybe her mind paints pictures. Maybe her life is one long hallucination. *A girl with kaleidoscope eyes.*

"See, when a pope calls a pastoral council he's calling a council on the *gestalt* of the Church—not on the *dogma* of the Church. But what Vatican II did was amend dogma. John XXIII (and Paul VI after him) had an agenda, which was *aggiornamento*, or modernization, of the Catholic Constitution, and he wanted Archbishop Lefebvre to follow it through, beginning with the Declaration on Religious Liberty. Well, the pope had another thing coming."

Mom says, "The speed limit is forty," and Dad accelerates.

"To modernize the Church, the Second Vatican Council attacked the heart of the Catholic belief system. Before Vatican II, the Church supported the principle of religious tolerance for all people. But the council threw out that doctrine and replaced it with the Declaration on Religious Liberty for all people. Lefebvre objected to this change, and rightly so. You don't need to look up 'tolerance' and 'liberty' in a dictionary to know there is no similarity between the two. One means 'patiently putting up with,' and the other means 'the unconditional freedom of.' In other words, what's the point in being Catholic, when all religions are equally fine? Huh? You've got liberty! You're free! Go on! Fly away! We *want* you to!"

Terry is twirling her hair around her index finger and smiling. I don't question what's on her mind—I know it's a boy. But which boy? She's been hiding a crush from me, but I think I know who it is. Aaron Schmidt had gone to Mexico for vacation and come back tan. With that blond hair and those blue eyes . . .

"Before Vatican II, the chair of Peter had supreme authority over all the bishops. After Vatican II, the Church entered what's called *collegiality*, allowing its bishops to disobey Church teaching as long as they do it *in good conscience*. In other words, if a bishop thinks abortion, birth control, homosexuality, or any number of other crimes against God are okay, he can go right ahead and say so without fear of excommunication."

Dad's voice is turned up, competing with the rumble of the engine and the noise of Danny and Nick fighting in the back. He looks at me in the rearview mirror to see my reaction. I raise my eyebrows in imitation shock.

Mom checks her watch and presses her lips together. "Six-fifty-eight."

"Now, combine *collegiality* with what they call *ecumenism*, which is just a fancy word for brotherhood, and what do you get? Catholics have always been forbidden to worship with heretics. After Vatican II, they weren't just permitted, they were *encouraged* to do it. 'Join in prayer with your separated brethren,' Paul VI said in the *Lumen Gentium*. In other words, don't discriminate against the Lutherans and Anglicans and whatnot. Let's all hold hands and praise Jesus in one voice!"

Vincent climbs over the front seat into the back, and is laughing at Danny, who is making farting noises with his armpit. I try to roll down my window, but after one revolution of the handle it stops at the nylon rope.

"Once Vatican II had destroyed the core of the Church, they opened the way for communism. And the way they did that was to leave out any mention of it. The number one point of a pastoral council should be to condemn communism. Catholics around the globe expected it. But there was no condemnation. Why? Because the pope made a pact with the Kremlin at the meeting in Metz promising that if Soviets sent Russian orthodox representatives (which was the KGB, and Pope John knew it) to be a part of the council, the Vatican would leave it out. And they *did* leave it out. And the omission was a big gaping hole. How do you gather an ecumenical council with twenty-five hundred bishops, five hundred theologians, and eighty orthodox and Protestant ministers to discuss the role of the Catholic Church in the world, and leave out communism? It's impossible! That's what the Fatima message was *all about*, for cryin' out loud!

"Communism is the most significant threat to Catholicism that exists or has ever existed in the history of the world, and the Vatican was pretending it was totally insignificant. And Pope John XXIII was calling the believers in Fatima 'prophets of doom'— which is like calling Our Lady herself a prophet of doom. Was that how the Vatican was going to consecrate Russia to Our Lady's Immaculate Heart? Was that how we were going to achieve the conversion of the Russian people? A move like that gave the clear and precise message to the world that communism didn't matter— and that Our Lady of Fatima didn't matter."

The tan skin of Dad's face has darkened to an unhealthy sunburned color. His voice is loud and argumentative, and the muscles in his jaw are straining. I wish I could ease his anger somehow and make everything all right, even though I know I'm helpless to do so.

Mom says, "Weren't you supposed to turn right on Snell?"

Dad's eyes flit from road to street sign. "Oh, yeah . . . I'll catch the Monterey Highway and circle around." He accelerates, puts on his blinker, and he's a driver again, but soon decelerates, and continues to talk.

"Vatican II was made up of two camps. The traditionalist camp, with the likes of Lefebvre, and the humanist (or progressive) camp, with the likes of Suenens, Blondel, Lubac, Balthasar, Ratzinger, and others. The traditionalists wanted to safeguard the holy canon, but the progressivists saw the canon as rigid and alienating to regular people. They wanted to make the Church a warm and fuzzy place, like the Protestants had made theirs. And what better way to do that than to redefine its precepts? Like the sacrament of marriage, for instance. Before the progressives got their hands on it, the Catholic Church defined the purpose of marriage to be the procreation and education of children. After Vatican II, marriage was suddenly for the good of the couple. What kind of progressive hogwash is that? What makes the parents more important than the kids? No wonder people are having affairs, and getting divorced. The Church is giving them *permission* to break up!"

Dad thumps his palm on the steering wheel and Mom says, "They certainly are."

"But what finally got to Archbishop Lefebvre and made it impossible for him to support Vatican II was the *Novus Ordo*. That was an outright sacrilege. And Lefebvre called it what it was: 'evil' and 'pandering to the Protestants.' And he called those responsible for doing it 'wolves, thieves, and mercenaries.' Nobody else had the guts to do that. Not even the Roman Curia."

Pressing my forehead to the cold window I can see the city changing as we approach downtown. I notice how the roomy neighborhoods grow closer together and the one-story houses become two- and three-story duplexes with long front stoops and decorative cornices, and the streets become shady with trees and buildings, their sidewalks crowded with newspaper dispensers and telephone booths, and their littered curbs lined with parked cars. I sense that St. Mary's Parish is around here somewhere, but I don't know where. I look up at the skyline for the border of palm trees that surround the school like feather dusters, and think I see one of them. I imagine Miss Rose entering the church building to change the altar linens and sweep up before the nine o'clock mass. I think how civilized that is. A church housekeeper sweeping up. Mass at 9:00 a.m.

As we roll at Dad's patently senior pace, he spots me in the rearview mirror to make sure I'm listening. I glance up to reassure him that I am. His eyes are ablaze with emotion and his cheeks heated, as if Vatican II were happening right here in this very car.

"So Lefebvre separated himself from the system and started his own seminary, which he named after Pope Pius X, who was the pope who defined modernism as 'the synthesis of all heresies' and issued an oath against it, which he commanded all the hierarchy—priests, teachers of theology and philosophy, bishops, and Church authorities—to swear to, threatening to excommunicate those who didn't. The oath was in place all the way up until the sixties, when Vatican II did away with it, which of course they had to do since they were propounding modernism."

"Are we there yet?" Danny asks, his legs hooked over the seat.

"Not yet," Mom says, looking at her watch.

"Well, when are we going to be there?"

"Soon."

"How soon?"

"As soon as your father picks up some speed."

"The Vatican calls Lefebvre's seminary a 'wildcat' seminary, because they don't know what he's up to, or what his ultimate plan is. Well, pure and simple, his plan is to keep Catholic tradition alive by ordaining traditional priests. If the pope and his friends the Freemasons weren't hell-bent on destroying the Church, Lefebvre wouldn't be forced to take emergency measures. But since the Church is in a state of emergency, the faithful have a right (and a *duty*) to override authority. Just like St. Paul did to St. Peter, the first pope, in Galatians 2:11. When he saw Peter behaving wrongly, he 'withstood him to his face,' setting a precedent that obliges us to resist the wrong conduct of any pope."

Dad says, "We live in a time of war. We have to take extreme action. We no longer live in the heroic age of the Constantinian

Church. We have to make our own age heroic. And for us as a family, that means recognizing our heroes and following their lead."

Suddenly Mom says, "I really think you've gone too far, Lyle," and I'm surprised she said that, and think maybe he has, when Dad says, "By gosh you're right, we're practically at Blossom Hill Road. I've got to turn around."

Slowing way down, he makes a smooth U-turn, rotating the steering wheel under his palm and then rotating it back. He looks again in the rearview to make sure I'm taking in and digesting his every word.

"I know what you're thinking. You're asking yourself the same questions so many Catholics are asking: Is the Catholic Church leading the faithful into heresy? Did the great apostasy begin at the top? Is Vatican II the Third Secret of Fatima?"

I nod for Dad, then glance at Terry, who rolls her eyes because she thinks I'm kissing up, and I look away because I know she's right.

"Well, those are good questions. And the answers are yes, yes, and yes. And the way they're doing it is with the disease of progressivism. It's like gangrene. It continues to eat away at truth until you can no longer see truth beneath the thick layer of rot."

Dad is semi-shouting now, as if he were a coach addressing his team that is losing. Mom is frowning at him with her *Oh good grief* frown, and Dad is ignoring her.

"And that is why Pope Pius X called modernism the 'synthesis of all heresies.' Because it obscures the objective truth. And if you deny objective truth, you deny dogma. And that's what René Descartes did. His *Cogito ergo sum* principle rejected the very idea of objective truth, asserting that truth is subjective, when it very well is not. 'I think, therefore I am' is at the heart of the problems we have today. It is the philosophy that is helping the Vatican destroy the Church."

"Lyle!" Mom finally says with exasperation. Mom always seems to vacillate between starry-struck admiration for Dad's brilliance and cynical exhaustion over it. "You're talking *way* over their heads. The kids aren't going to understand all that!"

He turns to look at her now and pretends to be surprised.

"Ronnie asked about SSPX, and I'm telling her."

"What has Descartes got to do with Pius X?"

"Everything. You can't talk about these things without bringing up *Cogito ergo sum*. You've got to start with first principles, Marty. You know that."

"It's not over my head," I muse offhandedly from my window. "I get what he's saying."

Terry gives me a look of exhausted patience.

"Well, I *do*."

I get the Society of St. Pope Pius X, because that's all Dad has talked about for years. The only difference is now it's got a name.

Dad rolls slowly by Caspers, Baskin Robbins, One Stop Liquor, and Dunkin' Donuts—all closed. The SSPX opens earlier than the shops because when you have mass in a department store you have to start early if you're going to avoid drawing the attention of window-shoppers.

Dad is sulking now, as he looks for the address. "Keep your eyes peeled, kids. It's here somewhere."

I roll down my window and search for street numbers. Churches are easy enough to find. Just look up and locate the steeple or bell-tower and you're there. Stores, though, can look a lot alike. We pass a tavern glowing with a *Coors* sign, and a shoe repair shop glowing with a *Keys Made Here* sign, and a Western Union announcing *Next-day MailGram Messages*.

Dad glances at his watch. "We're late." Mom huffs and looks away.

I scrunch my mouth, and hump up a shoulder—making an *oh well* expression. Dad might be right about objective truth and heroism in our age, and all that, but I'm not sure I'm going to like these SSPX people. Wherever they come from, they're not going to be everyday St. Mary's people, and I don't see what we can possibly have in common with them beside the fact that we're attending mass in a store marked "183."

"Dad!" Danny shouts. "Stop! It's 183!"

And there it is, a giant department store with mega-sized windows flickering from interior processions of bare fluorescent tubes, and eaves flapping with giant red and yellow banners that read: *Going out of Business! 50% Off and More! Sale, Sale, Sale!*

Dad groans, "Welcome to the Holy Church of Bankruptcy."

And he parks, taking a long time to back the car in, line it up with the curb, turn in the wheels, and switch off the ignition. And more time to pull on the hand brake, roll up the window, tap off the headlights, check his watch, and make a note of the time in his tiny spiral notebook (a habit picked up from the CHP). As he does all this, we sit in tense silence, and I become aware of the misery in the movement of his hands over the gadgets; of the despair in the slope of his shoulders; of the injury in his face. He looks like a man who's been robbed. And he is. He's a man who's been robbed of his Church. The look on his face remains as he locks up the car, places his keys in his suit coat pocket, and heads up the sidewalk, the rest of us lurching forward in our thick winter coats, the boys in slacks and ties, Mom and us girls in coats and long skirts.

At the revolving doors, a chain and lock bar our entrance. I'm heartened, and think maybe the progressives got wind of the SSPX mutiny and locked up the place. Maybe we can go home and say the rosary instead, and not pit ourselves against Vatican II and the entire Catholic Church. But Dad knocks with his knuckles loudly against the glass and shields his eyes against the reflection of the radiant gray dawn, and a figure inside points to the eastern portion of the building.

Dad says, "Ah. Side door."

We enter through the fire exit, and walk along a wide corridor with men's and women's restrooms and a refrigerated drinking fountain, veer around a dead escalator, and arrive in the main showroom.

It is a wide-open space, an asbestos cavity with acoustic ceilings and walls sprouting wires that have been disconnected from their circuits. The floors are littered with plastic hangers, flattened cardboard, price tags with string tails leading nowhere, balls of duct tape, garbage bags full of trash. Empty T-racks pose like skeletons forced into an upright position for a museum. And there in the center, sitting quietly, is a group of twenty or so people in four rows of metal foldout chairs.

So these are the schismatics that are just like us. I give them a quick once-over as I take a seat at the back, and breathe out a mute sigh over the realization that they actually do resemble us. No edgy or unpredictable-looking radicals. No one wearing a beret over deadly eyes giving us fixed, dangerous stares. Certainly no one that looks capable of slinging on a machine gun and robbing a bank for their ideology. The women are dressed in lace head scarves, buttoned-up blouses, plain knee-length skirts, opaque stockings, and low heels. The men are in jackets and ties, ironed slacks, and polished shoes. I notice a girl my age. She looks like a saint, with long golden hair and rosy cheeks, a ruffly blouse, and a long flowered skirt. Looking back, she notices me, too, and her face brightens. I look away, not wanting to encourage her. I put on my white lace head scarf and disappear like a moth against bark: one scarved head camouflaged among the other scarved heads.

Terry, whose expression is half-bemused and half-bored, sits beside me. *Well*, her angular jaw says. *Isn't this jolly?*

The schismatics couldn't be a more disappointing group. But my biggest disappointment is with the guerrilla priest. Secretly, and perhaps with a touch of self-delusion, I'd hoped he might be subtly bestial or savage-looking. With a word like "guerrilla" attached to a profession, the least you might hope for is a little extra hair. But this man is tall, clean-shaven, and bespectacled, even slightly elegant in his crew cut and ordinary black cassock. I sit heavily, and take out my rosary, and the activity triggers a throat-widening yawn. What good is being an anti-revolutionary if you have to be part of such a dismal group of deadbeats?

I watch the guerrilla priest, whose name is Father Heelan, putting on his vestments. For a priest, getting dressed is a ceremony just like saying the mass is a ceremony, requiring the kissing of each garb and a quiet prayer as he places it on his body. In a church this activity is usually done in the vestry, a semi-private room just to the left of the altar, so it's strange to see it being done openly, in the showroom of a department store, in view of all these laypeople. It seems wrong, both for him to be doing it, and for us to be watching, as if his secret identity were being revealed with the addition of each garment—like Superman or Batman. You know he's the caped crusader, but you don't want to watch the step-by-step transformation.

Father Heelan works quietly and methodically, beginning with the amice, which is a fussy-looking shoulder cloth with strings, then the alb, which is like a white nightgown, then the maniple, which is an oar-shaped cloth that hangs over his arm, then the stole, and finally the chasuble, which is a heavy outer garment like a poncho without sides. Despite myself, I like chasubles. They're swanky garments, and Father Heelan's is especially expensive-looking, with satiny white fabric embroidered with golden scrolls and green leaves and little red fleur-de-lis. Even an ugly priest can look stately in a chasuble, and Father Heelan looks positively kingly.

Now Father Heelan stands at his "altar"—a foldup table with a starched white tablecloth and a golden crucifix on top—and turns his back to the parishioners, the old-fashioned way. Without so much as a hello, or a wilted smile to acknowledge the extreme circumstance, he bows, kisses the tablecloth, makes the sign of the cross, and begins the mass.

In nomine Patre, et Filii, et Spiritus Sancti.

And just as in church, we stand, we sit, we kneel, we strike our breast three times, and we slowly turn the pages of our missals. And just as in church, my attention ranges over the pastures of life's inane surfaces: the bulbs' frenetic pulsing in the windows, the banners' gentle fluttering on the outside, the price tag at my feet that reads $49.99, $29.99, $19.99, $9.99!, the hangers, the racks, the ghostly feel of humanity departed. Where is my spirituality? My religious awe? It's the same every time I sit through a mass. I end up wondering where my faith is.

I look at Dad. He is totally immersed in a warm spiritual bubble bath. His lips are moving, his eyes are full, and his whole being is caught in the whirlpool of the mass. I envy his engagement. It is a mystery to me, bound up in the *explosion of faith* he experienced in boot camp—so different from the rote exercise of my own faith, learned along with potty training, walking, and talking.

Mom, who carefully articulates every syllable of the Latin liturgy, is a picture of concentration—the kind of concentration you see in the faces of musicians playing a difficult solo or test-takers at the DMV. I doubt Mom ever had an explosion of faith. You don't have explosions without fuel and something to set it off. Mom is steady and non-volatile, even slightly bureaucratic about her faith. She's a loyal follower of protocol and very good at dealing with the logistics of religion—with its day-to-day disciplines, routines, words, rituals. But I don't know how much she *feels*. Mom would never mistakenly say the Joyful Mysteries on a Tuesday; or miss a Holy Day of Obligation; or forget a religious feast; or cook meat on Friday. She makes the sign of the cross in sync with Father Heelan and nods her head when Jesus' name is spoken and never leans when she prays. She does everything precisely as she learned, as if religion were a formula for getting to heaven, and each forgotten word or missed genuflection might dilute the strength of the portion needed to get there. But what does it all *mean* to her?

It's a matter of *Weltanschauung*. And Mom's is different from Dad's. I know that if I were to ask her what hers is, she'd snort at the question and call it nonsense and say something like, *Oh, don't start that. You sound like your father. Faith is faith, I don't need to give it a fancy German word*. So I don't ask. Anyway, it's obvious. All of Mom's praying is for the family. And all of her penances and hard work; everything she talks about, worries about, saves for, and plans for has to do with family. Mom isn't really that torn up over Vatican II. What she *really* cares about is our family.

I become aware of how I am ranging, ranging, ranging, and pondering—what? I'm not sure. How everyone is more religious than I am? How I can't wait to get out of here? How sharp my sit bones feel against the seat? How I seem to have misplaced my *Weltanschauung*?

Dominus vobiscum.

Et cum spiritu tuo.

Sursum corda.

Habemus ad Dominum.

Traffic is picking up on the street. I begin to notice the high-pitched squeal of car brakes, and buses crisscrossing, their clouds of exhaust darkening the sunlight. A pedestrian walks by. It dawns on me that the donut shop will be opening. And the Baskin Robbins and liquor store. That will mean more people. They'll park their cars and pull out their strollers and scoop up their children and stroll along the downtown city streets, like people do on Sundays, and they'll notice the big windows with the flickering bulbs and the sale signs and wonder what's going on inside, and they'll peer through the plate glass and see Father Heelan in his dazzling chasuble standing at the foldout table with his hands lifted in prayer, and our little assembly of schismatics kneeling in a showroom full of post-market shrapnel, and they'll wonder, *Why are those people praying in that department store? Did their church burn down?* And the thought of this sends a cold blast of shame through my entire body.

I'm not ashamed of being a traditionalist, I'm ashamed of how traditionalism appears to non-traditionalists. I want the traditionalist cause to be cool-looking. Like punk rockers with their Mohawks and safety pins. We are as anti-establishment as they are; our attitudes should say "anarchy" better than our modest skirts and blouses do. That is what I want: to throw up my fist and say "anarchy." Not bow down under a scarf and murmur quiet prayers against modernism. I want to feel that I am actually fighting a fight. Being an SSPX traditionalist feels like I've already lost. Dad would be astonished and utterly dismayed if he knew how I feel. He'd say, *Is that what two thousand years of tradition mean to you? Anarchy?* And what would be my answer? *I don't want to be here and I don't want to be seen here. I'm embarrassed for us.*

Luckily for me, underground masses go much faster than regular ones in a church. With no altar boys to slow it down with their clumsy bell-ringing and book-transporting, and so few of us receiving Holy Communion, things move at twice the pace. Soon

Father Heelan is wiping his chalice and giving the final dismissal, and I'm heartened that I might not be seen by a window-shopper after all.

Ite, Missa est. (Go, you are dismissed).

Deo gratias. (Thanks be to God).

As Mom kisses her rosary and snaps it inside her handbag, I slide edgewise off my chair and practically sprint to the car. I don't want to risk being cornered by the saintly girl. I don't want her to think I'm one of her kind. I'm here out of desperate circumstances, not to join a stereotype. Terry understands the danger as well, but is less panicked about it, and takes her time to meander out after me. Slouching in the chilled interior of the Rambler, we stare dully at the scene behind the showroom glass.

She says, "SSPX people look human, but something is different. What is it?"

I say, "Who knows?", but I try to nail it down. They're sincere-looking, like voters with an important election at stake. They stand upright. They keep their shoulders squared, and center their chins over their Adam's apples and maintain eye contact, but many of them grip their wrists at their crotches with nervous energy. An air of readiness pervades the place. And misfortune.

And then it occurs to me. "They look like Mormons."

Mom is still wearing her scarf as she expresses some thoughtful point to a heavyset woman in a red coat. She looks like she has a load to share with the woman, and is eager to unburden herself. Dad is standing off to the side, staring down a professorial man with a thick crown of black hair. His face is eager, intense, watchful, and calculating. He wants to know exactly what this man thinks. What are his beliefs? Does he understand the Fatima message?

I sigh, fogging up a circle of my window. "*Oh my God,*" I blaspheme gently. "We're gonna be here *for-ev-er.*"

Terry doesn't acknowledge the blasphemy, but sighs and slumps lower in her seat. "You're not kidding."

"I hate this church."

"Me, too."

But what we can do about it? Nothing. We're helpless. We don't have a vote. We're the victims of the Blob.

So this is what we do now: awaken at the first hint of dawn on Sunday mornings and scurry like rats to abandoned buildings to have mass where no one would think of looking. Sunday after Sunday. After six months of Sundays at the department store, Dad gets a call from his "contact," who tells him that the owners of the building signed a lease agreement with J. C. Penney, and that our schismatic church is moving to a new location. Dad writes down the address. This time, it's a truck garage in south city.

"Oh, goody," Terry says as we round a pile of worn-out truck tires and pull up in the parking lot. "It's the Church of St. Peterbilt."

The place is like a hangar, only for sixteen-wheelers, with two huge corrugated metal doors that roll up on rods attached to chains. When you manually operate one of the chains, the whole building roars louder than the sound of a million ball bearings crashing. The irony here is depressing. If your priority as a schismatic is to avoid drawing attention to yourself (as it is for me), this is not the place to have mass. The fact that we are miles from a populated area (a dubious comfort in itself) and its built-in crowd of gawkers doesn't matter. What matters is the freakish way in which our odd tribe of Catholics conducts itself. It's outlandish.

Disembarking from the Rambler, we approach the massive structure, and because we're late the professorial gentleman from the department store (who seems to consider himself a kind of front man) sets the chain in motion, and against the background of nerve-rattling noise the movable wall rises slowly up like a reverse avalanche, drawing a bright square of early morning sunlight—which moves like a searchlight into the dark interior of the garage—to seek out what is hiding in there. As my eyes follow the light farther and farther inside, the door reaches its summit, the light stops moving, and there, framed in a stagy beam, are the altar, the priest, and a handful of worshipers kneeling in the center of an oily cement floor.

A spectacle like this is like a headline in bold letters on a newspaper: WAR! or PLAGUE! When you see it, you can't ignore it. Directly or indirectly, it concerns you. It's up to you to figure out what it means to you and your life. I feel the huge significance of this, yet my thoughts can't expand beyond the immediate concerns of this moment in time and place. This dress that I'm wearing, for instance, that Mom bought from Goodwill, with its flowers, and lace collar and cuffs, and bunched waistline, makes me look like a half-witted farm girl. It is *not who I am*. And these navy-blue old-ladyish shoes with their buckle and low heels are *not who I am*. And nylon stockings are for secretaries. And who thought this would be a good place to have a mass? Is the person insane? And how many people in those trailers across the street were just startled out of their sleep and are now peeping through their curtains at the pathetic congregation floodlit in the middle of a greasy garage? What are they thinking at this moment? Are they laughing at us? My thoughts plunge me into a state of sick humiliation and I feel the need to run and hide.

But I follow Mom and Dad into the chilly air inside, and because I'm a dutiful daughter I unfold a metal chair for myself, sit down, and take out my rosary as the metallic door crashes down again, swathing us in gloomy glory.

In nomine Patre, et Filii, et Spiritus Sancti.

There is nothing like the pain that you feel in your knees when you're kneeling for the Consecration on a cement floor in a dark truck garage. Or the cold you feel in your tush when you're sitting in an aluminum chair in a cotton-polyester blend skirt in a dark truck garage. Or the difficulty in reading your missal when the only illumination comes from a few panels of weak fluorescents high up in the rafters and from the slivers of daylight slicing through the gaps, seams, and riveted joints of the sheet metal walls. Or the desperate boredom that you suffer in your head when you give up trying to follow the mass and your mind ranges over whatever your eyes land on, which in this place is tool benches, oil drums, racks of tools, hazardous waste posters, and many, many truck parts. Or the unwilling bitterness that you feel for your parents when they insist on spending an extra hour socializing in a dark truck garage, leaving you waiting and hungry in the car. Or the doubt that you encounter in the middle of the night when it suddenly occurs to you that God is not where you think He is.

"God isn't at the department store. And He isn't at the truck garage. He doesn't hang out in dumps. What kind of a God would abandon St. Mary's and spend all His energy hanging out in Loserland?"

Terry is never in the mood to talk anymore, and as usual when I want her feedback, she turns her back on me and shuts me out. "You're just making it worse by thinking about it. Shut up and go to sleep."

I've stopped liking Terry's company. Lying there in the dark, I think I might even hate her. I toss this idea around for a while, and when she starts to snore I decide I hate her guts and can no longer bear to breathe the same air she breathes. So the next day I scoop my clothes out of the dresser we share, and with my stack of games and hamster cage move into Vinny and Jennifer's room, and move Jennifer's stuff to Terry's room. When Vinny comes to bed that night, he doesn't ask me why I'm there. He just looks happy to see me. And when the lights go out, we have an entirely different conversation than Terry and I ever had.

I say, "G'night, goofball," and Vinny says, "G'night, goofball." And I say, "No, *you're* the goofball," and he says, "No, *you're* the goofball." And it's the beginning of a long debate that will never quite end.

After several months of Sundays in the truck garage, we receive the joyful news that we can't go there anymore because whoever made it possible in the first place quit or got fired. But no one is having any luck finding another location, so Dad spends a couple of days searching the real estate pages of the newspaper for a cheap or free meeting place, makes some phone calls, takes a couple of trips to check out some places, but comes up empty. There doesn't seem to be any choice. Our small parish has to make do. So he invites the whole clan to come to us: to our small, wood-paneled, thin-carpeted living room with the smoke-stained fireplace, and drab curtains, and soiled, cat-damaged couch that Mom scored from a sympathetic Mrs. Gutto when the Guttos' new one was delivered from Montgomery Ward.

"In our living room?" I say from my post at the sink. I'm now convinced that my life is going downhill so fast that by the time I'm old enough to leave home, I'll be dead. "Mom, seriously. We can't have church in our *living room*. Look at our *furniture*. It's *gross*."

"People don't care what our house looks like. They're grateful to have a real mass to go to."

My neck feels snapped. My head is inches from the dishwater.

"Mom, we *can't*."

"Don't forget, Ronnie. Pride is a mortal sin."

"Can't we at least have it in our backyard? At least then people can go through the gate."

"The patio is covered in apricots. It's a mess back there."

It's true. The apricot tree dropped a gazillion apricots on the bricks and the sun baked them and Vinny rolled over them in his roller skates. It'll have to happen in the living room. So Mom picks up a card table at Goodwill for an altar, and the next morning the small crowd arrives early (Dad is still in the shower) and crams in, backing into the corners, the hallway, and the kitchen to make room for everyone. Our priest is now Father Lowell (Father Heelan has mysteriously left the parish), and I'm grateful to see that he likes privacy, and dresses in his vestments in Danny and Nick's bedroom, even though the floor is a mess with Matchbox cars and Rock 'em Sock 'em Robots.

That night, I gripe long and hard at Vinny in our bedroom.

"God must be laughing at us. I mean, come on. He was crucified on a cross two thousand years ago, and now we're praying to Him in empty stores and truck garages. It doesn't make sense. Do you think He actually comes down and hangs out in these places? Do you think He appreciates what we're doing? Do you think He comes to our living room? What do you think, Vinny? Does God hang out in dumps?"

Vinny snorts and covers his mouth with his fingertips and squints his eyes so tightly his eyelashes disappear. Vinny has turned out to be a great roommate. Not only does he not mind the rattling noise of my hamster running on his wheel at night, he's a good listener.

"You think that's funny, don't you?"

He doesn't answer, but keeps snickering into his fingertips.

"So, where does God hang out, Vinny? Come on . . . I won't tell."

"I say nothing."

"Ha. You're wise. You *say* nothing, but you *think* a lot. That's my policy, too."

Next week, the girl who looks like a saint comes, and I watch her carefully from my foldout chair beside the coffee table. She has a large family, too, and a father with intense eyes, and a loving but strict mother who carries a baby on her hip. Suddenly, I am intensely curious about the girl. I wonder what she thinks about, and if she has mass in her living room, and if she is home-schooled, and if she knows what a *Weltanschauung* is.

So after mass I sidle up to her and say "Hi," and she offers me her soft hand in an old-fashioned way, and I shake it with manly pressure the way Mom does, and she giggles a little, and says her name is Angela, so now I think she looks like an angel untouched by worldliness rather than a saint. Her mom is helping my mom serve coffee, so I invite Angela into my room and we sit on my bed in our almost identical long flowered skirts and lace scarves searching for something to say. I feel the need to be nice to her, as if her air of innocence demands it, so I say, "Your hair is really long," and she says, "Thanks," knowing I intended it as a compliment. Then I feel kind of ashamed for bringing up her looks, so I say, "Hey, I like your mom's chocolate peanut butter balls," and she says, "They're made with paraffin," and I say, "Cool," even though I don't have a clue what paraffin is. So I say, "Would you like to hold my hamster?" and she nods, so I snatch Rare from his cage where he was napping in a ball, and stand him up on his hind legs to show her the reason I named him Rare, and she agrees that he is indeed a rare animal with that white diamond on his chest. Then she tells me she likes horses, and spends a long time talking about Arabians and Appaloosas and Pintos, and says she wishes she could ride, but her family can't afford the lessons, and the reason for that is her dad quit his job at PG&E to attend meetings with the members of Pius X and discuss Vatican II.

"But someday," she sighs, "I'll get my own horse, and I'll be a professional horsewoman."

As Angela is talking, I am staring with unguarded frankness into her eyes. So she is not an angel untouched by worldliness but a real person with real fantasies, living the life of a schismatic like me. I've never met someone like me before. It's scary and interesting and also weird because I sense that when you have a lot in common with someone, you and that person have no choice but to be friends, even if it turns out you don't like each other.

"So hey," I propose offhandedly. "Do you want to write letters back and forth or something?"

"Sure, I guess so."

"Okay . . . So . . . Do you want to start *today?*"

"Okay. You write first."

It's like *Truth or Dare* and I have to accept both challenges.

"Deal."

I take out my diary with its tiny lock and key from its hiding place under the bed, find a blank page, and hand her my special purple pen, and she lightly applies her address with rounded, carefully proportioned letters onto the page. When she's done, I scrawl mine in decisive print and tear out the page and hand it to her. And then we smile as if we're the first people ever to come up with such an amazing idea as being pen pals.

And then it's time for her to leave, and I'm sorry because I don't know when I'll see her again. People like us move around a lot. We meet in obscure places, at unpredictable times, and the priests change and so do the faces. We don't have pastoral council meetings or choir practice or pancake breakfasts or any of the usual church events that bring people together. For confession we walk to our local New Order churches and confess to the modern priests. We hold marriages and baptisms in our living rooms and backyards. How do you carve out a corner of consistency where you can enjoy a steady friendship? You don't.

So it's no surprise that months will pass between our visits, and then years. We'll write, but our letters will be mostly filled with shy references to past letters and conversations. We'll talk on the phone, but the lack of privacy will make it difficult to say what we really think. Every now and then, at some family gathering, we'll exchange a smile, and we'll lean toward one another, and the air between us will dance with possibilities, but then we'll be interrupted by something—usually our younger siblings (whose business it is to interrupt)—and the opportunity will disappear.

12

counter-revolution 101

YOUR LIFE CAME down to an accident of timing. If you happened to live in the heroic age of Constantine, in the fourth century A.D., you had it made. Back then you were practically forced to be Christian (Christian being the word for True Catholic back then), because Emperor Constantine made Christianity the official religion of the Roman Empire and demanded that all pagans and heretics convert. So you had two choices—be Christian or be in danger of death. Once, around 325, when some Christians got the absurd notion that Jesus was created by God and not part of the Trinity all along (the Arian heresy), Constantine realized that one heresy could lead to another and soon Christians would be saying Jesus wasn't even God but only a prophet, so he called the First Ecumenical Council in Nicaea (Vatican II was the Twenty-first Ecumenical Council), summoning bishops from Asia, Syria, Palestine, Egypt, Greece, Libya, and elsewhere to put a stop to the waffly ways that Christians were interpreting Holy Scripture and to make the doctrine absolute, under the guidance of the Holy

Spirit. That way, no one could mess with Church doctrine, and if someone did start preaching nonsense like the Arian heresy, you, a Defender of the Faith, could grab your shield with the Chi Rho cross emblazoned on the front, leap onto your armored horse, couch your lance, and go galloping straight into that church, or house, or town center slicing off heads and no one would try to stop you. Because back then all Christians were expected to kill heretics, and if you killed a *lot* of them, people would praise you, and the Catholic Church would have a feast in your honor and maybe even canonize you for stopping the progressives and keeping tradition intact.

If, on the other hand, you happened to live in the positively *un*-heroic modern age of 1975, in San Jose, California, and you wanted to defend the traditional Catholic faith, you were thoroughly screwed. First, Christianity was no longer mandatory. Second, it was watered down to include so many Jesus-loving sects that it was impossible to get everyone to worship the same Christ. Third, Catholics themselves were confused. Where there used to be one way to say the Roman Catholic Mass—in Latin, the Tridentine way—now there were thousands of different ways to say it—all *Novus Ordo*, and all invalid. And fourth, the Vatican had just lifted the ban on Catholics to become Freemasons, which Dad said was Satan's church. Where was Constantine when you needed him? Pope Paul VI was no Constantine. In fact, he was possibly an anti-pope. Why else would he have forbidden priests to say the Latin mass? Why else would he have lifted the ban on Masonry? Because of him and his predecessor, there wasn't a single parish around that didn't practice every possible doctrinal heresy. And what were you going to do about it? You couldn't exactly grab your gun and get in your car and go around doing drive-bys of churches. You couldn't even break a window or throw a smoke bomb.

These days defending the One Holy Catholic and Apostolic Church wasn't a matter of what you did but a matter of what you *didn't do*. Instead of slaughtering heretics, you had to live among them peacefully and show them what you stood for by *not doing* what they did. Which meant that you *didn't* follow their fashions, or see their movies, or listen to their music, or swim in their public pools, or go to their schools or churches. And while you didn't do those things, you prayed for the souls of those who did, even though you knew it wouldn't do much good since most of them were going to hell anyways.

Dad said it was like your hands were tied. You wanted to do what was right, but you couldn't for the life of you figure out how to do it. What the world needed, he said, was an army for Our Lady. Not like the missionary-style Salvation Army that wasted all its time helping the poor, but an army like King Charlemagne had for Our Lord in the eighth century. Charlemagne was the king who set out to convert the Saxons in Germany to Christianity (Catholicism) when ninety percent of the population was pagan. To accomplish such a huge feat, he sent his army on a bloody campaign that ended with the heroic beheadings of 4,500 Saxon leaders for their paganism. That's the kind of devotion to the faith Dad was on the lookout for.

Every era in history since civilization began has produced a hero. Where was *our* hero? At times, Dad wondered if it might be him. He prayed for the grace to know Our Lady's wishes. He dedicated novenas to the question. He told us to do the same. "Pray to know your vocations," he said. "Every human has a role in the Age of Faith." The hero was out there somewhere. He or she had to be. And finally in that year of 1975, Dad discovered him. While perusing a newsletter on Harry Doten's desk, he happened upon an article about how the Vatican had helped the Chilean Catholic hierarchy elect the Communist president of Chile, Salvador Allende. Dad could have written the piece himself. He looked at the letterhead. The emblem was a golden rampant lion—the medieval symbol of a lion in battle. The name of the organization was TFP (the Society for the Defense of Tradition, Family, and Property—the anti-Communist trilogy). Dad grabbed the phone.

"*Nemo me impune lacessit!*"

Mom said, "What?"

" 'No one wounds me with impunity.' It's the motto of the Royal Standard of Scotland. Remember? The Scottish coat of arms?"

"Doesn't ring a bell."

"Come on, Mart! I told you about William the Lion, the king of the Scots, who charged the English invaders in the twelfth century. During the raid William galloped straight toward the English troops while his own troops lagged behind, and he shouted, 'Now we shall see which of us are good knights!' There's an anti-revolutionary group in Brazil that carries the standard of the lion rampant. Only it's gold on a red background rather than the other way around."

"No kidding."

"Would I kid about a thing like this?"

Dad wrote letters to the TFP and they wrote back, and within weeks representatives flew in from Brazil and came to our house. The men from the organization (Dad called them "The Group") were dressed in suits with red satin sashes draped over their shoulders, and wore little gold pins on their lapels with the rampant lion on them. You could feel a change in the atmosphere when they entered the house, an excitement of ions that scrambled in your hair. I've always felt that charge when strangers had an agenda, and these men had one.

They stood together on one side of the room. Their bodies

possessed an urgent muscle tone that drew their carriage upright, giving them added height and density. Their gazes, their military-style haircuts, their fine suits, and their polished shoes and faces claimed a readiness to impart the truth at the earliest opportunity, reminding me of political canvassers trying to influence an election at the toll booth. When Dad introduced Mom, the men did not say "Hello," but *"Salve Maria"* ("Hail Mary"). They also did not shake her hand, but bowed their heads at the neck as if she were a dignitary of some kind. As we trickled in shyly, Dad introduced each of us by our biblical birth names as if to emphasize our saintly qualities: "The oldest there is Theresa, the second oldest is Veronica. Then there is Daniel, Nicholas, and Vincent. And over there is Jennifer, Mary, and Bernadette." To each of us the men said *"Salve Maria,"* and gave the same at-the-neck bow. When dinner was announced, they stood behind their chairs, gripping the backs, and led Grace in Latin. Over dinner they spoke with accents, in low, serious voices, looking to each other for help with vocabulary. They talked about the coming Chastisement, although they called it the *Bagarre*, which was their word for the Chastisement. *Bagarre* was French for "Brawl" with a capital B. Uncontrollable chaos. Free-for-all fighting in the streets. When they talked about the *Bagarre*, they included Our Lady as if she was going to be right there with them, shouting from the rooftops, her robes flowing—"with Our Lady's help," they'd say, or, "by the grace of Our Lady," or, "if Our Lady wishes it," and I could see by Dad's expression what he was thinking: here was the army of Our Lady that he'd been dreaming of.

The representatives invited Mom and Dad to meet their leader, Professor Plinio Corrêa de Oliveira, in Brazil, and Dad accepted the invitation. He booked flights for himself, Mom, Harry, Gail, and the Dotens' two older sons, Randy and Jake, and flew to São

Paulo. At Dr. Plinio's nineteenth-century estate, called the Reign of Mary, the leader treated his rich American visitors to a fantastic display of militaristic Catholic spirit. Young militants dressed in suits, with red berets and white gloves, guarded the statue of the Pilgrim Virgin (the statue had wept real tears in New Orleans in 1972) that stood on a pedestal behind velvet ropes, and allowed the guests to venerate her one at a time. Militants also guarded a large crucifix that contained a first-class relic of the real Cross of Jesus Christ, inviting veneration one at a time. Later, Dad and the other men (the women were kept separate at all times) went to the St. Michael's seat and sat in a bleacher section with various other male visitors, where the procedings continued.

On stage, Dr. Plinio sat in a thronelike chair surrounded by armed bodyguards trained in karate—the kind of people you would see on graduation day from boot camp in dress blues, Dad said. (Dad was impressed that the members of The Group had a blanket permit to carry concealed weapons because of several attempted bombings by Communist supporters.) The meeting opened with the Prayers of the Group—a litany for the Catholic Resistance. Then the guests put on headphones, and a speaker gave a lecture in Portuguese that bilingual assistants translated into microphones. The lecturer talked about Dr. Plinio's history (as a former Brazilian congressman, professor of history, and daily columnist for a São Paulo newspaper), the history of the TFP, and the fallout over his book *Revolution and Counter-Revolution*. After the meeting, the guests were instructed to convene for the ceremony. In a protected courtyard, "warrior-monks" (as Dad called them) dressed in white tunics with the knee-length brown scapulars, the red cross of St. James, calf-length black leather boots, and red capes over the left shoulder marched a "Marine Corps–like step" modified with a sliding foot and heel slam, while carrying medieval broadswords and singing "O Rome Eternal." Dad was transported. The tears gushed. Harry cried, too. Unembarrassed. Nothing they'd ever seen could compare to this.

For the next week, Dad and Harry toured the rest of Plinio's facilities: the financial seat, the foreign relations seat, the journalist seat, the research seat, and other seats. The Group was like a fully operational mini-monarchy! Dad's only disappointment with the trip was having only enough time to visit seven of the twenty-six seats.

When they came home, Dad's pupils were two bullets of black light. All these years he'd dreamt of such a thing as The Group. But it had always been that. A dream. Well, this was no dream. It was *real*. The Group had the spirit of True Catholicism. The Group *was* Catholicism. They were the phoenix sprung up from the cold embers of the post–Vatican II pile of rubble. And their leader was a kind of prophet; a *witness*. God had promised Zerubbabel, the prince of Judah, two witnesses—one religious and one political—to the crimes committed by humanity against him and his Church. Archbishop Lefebvre was the religious witness. Now Dad had found the political one: Dr. Plinio. The Crusades of the twentieth century had begun. The war cry had been sounded.

Dad experienced the calling he'd been waiting for. There was a new certainty in his carriage and step. Finally he could be an active accomplice in the fight against the revolution. He would carry the standard of the rampant lion right into the *Bagarre*. The Group had an east coast seat in the United States; they needed a west coast division. Harry hatched a plan to lease a mansion on one of his properties and make Dad the chief secretary. Dad got right to work. He organized SEFAC (Specialized Education for Anti-Communism) seminars for large groups of men. He threw banquets, conducted international meetings, wrote lengthy articles, and recruited new members into The Group. He ran a think tank dedicated to counteracting statist communism, Gramscism, and the Vatican II Church. His job was to learn the strategic and tactical arts of war, and to dominate the field. At last, he was doing what he'd craved to do since Vatican II. He'd joined the fight against the revolution. There was only one thing more he could do: send his boys off to join Our Lady's army. Or *men*, really—Danny was twelve, and Nick was nearly eleven.

The Group's boys' academy in New York was a strict, focused, militaristic Catholic institution. The boys rose at dawn, made up their beds like soldiers, attended the Tridentine Mass, raised the red standard with the rampant lion as they chanted the Nicene Creed in Latin, ran a mile, showered, prayed the rosary, marched to the refectory while singing St. Louis de Montfort's hymn "We Want God," heard the life of a saint read aloud during breakfast, raised the national flag, said a short prayer before class, then began their school day with Religion. Dad said it was like the Marines, only Catholic.

The morning Danny and Nick left for New York, I stayed in bed and faced the wall. I knew by the sound of their breathing that they were standing in my doorway wanting to say good-bye, dressed in their new dark blue suits with the little rampant lion pins on their lapels, and their polished black shoes, and their hair newly buzzed, but they didn't speak, and I didn't turn to look at them, because if I looked, I'd start crying, and I couldn't cry in front of my brothers. That would be too weird. It had been like this since I found out they were leaving. Their absence—the anticipation of it—was like watching a train about to crash into them and being unable to push them out of the way. Danny and Nick were going off to war. Their lives were about to change. *They* were about to change. If the *Bagarre* came when they were gone, I'd probably never see them again. Mom called from downstairs telling them to hurry up, they'd miss their plane. Danny said, "Okay. Well, see ya, Ronnie," and the last thing I heard was the soft sound of their shoes on carpet as they walked away. And then they were gone.

HARRY PAID DAD the equivalent of his CHP salary to run the counter-revolutionary think tank, and we were soon *back on our feet*, as Mom put it, so that Dad could quit Hamm's Beer and Cut 'n Shoot and buy a two-story house on Grey Ghost Avenue. For a housewarming party, Dad bought a dartboard, hung it on a prominent wall in the kitchen, and attached a photograph of Jane Fonda over the bull's-eye. When the Dotens arrived, he doubled over laughing at the looks on their faces. "It's for target practice," he said. "Hit the peacenik and win a prize."

If you could pick a house in California that resembled what we had in Portugal, the house on Grey Ghost Avenue would be the closest thing you could find, with its miles of surrounding hills waving their golden manes, and orchards blotted with Bing cherries and bursting with apricots, and the nearby Union Pacific Railroad cutting through as straight as a carpenter's chalk line. Walk in any direction and you'd run into a creek or stream overgrown with blackberry bushes and teeming with snakes, frogs, leeches, dragonflies, and centipedes. Moving there, I was sure we had found our niche, and would never have to move again.

But after the first year at their counter-revolutionary seat, relations between Dad and Harry grew tense. Harry was controlling and argumentative, and constantly made petty complaints about The Group, and Dad began having philosophical disputes with him over lunch. The thing that had originally brought them together seemed to be wedging them apart. They just didn't see eye-to-eye on things anymore. And for various reasons Dad suspected Harry of being a Hitler sympathizer and possibly even communicating with the pro-Nazi *Los Tecos* organization in Mexico. And then one day the dam burst.

"Hitler didn't kill a single Jew. It's a myth," Harry said.

Dad, who had strong opinions about the Holocaust, lost his temper, which caused Harry to lose his. Dad called Harry "myopic and unlettered," and Harry called Dad "literal and pigheaded." Harsher words were exchanged, Dad later told Mom, but he wasn't going to repeat those.

"Harry must have been waiting for the opportunity to bait me in order to get to The Group. They're too militant for his liking. Too above board. Too Catholic. They've been kept out of the World Anticommunist League. Harry wants more bang for his buck. I'll bet he wants The Group to be like *Los Tecos*, and for all I know carry out death squad murders and assassinations. There's no other explanation. He wants out."

That day, Harry fired Dad, pulling the rug out from under Dad and from under The Group's west coast headquarters, and stranding Dad for the second time.

"It was bound to happen," Dad said to Mom by way of excuse. "Anyway, we don't need his money. We can still run the SEFAC seminars. We'll just have to do it out of people's homes."

But his first concern was work. With very little in savings and high monthly expenses, he didn't have time to go through weeks of paperwork to get reinstated in Sacramento. So he sent out nearly fifty résumés to corporate security offices throughout the United States and sat back to wait.

Our savings went dry in less than a month. Mom applied for food stamps. She was ashamed, she said—not for using food stamps but of a country that would allow the family of a former police officer to become dependent on food stamps. She concocted new ways to stretch the budget. A two-day-old loaf of bread from the Wonder Bread outlet cost twenty-five cents. Soaked with eggs, milk, and Velveeta, it made a cheap cheese soufflé. By doubling the water in the powdered milk and blending it with ice and a little white sugar, the milk foamed, and hid the thin flavor. You could add twice the usual amount of oats to meat loaf and effectively double the recipe. She tripled the potatoes in the slumgullion and goulash. The generic food store sold canned food without labels at a third of the price, slashing off a few more pennies if the can had a dent.

Finally, Dad got a call from United Parcel Service. The head office in San Francisco needed someone with a background in law enforcement to oversee loss prevention for the west coast.

They interviewed Dad. They said Dad was tailormade for them. Dad perked up. It was a well-paying job—just what he needed to make a new start. They asked for references, and Dad gave them several, including Harry Doten. UPS called Harry, but he refused to take their calls. Days went by. Dad was getting impatient. "What's the holdup?" he asked. "Harry Doten won't talk to us," the personnel manager said. Dad's rage grew. "Try him again," he said. They tried again. And again. But Harry hung up on them.

Dad had to hold himself back from grabbing his gun and going after Harry with intent to kill. Instead, he grabbed the rosary, gathered us in the living room, and told us to pray for his intentions (a job) and for sinners (Harry Doten). Then he said, "We've got to sell the house. In fact, we've got to get out of San Jose altogether. I can't bear to live in the same city as Harry Doten. I never want to see him again."

Now Mom stepped in. Enough was enough. Harry was no friend. He was a traitor. A phony. A hypocrite. He made empty promises, led Dad on, took advantage of his enthusiasm. She couldn't chance Dad going to talk to him, so she would have to go herself. Marching out of the house she drove straight to The Fun Spot and banged on the office door. When Harry came to the door, she looked him in the eyes. "Don't do this to us," she said. "For my sake." Harry must have been ashamed, because he stuttered a short apology, telling Mom he had no animosity toward her or the rest of us. Things had gotten out of hand. He promised to give Dad good references.

So Dad got the job and started looking for a new place to live— preferably closer to Holy Innocents and San Francisco than where we lived now. Mom started packing. With no place to go, her packing went slowly. She didn't say what was on her mind, but I guessed what she was thinking. First Noreen Poole, and now Gail Doten. The counter-revolution had a way of putting big distances between people and the ones they loved.

NOW, INSTEAD OF Travis rocketing us up 680 to Holy Innocents, Mom freighted us there in the Rambler, effectively removing the one incentive I had for attending the school in the first place. Settled in the slow lane she drove *slowly*, and made us say the rosary, while Mary and Bernadette crawled all around the car, and Vinny had to be held and played with, and Jennifer fussed and got carsick, and Terry—who spent the whole ride reading novels by dead English women—was no help at all. Gone was the thrill of speed, the cop-dodging, the music, the cherry cigars, and most of all the exciting proximity of Travis Doten.

What nobody knew was that love had infected me quietly, like a virus, and I suffered badly from it. It began as a growing discomfort whenever Travis was around—a jittery anxiety centered in my solar plexus. The actual pain started when I began noticing how Travis's eyes would linger on mine for an extra few seconds and a smile would creep across his face. Then he began leaving little reminders of himself in my brain, usually at the most awkward times. Suddenly, in the middle of the rosary or a tie-breaking exam, I'd see his ocean-blue eyes, his cleft chin, and his sleek, comb-sculpted waves of blond hair, and my pulse would rapid-race in circles like a whirligig pump toy. I tried to shake him off. But there he'd be, as real as life: the tease of his smile, the cracked tenor of his laugh, and the near-blasphemous *Jaysus!* that he'd always shout after a close call on the freeway. Or, *Muthu!* He didn't have to be near. I could smell the spicy cologne he wore, and taste the wet tip of his cigar, and imagine the feel of his freshly shaven cheek, and see the drape of his white cotton shirt against his flat chest, and my heart would go wild like the whirligig and I'd have to take large breaths for adequate oxygen.

And now this. Days before, Travis and I were passing notes and exchanging promises to meet after school. Now our families were enemies. Now I couldn't say "Doten" without Dad having a conniption that lasted for an hour as he marched around yelling about Hitler sympathizers. Travis called me on the phone and whispered that he *had* to see me, so we met secretly, late at night, in his Buick. I slid into the familiar leather of the passenger seat, my heart banging away inside me, and kept my gaze on the dashboard while we made small talk, but somehow in the middle of it Travis leaned over and kissed me, and I kissed him back. It didn't last long because I made an excuse and bolted from the car. I couldn't bear the emotional overload. But that kiss told me what I needed to know. Travis loved me. And now I needed a plan. Nothing else mattered. Not Hitler, not the Jews, not Dad—nothing. Just a plan. I thought about staging my own death (Terry had told me the *Romeo and Juliet* story). I thought about running away with Travis, stealing away in a Union Pacific train car, changing our identities, and disappearing forever. I thought about elopement. Marriage. Wow. Marriage. Unimaginable. I was barely fourteen. Could a person get a marriage license that young? My life was either about to get really exciting or really messed up. I didn't know which. All I knew was that I could not stop the thought, *He's a Doten. Dad would never forgive me.*

A month later, we moved out of San Jose. The Dotens stayed in San Jose. Neither crossed the line.

I did not cry openly to Mom or Dad, who had the *Bagarre* in mind and had made huge sacrifices for it, or to Terry, who'd gone through an infatuation of her own with Travis and degraded it to puppy love when she found *real love* with John Armour. I cried quietly into my pillow, alone with my heartbreak. It wasn't fair. Travis and I were the victims of our parents' principles. It was always about that: principles. And if there was any doubt over which direction my parents' principles were taking us on the ladder of prosperity, it dissolved when we left our house on Grey Ghost for the last time and pulled up in front of our new house on Richie Drive.

Looking out the car window, my eyes pinballed from the weedy front lawn to the peeling brown paint to the sagging garage door propped by a rake handle to the gutters overflowing with pine needles, black walnuts, and acorns dropped from various untrimmed trees, and finally landed on the house's one surprise feature. A giant stump—left over from what must have been a magnificent oak tree—rose sixteen feet in front of the house like an amputated limb.

"Well, kids. Here we are," Mom said. "Welcome to your new home."

Small, single-paned windows blinked in the dreary winter light. Leaves blew past. The silence in the back of the Rambler spoke volumes. I looked at Terry, who seemed to be experiencing a bout of dizziness, and knew we'd reached the bottom rung and could go no further.

Pleasant Hill (a town which was "neither pleasant nor a hill," as Terry later pointed out) seemed to be one big parking lot of low-income tract homes mixed with car repair warehouses and fast food restaurants, and our three-bedroom one-bath house was probably on the low end of the scale of low-income houses. There was no front step up or down; you walked straight into a house with no flooring, or even subflooring: just a concrete slab onto which the last owner, a former naval engineer, had tacked a beige, low-pile carpet. In the bedrooms there were no carpets, only squares of dark brown industrial linoleum glued with epoxy onto the concrete slab.

"The man who lived here before us was kind of eccentric," Mom said, doing her best to put a positive spin on what was clearly our final disgrace. "Isn't that neat? Everywhere you look you see his handiwork."

His handiwork included walls that were painted in stunning colors of dark purple, vivid green, and electric orange—discontinued government-issue paint that he'd inherited from the U.S. Navy (dozens of cans still occupied shelving in the garage)—and sections of walnut-finished veneer paneling.

"As soon as I walked in the place, I knew we were meant to live here," Mom added, just in case we had any doubts.

What Mom didn't say was how she thought our growing family was supposed to fit into this tiny house. Six months' pregnant with her ninth, she must have had visions of harmonious family closeness. And truly, living in that house we were as close as kittens in a shoebox, bumping into each other in the narrow kitchen, cramming three at a time into the minuscule bathroom, climbing over one another to get in and out of the bathtub, the noise a constant caterwaul of bickering and tattling and shouts from Dad to *tone it down*. When Lyle III was born, and Mom became pregnant with Bernard, the only logical thing Terry and I could do was to volunteer our bedroom and move to the back porch—a primitive space with a flat, tar-papered roof tacked through with roofing nails. Since we'd entered a new level of mutual loathing, we subdivided the back porch into two private cells using flexible bamboo fencing (which we discovered under a tarp in the backyard) for the walls, and hung old blankets for doors.

Terry and I had similar rules of entry. To enter, you were required to say, "Knock, knock," at the blanket-door. When one of us responded, "Who is it?" you had to say your name. When we asked, "What do you want?", unless you were Vinny, you'd better have a very good reason for wanting to come in.

WHEN YOU FEEL frustrated with your life, it helps to step back and look at the big picture and remember that things are the way they are for a good reason. Now that I have a room of my own, I lie on my bed and contemplate the facts on a regular basis.

The world began on Saturday, September 22, in 3760 B.C. This is the first day on the Hebrew calendar, and the Hebrews wrote the oldest history book in the world, the Old Testament, so you have to trust they know their dates. On that day, 5,737 years ago, God created Adam from a handful of soil, and Eve from his rib, and God placed these two perfect specimens of man and woman in the Garden of Eden, and for the first time ever in the history of the world there existed pure human happiness. But then God gave His creatures free will, because what would be the point in creating people and not giving them minds of their own? And then He decided to put His creatures to the test, because why give people free will but no opportunity to express it? For the test, He planted the Tree of the Knowledge of Good and Evil, gave His creatures strict orders not to eat its fruit, then allowed His archenemy Lucifer into the garden to tempt them to do just that. Now, as an omniscient creator, God knew perfectly well what the outcome of this test would be, so it must have been with some small measure of Machiavellian sport that He sat back and watched His creatures succumb to temptation and eat the fruit. And it must have been with a touch of irony that He approached them in the garden and asked, "What is this that you have done?" And when Eve answered honestly, "The serpent beguiled me and I ate," it must have been with at least a slight pang of sympathy God threw our first parents out of the Garden of Eden to begin the long, hard saga of the human race.

And things have been pretty miserable ever since. War, hunger, viruses, disease, the pain of childbirth, murder, torture, slavery, depression, suicide, rape, insanity, developmental disabilities, allergies, tooth decay, boring office jobs, taxes, and death are just some of the result of Adam's and Eve's original sin. For almost six thousand years humans have been paying for that single momentary lapse of conscience. And why? To win heaven back, of course, because that was God's plan from the start. To give us a higher purpose, the individual quest for salvation. It was an act of mercy, not cruelty. The ultimate challenge. Life only lasts so long, but your soul lasts forever. Your soul is the one thing in your transient life worth fighting for, worth suffering for, even dying for, and the sooner you realize that, the sooner you can get over yourself and get on with the task at hand.

It's a comfort to know all this, because when you are living at the pinnacle of history, in the time of the Apocalypse, in a tumbledown shack that lacks even a trace of aesthetic appeal, in a town that will never achieve the beauty and sophistication of the city from which you came, and have had your dreams of future happiness with the man you love forever shattered, you want to know that there is a reason for all the trouble. You want to know that God had a plan from the beginning, and that the plan includes you, and that things are moving along as expected. You want to feel assured that the efforts you are making to reject the modern world and remain loyal to the True Church are important and worthwhile and not a waste of time and energy. Otherwise, you'd feel like you got your facts wrong, and are not required to fight with the counter-revolutionary crusades, but should be having a good time like other teenagers, going to public school, dating, and going to the disco.

OUR HOUSE ON Richie Drive soon became a counter-revolutionary meeting center for traditionalists, and a stopping point for members of The Group who traveled from house to house caravan-style bringing news of the fight and drumming up financial support. To create a traditional atmosphere, Dad did the decorating. Over the couch he mounted two silver broadswords in the crossed position to denote two armies forever clashing in battle. On the opposite wall he mounted a wood-carved panel depicting the scene of a battle in the Crusades in which horses, knights, foot soldiers, and pagans were crammed so tightly in hand-to-hand combat that they were practically in a dogpile of bloody carnage. A life-sized painting of St. Thomas More stared out of its frame to remind you of his beheading by Henry VIII. On other walls were the Sacred Heart of Jesus, Our Lady of Fatima, several large crucifixes, and burning votive candles, and beside the front door, a holy water font that underwent such heavy use (even the neighborhood kids dipped their fingers) that Mom was obliged to refill it daily.

And finally on a wall all its own hung a replica of a medieval shield bearing the words of St. Bernard, *Maledictus qui prohibit gladium suum a sanguine* (Cursed be he who fails to bloody his sword)— Dad's favorite counter-revolutionary motto.

We did not have a dining-room table but a conference table that sat fourteen. Dressed in their suits, pins, and sashes, The Group members would come in rented cars (sometimes two or four, at other times ten or more), humbly bow at the neck, greet everyone with "Salve Maria," and file into the living room/dining room. The meetings began with the Prayers of The Group, which Dad would often lead, while in the kitchen Mom would prepare a three-course meal which Terry, Jennifer, and I would serve on her best china dishes (slightly chipped after their trip to Portugal and back). While the men ate, we girls would sit with the kids in the back porch and eat on TV trays. We preferred this, since in the other room the talk was always the same. The Church was in a crisis. We must continue to pray. The *Bagarre* was near. Our Lady's Immaculate Heart would triumph. When dinner ended, Dad would write a check and hand it over, and with "Salve Marias" all around, the meeting would be over.

When Danny and Nick came home to visit, Mom filled the candy bowls and cooked pot roast and scalloped potatoes and baked apple pies. Having Danny and Nick home meant late nights around the table asking them questions. And when they talked, we listened. They had insider information that we didn't, and we felt privileged to hear it.

"Want to know what hell is like?" Danny asked. "Think of an inverted mountain whose peak rests on your pinky. That pain in your pinky will be the pain your whole body will feel for eternity.

"When you're thrown into hell, you're flung with so much force that you fall fast and hard for a long time. When you finally hit the ground, whatever position you land in will be the position you will stay in for eternity, with all your bones broken, your limbs twisted, and your guts spilling out. In that position, you will either freeze or burn. If your punishment is to burn, what will happen is your skin will burn off first, and the rest of you will just sizzle away forever, never being destroyed, but always burning on the meat under the skin. It's hard to say what's worse, burning or freezing. In a way, they both feel the same."

They talked about eternity.

"If you want to know how long eternity is, think of a spider. He strings a web from the earth to the moon. Then he comes back to the earth and waits. After a thousand years, the spider transports a single grain of dirt from the earth to the moon. Then comes back and waits for another thousand years. By the time he's transported the entire earth, grain by grain, to the moon, eternity hasn't even begun.

"Imagine the moon is made of solid steel, and once every thousand years a giant seagull flies from the earth to the moon and sweeps his wing over the moon. Then he flies back and waits for another thousand years before he does it again. By the time the moon is worn down to the size of a BB, eternity won't even have started yet."

They told us more. The *Bagarre* would happen sometime in the 1980s. No one knew which year exactly. St. John Bosco had written the date on his own tombstone, but the last number was marred by vandals. There was some confusion over when the Three Days of Darkness would come. Some, like Nostradamus, thought it would come around 1999, but no one knew for sure. A giant cross the color of blood would appear in the sky as a warning. The temperature on the planet would drop to freezing. And then complete and utter darkness would fall. Hell would be emptied and the demons would roam the earth. The winds would blow and earthquakes would shake and a hurricane of fire would fall from the sky. No electric lights or candles would function. Only blessed candles would accept the flame of a match, and nothing would have the power to snuff those out.

"You should not look out the windows," Danny said, "because the sight of a demon is so terrible that you will die of fright on the spot. You should lock the doors and windows and pull the curtains and pray over blessed candles. The demons will come right up to the house and imitate the voices of people you know and sound convincing. They'll sound just like me talking to you right now. They'll say, *Terry! Ronnie! It's Danny! I caught the last plane out of New York and took a taxi! Let me in! Don't leave me out here to die!* Trust me, it'll be a temptation. Don't be fooled. Pray constantly for three days, and don't give in to the temptation."

Along with physical darkness would be spiritual darkness. People would give in to despair. They'd die of terror and suicide. Only the truly faithful would survive. Then, when the Three Days of Darkness were over, we could open our windows and witness the devastation outside. It would be horrible. The whole world would be covered in cadavers. But the world would be purified, and the believers would bury the dead and rejoice to be among the living. It would be the beginning of a new era of peace and tranquility— literally a heaven on earth. God would give the world a lustrous physical beauty that we couldn't imagine. New elements would appear that we've never seen: diamonds that acted like fire, liquid emeralds, rubies that you could eat. And all this would happen in *our* lifetime. That's why it was so important to be prepared. Our Lady would keep Satan chained up for a thousand years, and at the end of that time hell would open its gate once more, and there would be a final battle between the forces of good and evil. And when *that* was over, it would be the end of the world. But we would all be in heaven by then, so we didn't have to worry about that.

When my brothers imparted knowledge, they didn't falter or hesitate. They spoke seriously, and with absolute confidence in what they were saying, and Mom and Dad nodded and made sounds of affirmation and never questioned the authenticity of their words. No one did. Their information was sacred, passed on, obviously, from the visions and prophecies of saints. You couldn't read it in a book. It had been covered up by modern society. Just like the Third Secret of Fatima had been covered up by the Vatican.

On top of that, we'd been told by someone in The Group that Danny had *Thau*. This was an invisible sign that Professor Plinio could see on the foreheads of those with saintly vocations. If you had *Thau*, you had a spiritual vocation. The word, which named the last letter of the Hebrew alphabet that had the shape of the cross, came from a passage in Ezekiel in the Old Testament (9:4), in which God orders a man to "Go through the midst of the city . . . and set a mark [*Thau*] upon the foreheads of the men that sigh and that cry for all the abominations that be done in the midst thereof." People with *Thau* saw through the decadence of Western civilization and suffered like martyrs because of it. And Danny, it was said, was privileged with *high Thau*, meaning he was one of the elite.

13

fissures

I WAS PREPARED for almost anything when it came to the counter-revolution, but I was not prepared for what happened next in our household.

It was a regular busy day. Mom was yelling orders from the kitchen, the kids were racing around and making a mess, and Terry was helping with the babies. At one point, Dad was walking one way and I was walking another, and we intersected in the living room. "Stop," Dad said, and I froze. "Look at you." I looked down at myself. I was wearing a T-shirt and jeans as usual. "The way you girls dress is scandalous," he said. "Pants, shorts, sleeveless shirts. What's your plan? Are you on a mission of seduction? Do you want to bed down the entire male population?" I glanced at Terry. She was wearing a low-cut blouse and tight, embroidered, ripped-at-the-knees jeans. Neither of us knew what to say. "You're smart girls," Dad said. "You know what's going on. You know the Church is in a crisis. And yet you dress like . . . like . . . *fasudas*."

Fasuda was TFP-talk. It meant "slut." When you said "slut," you were voicing a modern insult. When you said "*fasuda*," you were voicing a distinctly counter-revolutionary insult.

Dad said maybe the blame belonged to him and Mom. Maybe they hadn't guided us from the start like they should have. With all the troubles in the Church they'd let some of the important things slip by, like a proper dress code. Anyway, he was sorry if he'd been lax, but enough was enough. It was time to stop wearing modern clothes.

"We live in the blackest, most vile century in the history of mankind," he said. "I know it isn't pleasant, but we all have to make sacrifices. We have to stand up. You can't win a fight if you fight with half a heart."

As I listened to Dad, my heart pounded heavily and my eyes saw double images. *This is it*, I thought. *It's over*. And I realized at that moment that I'd intuited long ago that it would come down to this. Clothes. Ever since that day in Portugal when I stuffed my hated dress into my carry-on bag and shoved it deep under my bed, I knew I'd be pulling that dress back out and wearing it, and others like it, for the traditional Catholic Church. That for me to be part of the counter-revolution I couldn't escape wearing a goddamned dress. You can't fight with half a heart, Dad said. And therein lay the problem. I believed in the fight, but did I have a whole heart to fight it?

"No more pants," he said. "And that's final."

I looked at Mom with eyes that pleaded for mercy, but Mom had begun dressing in knee-length skirts and shapeless blouses back at the Jeffrey Street house. She wasn't likely to sympathize with my dilemma. Anyway, Mom would never betray Dad. Whether she agreed with the dress code or not, Mom was the steel backbone that gave Dad strength. How many times had I heard him admonish her, *You've got to back me up on this, Mart. You know I can't do it on my own.*

"You should be *proud* to dress modestly," Mom said. "Proud, because you're giving glory to God."

I looked at Terry, whose floor-slanted eyes said, *Whatever. I'm tired. Leave me alone.* She probably had something up her sleeve, but she wasn't going to fight Dad out in the open. Not now, barefisted in the ring, with Mom refereeing.

The problem with the counter-revolution had always been that it was tedious, and I was beginning to build a long list of grievances against it. First Danny and Nick going away. Then Holy Innocents. Then the bustup with the Dotens. We weren't allowed to go to discos or movies. We weren't allowed to listen to rock 'n' roll music. And now, no pants. The no-pants rule was a massive, colossal, gigantic setback almost too big to conceive. No pants meant no shorts, no cutoffs, no exercise leggings, no Capris, no gauchos, no ski pants, no bathing suits, no wraparound bellbottoms, no wet suits, gym shorts of any length, culottes, overalls, or leisure slacks. It meant no lederhosen for Halloween, or jodhpurs should we take up horseback riding, or leotards if ballet grabbed our interest. No pants meant no clothes of any kind with any style, flair, grace, or elegance. No pants meant *dresses.* Period. And not cute, short dresses that zipped up the back or side, but long, fulllength stage-curtain types of shrouds that descended, pall-like, to censure everything underneath in a thick cloth with some heavyhanded pattern that looked pathetically paranoid and old-fashioned (like flowers, or checks, or paisley, or fleurs-de-lis), all of which had the opposite of sex appeal.

Terry, Jennifer, and I (and Mary and Bernadette, too, who were old enough to know what was happening) absorbed this change in lifestyle with wide, unblinking eyes that stared into reality and saw horror there. Me: I rode my skateboard to school. What idiot rode a skateboard in a long skirt? Terry rode her bike. How was she supposed to strap down the billowing yards of modesty so they didn't get trapped in her back wheel? Jennifer did cartwheels and ran through her friends' sprinklers. Mary and Bernadette climbed trees and fences. All of us got invited to go swimming in the Selways' built-in pool. Have you ever seen a girl swim in a long skirt and not drown?

The day Dad made the no-pants rule, Mom appeared at my blanket-door and held out a big green garbage bag. "Just throw your pants into the bag," she said, "and get rid of them before they cause temptation." I'd anticipated the garbage bag. Mom never gave an order without following it straight through to its extreme conclusion. Knowing this about her, I'd gone to my room ahead of her and removed my favorite pair of jeans from my dresser drawer, shouldered up my mattress, and laid them lengthwise underneath. I did not think *deception*. I did not think *sin*. I thought *backup*. And then I changed *backup* to *self-preservation*. Keeping a single pair of pants was like having a fire extinguisher on hand. Or keeping a spare tire. Who drove through life without a spare tire?

Storing a single pair of pants was the beginning of a long series of self-preservations for years to come. From there followed a secret collection of funk-soul records—Earth, Wind, and Fire, the Ohio Players, Wild Cherry, and Parliament for starters—nasty, sexy, suggestive music to which I listened on the headphones late at night and to which I quietly performed some of my own dance moves. There was some experimentation with drugs—pot and mushrooms, mostly, which Terry would score from the down-the-street neighbor, and which would get the two of us laughing so hard for so long, it would be dawn before we'd finally collapse from exhaustion. There were also one or two clandestine trips to the disco where I'd try out my dance moves, and some kissing with a non-Catholic boy I'd meet up with at the park.

Terry had the same self-preservation policy as me, although Terry took it to the extreme. She wasn't content to get high on pot or shrooms, she wanted to try cocaine and rush. Discos were too straight, she wanted to hang out with the transvestites at *The Rocky Horror Picture Show*. She drank, but didn't stop at the buzz. She got totally fall-down puke-her-guts-up drunk. And she didn't just kiss boys. She went *practically all the way*, and then bragged about it.

I preferred a more moderate approach. I wanted to have fun, but I also wanted to be nominally counter-revolutionary. I was a fence-walker. I wasn't proud of this. There was a term for someone like me: *nho-nho* (pronounced "nyo-nyo"). This was a term The Group used. It meant you wanted it both ways. In Brazil in centuries past, the African slave wet nurses who took care of the children on the sugar and coffee plantations often called the children *nho-nhos*—a diminutive for *senhor* (lord of the plantation), as in "*nho-nho* Fabio" or "*nho-nho* Domingo."

Dad despised *nho-nhos*, because *nho-nhos* had only their personal interests in mind—like children. In history, this type always "tilted the scales toward corruption," Dad said, and he'd rattle off the primary offenders without taking a breath. "In sixteenth-century England it was the Catholic hierarchy who caused the self-destruction of that nation with the Protestant Revolution. In 1789, it was the bourgeoisie who followed the ideals of Voltaire and Rousseau. In 1914, it was the upper classes who followed the military in almost all countries. In 1917, it was the Russians who followed Lenin and allowed his revolution to happen. In the early 1930s, it was the higher classes in society and the upper military ranks who followed Hitler. From the first years of the Communist regime, it was Western capitalism that kept the Russian and then the Soviet Union alive. Those were the *nho-nhos* par excellence. And then of course it was the sellout of the Catholic hierarchy at Vatican II that brought about the Vatican ostpolitik."

Dad theorized that only two percent of Catholics were counter-revolutionary. The other ninety-eight percent were either *nho-nhos* or they were the other kind of liberal Catholic: a *nane*.

Nane was an acronym for the phrase *nada aprendido nada esquecido*, which in Portuguese meant "nothing learned nothing forgotten." The phrase, Dad said, had been uttered by Talleyrand in the eighteenth century when the Bourbons returned to France after the fall of Napoleon. "They have learned nothing and forgotten nothing," Talleyrand said. If you were a *nane* in the twentieth century, you were someone who didn't want to change your easy lifestyle, but insisted on carrying on exactly as you always had, regardless of the moral collapse of your leaders.

Nho-nhos and *nanes* were the kind of Catholic who might hide a pair of pants under a mattress (for emergencies), and make out with non-Catholic boys (but not go too far), and drink beer (but not enough to get wasted or caught), and still feel self-righteous enough to call herself a counter-revolutionary.

WHEN POPE PAUL VI died on August 6, 1978, Dad reacted the same way he had when Stalin died in 1953: with scornful indifference. And he was not surprised to hear the rumor that Paul VI turned over in his coffin, and that the stench around him was unbearable. He reacted with equal indifference when twenty days later Albino Luciani took the throne and showed his allegiance to Vatican II by assuming the name of both previous progressivist popes, John and Paul. Why should Dad care who was pope? The damage had already been done. To impress Dad, Pope John Paul I would have to reveal the Third Secret of Fatima and come clean about the evil council, and he wasn't going to do that. Thus, Dad's indifference remained when thirty-three days after his coronation John Paul I died (murdered by Vatican stooges, most likely, to usher in a more progressive pope), and Cardinal Karol Wojtyla, taking the name John Paul II, stepped into Peter's chair. Things were moving along nicely for the enemies of the Church.

What Dad did do was to step up preparations for the *Bagarre*. First, he cleared out a section of the garage and stocked it with emergency supplies: thirty gallons of drinking water stored in Clorox bleach bottles; a first-aid kit with a tourniquet and sterile needles; matches, dry goods, canned goods; and a three-year supply of toilet paper. He sent dozens of pure wax candles to Archbishop Lefebvre to be blessed, and sent away for more holy water from Lourdes. He ordered new larger brown scapulars for us all, which he gave to Danny and Nick to touch to the statue of the Pilgrim Virgin if they ever got the chance.

There were many ways to prepare for the *Bagarre*. Mom's way was to be a powerhouse of positive energy. To mix strong cocktails for the constant guests that walked through the door—the lonely ex-wives, and alcoholics, and discouraged Trads who stuck with their unhappy marriages because divorce was *Novus Ordo*—promising them her prayers and in the same breath telling them to grow a backbone and stand up to what ailed them; and to cook meals large enough to feed our family and the odd acquaintance who might happen to stop by, like the runaway teenagers of friends and the quietly hopeful bachelors from church at the Walnut Creek Veteran's Hall who had crushes on Terry; and to adopt whatever stray animals I brought home, such as the gopher snake, the mother cat and her three small kittens, the mallard duck, and the tarantula; and to refuse to tolerate depression in her children. "Blow your bad mood into this paper bag," she'd say, and then she'd pop the bag. "There! Whatever the problem was, it's gone. Now get back to business."

Reinforcing the importance of a vigorous prayer life, Mom bought a big brass ship's bell and installed it on our porch to ring when it was time for prayers. With a clang that covered a full square mile and hung in the air for almost a minute, the bell guaranteed that no Arnold, or non-Arnold for that matter, would lose track of the time or forget about the Angelus at noon and the rosary after dinner. Every day the bell's sharp but wobbly note materialized on the porch and radiated outward, drowning out cars, barking dogs, airplanes, and television, and penetrated the doors and windows of neighbors' homes, to force us to stop whatever we were doing and get home or face a look from Mom that said, *Is this the thanks I get for installing the bell and helping you keep track of your prayer life?*

Terry prepared for the *Bagarre* by taking (what else?) the extreme approach. When civilization collapsed, fashions would revert back to the Middle Ages. So Terry sewed capes for the women of the family. My cape was floor-length, made of purple velvet lined with white satin, and had a full hood and a fancy woven golden clasp. I wore it around the house, and to bed, and sometimes when I rode my skateboard, until the hem began to fray. This bothered Terry. "The cape is for the *Bagarre*!" she said. "Stop wearing it like you're in a *Prince Valiant* comic."

Reasoning that we would need to sew our own clothes out of whatever cloth was available, Terry taught herself how to design dress patterns on butcher paper, cut them out, and sew the dresses out of old bedsheets on Mom's pedal-powered Singer machine. The sheets had bright, cheerful flowerprints that made us look like walking tissue boxes or bathroom air fresheners, but I liked how cool they felt against my skin on hot days. With the cape over the top, you could close your eyes and imagine you were lying comfortably in bed.

Since we would have to substitute honey for store-bought sugar, she taught herself to bee-keep. The bees buzzed in and out of two big white boxes in the backyard, and Terry doused them with smoke when it was time to check the honeycombs. The only problem with keeping bees was the amount of stings the babies received. It got so bad that Mom had to keep them inside during the active spring and summer months, and let them out during rainy or cold weather days.

And finally, Terry taught herself archery, installing a hay bale target in the backyard beside her bee boxes, and target-shooting every day until she became a tolerably good markswoman. Archery, she said, would come in handy when Dad's bullets ran out.

Dad's bullets were not likely to run out, since he'd been preparing for the *Bagarre* for decades and had assembled a first-class collection of firearms and knives, which he kept in a fireproof safe in his bedroom. Every so often I'd ask to see his collection, just to watch him lay each piece out on his bed—something he did happily.

"This one's my favorite handgun of all time: a Colt .45 automatic. Feel the weight and balance of it. It's a perfect killing machine . . . When your enemy is within range, what you want to do is aim for his center. You don't want to try to disable him by shooting at his legs . . . This one here is my second favorite—the Colt Trooper .357 with the six-inch barrel. I carried this one as a regular sidearm in the Sheriff's Office and in the CHP. It's a good solid revolver . . . notice the heavy barrel, and the adjustable sights. It's cheaper than Smith & Wesson's .357, and a bit lighterweight. Perfect for policework . . . Ah, look at this. Remember the movie

Getaway, with Steve McQueen? He used this one: a high-standard twelve-gauge seven-shot police pump shotgun. And of course this one . . . *Dirty Harry* used the Model 29 Smith & Wesson .44 Magnum, although his was a six-inch barrel, not a four-inch barrel like mine. Take a look at this rifle. It's a Mini 14 .223-caliber Ruger, named after its cousin the M14. See? It uses a rotating bolt, and has a fixed, self-cleaning piston and moving cylinder rather than the M14's captive piston. Hold it up and look through the aperture sight. Nice, huh? Its action is the same as the rifle I used when I was in the Marine Corps."

I enjoyed how much Dad enjoyed his guns and felt closer to him when he shared them with me and thought about how wonderful it would be to see him use them. His knives had a different sort of fascination for me. I liked the way he would pick each one up, flip open the blade, and weigh it in his hand as if he were a Jet getting ready for a rumble with the Sharks. He had a Fairbairn-Sykes stiletto that had "the feel and balance of a surgical instrument," and a KA-BAR Mark II used by the U.S. Marine Infantry, and a Blackie Collins boot dagger, and a custom hunting knife made by James B. Lile, and a Bowie knife made by A. G. Russell.

"Is it sharp?" I'd ask, laying the pad of my thumb on the edge of the stiletto.

"Is it *sharp*!" Dad laughed, and slid the flat edge along his hairy forearm, shaving it shiny bald. "I keep all my weapons in perfect condition, ready for deployment."

My way of preparing for the *Bagarre* was to do nothing special. The end was coming, what was I going to do about it? Brush my teeth an extra time every day? Pack an extra pair of underwear? It was on its way—just around the corner. I was ready. Or almost ready. There was only one thing I could think of that I would possibly need for the *Bagarre*. Just one thing: a car. Danny and

Nick had talked about cities being prisons of death and destruction, public transportation being inundated by millions trying to escape, bridges going down under the weight of too many cars, and panic and terror on every street. I thought about Mom's Rambler. It overheated. And Dad might be stuck in San Francisco with his Toyota, unable to get home. We'd be sitting ducks on Richie Drive when the bombs started falling.

Terry had a 1963 VW Bug with engine problems that had been sitting in front of the house for over a year and I began eyeing it. The car had never run right. It had a flat tire. A dead battery. A broken headlight. Bad brakes. No blinkers. Windshield wipers that didn't move. A heater that stayed on permanently. A useless emergency brake. "If I was to buy your Bug"—I introduced the idea to Terry one day—"like . . . how much would it cost me?" Terry shrugged. "It's a piece of crap," she said, "but I'll sell it to you for a hundred and fifty bucks." My heart lifted. I said I could pay in twenty-dollar increments. She agreed, and we had a deal.

I spent that summer underneath the VW, my knees childbirth-wide, my voluminous skirt tenting my ankles, my blouse wicking up gasoline, my elbows carving themselves red into the pavement, my fingernails scratching up black dust, my knuckles bleeding from being bashed against rust and steel. I had a goal, and it was to get that car running. I read John Muir's *How to Keep Your Volkswagen Alive*, and studied the comics and followed the instructions. "If you have long hair, please get out your stocking cap and tuck your hair into it." I mean I *really* followed the instructions. Changed the plugs. Filed the points. Flushed the lines. Charged the battery. Nothing I did worked. "Low compression," said Pete-across-the-street, meaning it didn't have the power to turn over by ignition alone but would run with a push start. He helped me give it a shove, and sure enough he was right. My next task, logically, was to maintain the car that I'd resuscitated, so I accepted Terry's old job that she didn't want anymore—the job of full-time nanny for a single father with two kids—and every day push-started the car and drove to Emeryville twenty miles away.

Marshall Webb was an acquaintance of Dad's, a mutual friend of some people he knew in law enforcement. A divorced father with full custody of his two kids, Marshall Junior and Marcia, ages six and eight, Marshall repaired copy machines for a living. He was tall, slender, balding, fifty-five, black, and looking for love in the want ads of the *Oakland Tribune*.

I didn't see anything unusual in Marshall's treatment of me. I simply thought he was being nice. When he came home from work, he always brought something fun to eat: Chinese noodles, or pizza, or TV dinners, and as we ate he asked about my day and treated me like an adult, making me feel like I was a loved member of this wonderful black family that had no mother. I decided that I could live like this for quite a while *and* maintain my car. Then, at the end of summer, on my last day of babysitting before the kids started school, Marshall came home early from work. Seeing him standing in the doorway in his dark blue repairman's uniform, I said, "What happened? Were you fired?" He shook his head. "I have to talk to you." I said, "Okay," and followed him to the kitchen.

In the kitchen he opened the refrigerator, took out a bottle of white wine, uncorked it, filled two glasses, and handed one to me. I accepted the glass with a catch in my breathing. This wasn't like eating Chinese food. Something about drinking alcohol in the middle of the day together changed our relationship. Marshall tinked my glass with his, and I took a swallow, thinking, *Don't be so paranoid. We're just celebrating my last day with a glass of wine.*

But then he leaned across the table and took my hands in his. The firmness of his grip sparked a conflagration in my chest. My face burned on the surface. I looked down at his large, aging, coffee-colored hands and back at him. If this was a joke, I couldn't wait for the punch line.

"Ronnie Arnold," he said in his deep voice. "I don't know how to tell you this except straight up. Girl . . . I *love* you. I've been holding back for so long . . . I can't hold back anymore. I love you so much, baby. It's killing me. I'm *dying*. I—I want to *marry* you."

The idea of Marshall in love with me and wanting to marry me was so bizarre that I could do little more than stare at him with eyes flash-blinded, and listen to the words skipping in the record of my mind. *Love-you-baby-holding-back-so-long-killing-me-I'm-dying-marry-you.* He kissed the tops of my hands, turned them over, and kissed my wrists and forearms. His powerful lips pecked at me like a koi fish plucking food—hungrily, efficiently, mechanically—bringing goose bumps to my flesh. I thought that if he kissed me with that muscular nip anymore I'd faint, so I pulled my arms away.

He stopped then, and knelt on the floor. His face was level with mine. I could smell his old-man cologne. "Ronnie. Listen to me. I love you. *I love you.*" He leaned so close I could see my blanched face reflected twice in the mirrors of his black irises. Cradling my face in his hands, he kissed my lips. Out of genuine surprise I let him, although I didn't want to. He breathed loudly through his nose, and his cheek brushed mine, reminding me of the smooth but prickly belly of a dog.

Then he stood up and offered me a hand. I took it because I didn't have a good reason not to. He led me across the house to the bathroom like a dancer leading a partner to the dance floor. In the bathroom, he locked the door. At that point I knew why he'd come home early. I looked at him, and he met my eyes with sad tenderness.

"Uh . . . Marshall? What are we doing in the *bathroom*?" I asked, hoping sarcasm would disarm him.

He answered with another kiss. Then he began to undress me. If I weren't disabled by disbelief, I would have laughed at the stupidity of what he was doing. Did he actually think we were going to have sex? The look on his face said he absolutely did, but I was sure that any minute Allen Funt would appear and say, "Smile! You're on *Candid Camera*," and Marshall would slap his thighs and bellow, "I really had you fooled!" But Allen Funt didn't appear, and there were no cameras. Just Marshall and me in the bathroom. And I was naked, and Marshall was naked, and on top of it all he was trying to enter me. Why didn't I stop him? Protests were pounding fists on the door of my mind, screaming out furiously, ordering me to take action. Marshall was breaking into my body, trespassing, entering by force. And I was staring in open-mouthed disbelief at the ceiling.

Mom had never talked about body-related things. She'd never said the words "sex," "intercourse," or "rape." She'd never said "masturbation," "genitals," or even "menstruation." I had learned about my period from Terry—and her joking description had left me puzzled and doubtful. When my period arrived, the logic sunk in, but vaguely. I thought, *So that's what it's all about*, and went to tell Mom, but there was no dialogue or words of advice. I found the instructions to the pads on a folded-up piece of paper in the Kotex box. I was grateful to the Kotex people for putting it there.

Mom's lack of instruction spoke loudly that the topic of sex was not on the table. Home was no place to discuss it, nor was school. A book should not deal with it, nor television, nor music. Friends should not discuss it, neither should siblings or their parents. Sex should not exist in thought, word, or deed until the marriage vows had been made, and then it should be secretly shared between man, wife, and God.

Marshall didn't ejaculate. The strange end to this was Marshall losing his erection, and looking sad. "I've never done anything like this before," he said, an actual tear rolling down his cheek. I rose to my feet and stared at him. I'd never seen a man cry and I didn't want to. I looked down and saw a trickle of blood on my thigh. Unrolling a handful of toilet paper, I dabbed it up. I said, "I have to go," and started to get dressed. Untangling my scapular from the pile of my blouse, I kissed it, crossed myself, and put it on. I did the same with my miraculous medal. Then I started to put on my bra. "Wait," Marshall said. He wrapped his arms around me, and we did a sad, naked slow dance for a long minute. Then he let me go, and I finished dressing and left.

Back at home, I entered the house like a squirrel crosses a busy street, dodging the clutter and furniture to get to my room before I got hit with questions. Mom was standing at the kitchen sink peeling potatoes. "Well, hi!" she sang to me. "You're home early." I said, "Yep!" I didn't want her to see my face. I was sure she would see the imprint of Marshall's kisses on my lips. I didn't want her to hear me speak, either. I was sure my guilt would blare out of my mouth like a siren. I didn't want her to be near me. I was sure my skin, hair, and clothes reeked of old-man cologne.

Slipping through my blanket-door, I leaped onto my bed, covered my head with my pillow, and listened to my breathing. Had I been raped? I didn't know. For it to be rape, a girl has to say no. I hadn't said no. I'd been too slow. Too surprised. Did that mean I was complicit?

"Silence gives consent," Thomas More said in *A Man for All Seasons*. I knew the scene well: "If you wish to construe what my silence betokened, you must construe that I consented, not that I denied."

The noises in the house were as loud as ever. Mom shouted from the kitchen: *Mary, put the laundry away, Jennifer, set the table, Bernadette, pour the milk. Someone put Bernard in his high chair.* Jennifer screamed that Lyle was locked in the bathroom, and couldn't get out, and Mom shouted, *Who took the screwdriver out of the junk drawer?*

Suddenly, Terry appeared at my door. I looked at her, startled.

"Knock, knock," she said, even though she was already inside.

"What do you want?"

"You're home early."

"So? What's it to you?"

Terry had an extra sense that other people didn't have, an intuition that led her straight to a problem. She was so perceptive about things, she'd probably read my mind from the other side of the house.

"What happened?"

I let her wonder. It gave me power. But then I handed the power straight back. "Marshall kissed me."

"So what? He kissed me, too. Big whoop."

I stared at her. "He kissed *you*?"

"Sure. He would've gone all the way if I'd let him."

"And you didn't?"

"*No.* You think I'm dumb?"

I swallowed. I felt sick. "He said he's in love with me."

"And you believed him?"

"Yes."

"Don't you know a guy will say anything to get you to go all the way? *Duh!*"

"He wants to marry me."

"Marry you . . . Right." She waited. She was reticent, cool, and thoughtful. She wanted details. But she already knew them. Probably better than I did.

"So?" she finally said. "Did you?"

"What?"

"Go all the way?"

Terry and I hadn't yet reached the civil stage of our relationship, but I trusted her with the information. Anyway, I needed to tell *someone*, so I nodded.

"Big mistake," she said.

I could feel my throat tightening. I knew perfectly well it had been a mistake. She didn't have to shove my nose in it. "What makes you such an expert on my mistakes?"

Something in her face gave me pause. This wasn't just about me. She had something on her mind, too. She looked away. Then her eyes met mine. There were tears in them.

"I'm pregnant."

I stared. I wanted to burst out a dozen exclamations—*Not good! Bad! Stupid! Dumb! Calamitous! Terrible! Take it back! Make it not be true!*—but I sat there, silent, tense, and sorry. I didn't even like my sister at this point, but I wished I could undo what she'd done. It was the wrong move, wrong choice, wrong fate. It couldn't happen. Shouldn't have happened. Should not be. Could not be.

Finally, I asked, "Who's the father?"

"I don't know."

"You don't know? You don't *know*? How could you *not know*?"

"I just don't. Okay?"

TERRY HAD A secret, and I had secret, and Mom knew we had secrets and wanted to know what they were. Since the no-pants rule, she'd been stalking us with her eyes, as if she could tell we were up to something. Her attitude was upbeat as always, but her eyes said that even though she couldn't nail us down on any particular fault, she didn't trust us. She didn't insinuate or ask any questions or probe in any way or lecture or pry. She just watched us, looking for clues, and waited to catch us at something. Then one day while we were at school, she took matters into her own hands.

I'd kept a journal ever since Portugal. Every night I wrote the day's report, tackling life's problems—such as how much money it would take to bleed the VW brakes or replace the fuel filter, plugs, and distributor cap (my life revolved around car repairs)—which I tried to make more interesting with the use of caps, exclamation points, and underlines. I didn't hide my journals. The word PRIVATE was inked large on every cover. To me, the word PRIVATE meant that my journal was automatically off limits to all eyes but mine. To Mom, PRIVATE meant she'd finally secured access to all my secrets.

Soon after the Marshall incident, a paper fire was burning in the fireplace. Mom often burned paper, so I didn't think there was anything unusual about it happening on that day. "Howdy, Mom," I said, as I walked through the kitchen. Mom was at the sink doing dishes. She didn't look up. That wasn't like her. She always greeted me with a smile. Confused, I continued on to my room. Then, hit by a sudden premonition, I knelt down beside my bed and reached my hand underneath, feeling around for my secret stash of self-preservations. My hand encountered space. I looked under my bed. My stack of albums was gone. A quick scan of the room revealed them broken in half and stuffed in my garbage can. My heart began to slam against my ribs. I bent down and peered again into the empty darkness. My journals were gone. My *journals!*

All those pages of . . . of . . . I raced around my room, pulling open drawers, throwing back the bed covers, then stopped and stood panting. The fire in the fireplace! In my mind I flipped through the notebooks, seeing the poems, the confessions, the creative sketches, the blasphemies. But the calamity only really began to sink in when I remembered one particular entry.

Dear Diary,

Well, today held TWO new surprises. Yes, TWO! You won't believe it, but get ready 'cause here they are. First surprise. I'm having an <u>affair</u> with Marshall Webb. I'm not kidding. We <u>did</u> it in his <u>bathroom</u>. NAKED. I know. Unbelievable. But Marshall is in LOVE with me, and we might even get <u>married</u>, although I'm not sure about the last part. And the second surprise is . . . brace yourself . . . Terry is PREGNANT. Mom and Dad still don't know, but when they find out, boy is she gonna GET it!

I struggled to breathe. My life was over. Mom would take every word I wrote literally. She'd believe every syllable. She wouldn't understand that I hadn't written those things for her to read. She would think that if I wrote it down, it must be true. And then there was the drawing! I'd sketched a scene of Marshall and me naked together. Me as a Sleeping Beauty–like character, and Marshall as a giant black bull-like creature shooting steam out his nostrils. Me pale, shadowless. Marshall as black as coal. My eyes closed, my hair long, my lips soft. Marshall's eyes wide open, his hair nappy, his thick lips modeled after the Rolling Stones insignia.

I stood up on wobbly legs and stumbled around the bedroom. I leaned against my dresser. I blinked over the little lights pricking my vision. I thought about running away. I thought about suicide. I had to tell Terry! I walked to her blanket-door. I stood there. My mouth was dry. There was no way out.

"Knock, knock."

"Yeah?"

I stepped through. She was sitting on her bed, swathed in a shawl, reading the novel *Rebecca*. This was her second time reading it. I never read books twice. I barely read them once halfway. It was one of the things about me that Terry despised the most. She'd recommend a book and then ask if I'd read it, and I'd say, "Some of it."

She met my eyes. She put the book down.

"What's wrong?" she asked. I must have looked like Mrs. Danvers standing in her dark doorway.

I said the words I still couldn't believe. "Mom read my journal."

"And?"

I opened my mouth. Terry's death sentence hung in the air. I didn't want to tell her. I felt so responsible and sorry. Terry's eyes were wide, as if she could hear the pronouncement.

"She knows you're pregnant."

WE SPENT DINNERTIME in our bedrooms, rattled half to death, waiting for what would come next. Mom was in the house, doing Mom-stuff. What were her plans? I didn't have a clue. *If only she'd talk to us*, I thought. *Ask some questions, help us figure out what the next step should be.* She stayed away.

When Dad came home from work I was lying on my bed staring at a patch of moonlight on the bamboo fence wall. My eyes were wide, and my ears wide, too, listening for a signal—a sound, a tone of voice, anything that would give away Dad's mood. Did he know? Had Mom told him? What had she said? How would he react? The house seemed unpromisingly quiet. They must be talking in their bedroom in very low voices. Maybe that was okay. Maybe that was a good sign. Better silence than an outburst of some kind—slamming doors, or breaking glass. Terry's light shone between the thin bamboo slats. She must have been listening too.

After a tortuous span of time—a quarter of an hour? an hour?—Dad came to the back porch and called Terry and me into the living room. Mom had put the kids to bed early. When we entered the living room, we stood side by side. I felt doomed. The grandfather clock ticked a condemning *tut-tut* sound from its wall. Mom was standing beside Dad, holding a handkerchief to her face, which was puffy from crying, and Dad was sitting slouched in a chair. "Sit down," he said. He didn't look at us. His expression belonged to a man who was preparing himself to shoot his old dog. He wove his fingers together as if in prayer. His head dropped.

"Your mother is devastated," he began. His voice was hoarse. He clenched his teeth. "And I am, too. I would rather you'd stuck a pickax in my back than do what you've done."

I looked at Terry. Her face was the color of an oyster, her mouth slack, her eyes locked on nothing.

Dad's voice was half-choked.

"Ronnie, having a sexual affair with a *married man*—and he is married, don't kid yourself. Divorce is an illusion made up by modern society. It doesn't exist in the Church . . . the *real* Church, that is. And Terry, sleeping around with . . . *whoever* . . . and getting *pregnant*—don't even tell me who the father is, I don't want to know. It doesn't really matter, anyway. You've betrayed the Church and your own family."

A ferocious heat lit up my insides, but my skin went cold. I knew the consequences were going to be worse than I'd imagined.

"But *why?*" Dad continued. "*Why* are you willing to throw your soul away for such low-level escapades? Hell is eternal. Have you pondered what eternity means? Are you willing to suffer *in hell* for eternity?"

My heart raced. I rallied my nerve. I would explain. I would tell him about journals, how they weren't made up of facts per se. How they tended to be fictional interpretations of real events. Word games. Plays based on half-truths. Colorful life dramas. Reality stretched into a different shape. That journals were supposed to be places of free expression where a writer got away with impossible things, dreamt-up stuff, pretended, wished, invented, and acted in ways she never would in real life. I would tell him. I would make him understand. And when he realized his mistake, we'd all relax and discuss what really happened, and deal with it rationally. No one wanted to put a pickax into anyone's back. The situation didn't call for such talk.

"Um . . . That stuff I wrote"—I said, my voice shaking and my heart pumping like an overburdened sump pump—"in my journal, well, it's not all exactly *true*. It's just . . . stuff I *wrote* . . . I mean . . . sometimes I write things . . . in a way that *looks* bad, but isn't quite that bad."

I wasn't articulating my point of view very well. I glanced at Terry. She was staring at the floor, not feeling, not computing, drifting downstream. It was up to me to rescue us both.

"What I mean is, I'm not really having an *affair* with Marshall, exactly. I . . . He . . ." I shrugged helplessly. I still hadn't settled the rape question. I didn't know how to discuss such a complicated thing.

Dad seemed not to have heard me. "I've searched for a way we might still forgive you. I've prayed. But the deception—right under our noses, and with the younger ones watching—and believe me, they're watching everything you do. That we can't forgive."

I could feel my heart swelling like a sponge inside me, thickening, growing heavy, sinking, and the rest of me sinking with it, and Terry up above being pulled away by a different tide, too late for me to grab hold of.

Dad stood up. "It pains me to say this, but you are no longer my daughters. You are dead to me. You will both leave this house immediately. I want you to go, and never come back. I don't want you to contact your mother or your siblings or any of your relatives. Do you understand? Go. And I don't ever want to see either of you again."

He turned and walked out of the room. I turned to Mom. *Mom!* She was standing by the couch, leaning a little. She looked crippled. At the sight of her, I knew she was surprised by Dad's decree. But Mom. *Mom!* No. She wouldn't challenge Dad in front of us. Her duty was to him before us. She gripped the wall, turned, and with each step calculated to keep her upright walked to her room and shut the door.

14

infant ponderings

I WAS ANCHORED under the weight of oceans. Terry floated
on the surface, swaying, unanchored, broken, bobbing against the
shore of the armchair. She had it worse than me. She had a baby
coming. It sucked to be her. That didn't make it any easier to be
me. I stood up and traversed the floor on ten-ton legs. The room
stepped back to let me through. The grandfather clock swung its
finger. *Shame ... shame ... shame ...* Our Lady of Fatima watched
me sadly from her frame. *You heard your father. You are no longer his
daughter.* The statues glared down from their pedestals. *He tried,
but he can't forgive you.* Thomas More frowned behind glass. *Do not
contact your mother or siblings. Never come back.* The Sacred Heart
of Jesus. *Leave this house. Immediately. Go.* The kitchen held its
breath. *Go.* The back porch. *Go.* My bed. *Go.* My dresser. *Go.* The
cactus. *Go.* The snake in his tank. *Go.*

It sounded so simple. *Go.* There wasn't much to *going* if you
took the right steps. All you had to do was take the right steps.
Buy a ticket. Board a train. Take your seat. The whistle would

blow. The train would lumber down the tracks. You'd look out the window at the passing landscape. It would be a friendly landscape, with a wide sky stretching far out over flat plains with mountains in the distance and telephone lines curtsying beside you as the train passed. The train would rattle on for a long time, and finally stop at some exciting destination. Alaska, Canada, Mexico, Peru. People saved up all year to go to those places. They wrote post-cards home with colorful stamps and lots of exclamation points. Nobody saved to come to Pleasant Hill. Nobody wrote postcards from Pleasant Hill. That must mean that Pleasant Hill was not worth coming to.

Leave. Go. Never return. I stood in the middle of my room. How did one do it? There must be a list of do's and don'ts. A method. A book of rules. Novels were full of stories of leaving. That's proba-bly why Terry read them so much. In novels, girls were always dis-owned for something. Terry probably knew how to take the next step. Once she stopped swaying and started packing her things, I would watch how she did it. She would take banishment with style, grace, and the right amount of drama. Me?

I'll probably make a mess of it. I know I will.

My chest overinflated, stalled, and leaked air. Tears rolled in two straight lines. I looked around. *Well, time to pack. Time to find a new home. A new family.* I didn't own a suitcase. *How do you pack without a suitcase?* I parted my blanket-door and walked back through the house past Terry—still bobbing, unmoored—to the garage, flipped on the light, and peered into the rafters where I knew some suitcases were stored. They were huge. They looked like they belonged in the hold of a cruise ship. They still had their Portugal tags on them. *Shit—fuck—damn!* I walked back through the house, searching for something, anything, that would serve as a carry-on. My eyes landed on Beau's dog food bag. I picked it up and shook it. It was lined, strong. *This is good. Actually, this is perfect.* I dumped the remaining kibble out by the back door, and filled it with my clothes and shoes.

Leave. Go. Never return. What did that mean in real terms? It meant I'd never see Vinny (Bean Bag) again, or Jennifer (Keebie), or Mary (Mow Mow), or Bernadette (Beandip), or Lyle (Lunky), or Bernard (Winnie Woo). They were *my* kids, too. I was half their mom. I couldn't imagine life without them. My throat cramped and burned. I wiped my eyes with my sleeve. I took in large gulps of air, trying to even out my breathing. I thought about Dad, the man I'd loved all my life. He hated me. I was unforgivable. I thought about Mom. She was so strong, so take-charge. She should have given me a hand. She should have talked to Dad.

I could hear Terry moving around in her room. I went to her flowered door. "Knock, knock."

"Come in." Terry rarely tolerated me in her room. At the moment she was beyond those petty irritations. "What do *you* want?"

I looked around her *boudoir*, as I thought of it—its pillows, flowery wallpaper, lamp with the rose-tinted shade, shelves crammed with novels by Austen, the Brontës, Dumas, Hardy, paintings of sad women, the fountain pen in its ink jar, the decorative jewelry box that contained bracelets, earrings, charms, and necklaces given to her by boyfriends.

"Where are you going to go?" I asked.

"Hugo's."

Hugo was one of her boyfriends—maybe the father of her child. He was from Canada. That was probably why I'd included Canada on my list of potential destinations. Hugo's citizenship there had made it seem accessible to someone like me. Hugo came to our house once. But only once. He wasn't into God, he said; he was into David Bowie. And he was scared of Dad. No offense, he said, but your house is spooky. Like a goddamned mortuary. Dad hadn't liked Hugo, either. Hugo wore tight pants and had bleached his hair. Dad asked Terry, "Is that guy a fruitcake or something?"

"Can I come?"

"*No.*"

I waited for her to ask me where I was going, to which I would reply, "Shane's"—the in-joke name of my make-believe boyfriend—but she didn't ask. She unbuttoned the top three buttons of her blouse, exposing the lacy edge of her bra from which her breasts overflowed like the contents of two overstuffed bureau drawers, brushed her already smooth hair, and put on her floppy velvet hat. Licking the corner of a tissue, she tidied the edges of her eyeliner, applied fresh blue pencil to her upper lids, and slipped her big hoop earrings into the holes of her earlobes. Taking a wad of money from her jewelry box, she put it into her purse and glanced at me in the mirror. "Is there something you want?"

If I'd told the truth, I'd have said, *As a matter of fact, yes. I want you to like me. I want you to hug me. I want you to take me with you.*

Instead, I said, "No."

"Good."

I backed out through her door and in through mine, and stood looking around at the cactus plants, the comic books, the desert scene in the terrarium, the light-up goose lamp, the single crucifix, and thought, *Look at this ugly place. God, I am such a loser. No wonder Terry can't stand me.* Dropping my dress, I put on a sweatshirt and my emergency pair of pants, rolled the top of the dog food bag like a lunch sack, pulled on my stocking cap, and with one last look around my room walked out the back door.

Your mother is devastated. And I am, too.

Climbing over the back fence to the empty dirt lot with the

blackberry bushes, I looked to the left and right. To the right, the street curved and darkened to smaller neighborhoods and the public high school. To the left, the streetlights painted individual rings of cool white: stepping stones of light for city-crossers. I picked up my bag, turned left, and walked through them, following the road from glowing stone to glowing stone. I needed to think. And to think, I needed a quiet place. A place where no one would bother me. I came to the edge of Pleasant Hill Park. Under the moonlight the colors of the park merged into dark purple—a somber color, the color of Lent, the color of fasting, silence, waiting. In the center of the park was a grassy mound. I sat on it. There my body and mind seemed to blend in with the purple.

I would rather you'd stuck a pickax in my back than do what you've done.

In the sandbox, a mother finished collecting her toddler's toys, lifted the child into a stroller, and dusted the sand off his bare feet, talking baby talk to soothe him. Pushing the stroller ahead of her, she disappeared down the path.

A pickax in my back.

Across the park, floodlights lit up the baseball diamond as bright as day. Players in white uniforms and long red socks began to arrive with mitts and duffle bags. A game of catch was initiated by a potbellied man with a loud voice. Friends filled the bleachers, pulled sodas from an ice chest, and opened large bags of potato chips.

Hell is eternal. Have you pondered what eternity means? Are you willing to suffer in hell for eternity?

At the other end of the park a man flung a Frisbee. His dog bolted ecstatically after it, swung back around to deliver it, but refused to loosen his teeth from the plastic. The man pried it from the dog's jaws, and threw it again. Their game never varied. The pattern was always the same—throw, retrieve, fight—and always wonderful.

Hell is eternal. Hell is eternal. Hell is eternal.

On the sand-filled playground was a large cement pipe that kids used as an echo chamber. Taking my dog food bag, I crept inside. It was a good place to think. And so I thought.

Catholic doctrine said there was no salvation outside of the Catholic Church: that every single person on the planet without exception had to be baptized or his or her soul could not enter heaven, but would go to either hell or limbo. There were some loopholes, such as in cases of emergency, but for the baptism to be valid, water must be poured over the person's head (or sprinkled) and the exact words spoken: "I baptize thee in the name of the Father, and of the Son and of the Holy Ghost." If this did not occur, the soul would retain its original sin (a sin committed, by the way, by two complete strangers thousands of years ago), be barred from heaven, and suffer for eternity. The list of potentially condemned souls boggled the mind: Hindus, Buddhists, Jews, Muslims, pagans, atheists, Eskimos, hillbillies, natives in the Amazon, cannibals in New Guinea, Aborigines in Australia, Communists in Russia, traders on Wall Street, drug addicts in Oakland, astronauts in space, Romanian Gypsies, Mongolian nomads, Arabian tribal people, African goat herders, Native American whale hunters, old people who died in their sleep, drunk drivers killed in head-on collisions, residents of Hiroshima on the day we dropped the atom bomb, unbaptized babies who died of crib death, aborted babies, miscarried babies, victims of suicide.

Who was left?

Once, discussing the hell topic, I estimated that because of the baptism rule, probably less than ten percent of the world would make it to heaven. Dad's response had been, *If that.*

"But that's not logical!" I said. "What kind of God would willingly create souls with the full knowledge that they would suffer for eternity? Only an evil God would do that."

"Check your premise," Dad said. "The premise is: God is good. Let's extend that into a simple syllogism. If God is good, then everything God does is good. Therefore God sending souls to hell is good. This is logic. Pure and simple."

My mind whirled in circles. How could hell be good?

In cases of emergency, Catholic doctrine allowed anyone to perform a baptism, even heretics and infidels, but they had to pour the water and say the exact words. (Mom had baptized a baby she miscarried at twelve weeks by holding it in her hand and sprinkling water.) If there was no water and no one to say the words, a person could be baptized by his own blood (martyrdom), or by desire (a state of mind in which he or she felt perfect contrition and the intention to do God's will). But in order for it to be real, he or she had to understand the doctrine of salvation. No matter how ignorant the person, or remote his location, God would give him the opportunity to choose salvation. If that person refused, he would burn in hell for eternity.

Even so . . . probably less than ten percent would make it through the gates.

Catholic doctrine also said that if you were baptized a Catholic, you could never be unbaptized. No matter that you were only three days old at the time of baptism and didn't have a choice whether you were baptized or not: once a Catholic, always a Catholic. You were locked in, and should consider yourself lucky that your parents had had the foresight. The hitch: as a Catholic you were compelled by dogma to uphold the Church's teachings. To not uphold them would be an apostasy. And apostates went to hell for eternity.

I would rather you'd stuck a pickax in my back.

An argument was building in my heart. It was an argument about equity. It was an argument about fairness. It was an argument about absolutism. It was an argument about truth and perception. It was an argument about *Cogito ergo sum*. It was an argument contesting that Descartes might just be right. That the intellect can only know itself. That it cannot be objective. That it cannot know *truth*. If Descartes was right, Dad threw us out for perceived sins, not real sins. Would God throw a person into hell for perceived sins?

Have you pondered what eternity means?

The baseball players collaborated on the field. The friends in the bleachers hooted and whistled their appreciation. What a simple pleasure, I thought. Baseball. Dad hated most spectator sports. He said football games had the atmosphere of the Roman Colosseum. He always said the noble sports were one-on-one. Fencing, judo, boxing. Especially boxing. *There's nothing egalitarian about a professional fifteen-rounder*, he said. It was symbolic of the individual's self-reliance. It was a call to heroism. Teams were like safety nets. One for all and all for one. *Like a family*, I thought. *Until the game is over. And then you split up and go your separate ways.*

At the end of the game, the players shook hands and went off to their homes and lives. I was sorry to see them go. Without them, I was alone in the world. The floodlights switched off. The park closed its eyes. The world went to sleep. Were Mom and Dad asleep? I zipped up my jacket, wrapped my arms around my legs, and let the heaves take me over. The pipe sobbed back at me—two sobs for every one of mine. Hearing my own voice echoing back with such sounds of distress, I thought my heart would break from sorrow.

It isn't fair. None of this is one bit fair. That thing with Marshall wasn't even my idea. It was Marshall's. Why didn't Dad pick on him?

Why didn't he take him to task? That was rape. I didn't want him to touch me. I just didn't know how to say no. Mom didn't teach me. You didn't teach me. All you taught me was to wear a fucking dress and say my fucking prayers.

After a short eternity the sun came up, and like the dawn of civilization the park filled with happy families and their friendly picnics. Retiring to the shade of a tree, I watched them with envy. All that happiness, and none of it mine. Even dogs had a better life. That day I ate an abandoned bag of potato chips, fell asleep in the sun, got sunburned on one side of my face, and crawled back into the pipe at nightfall, where the arguments took up where they left off.

I have to say, God, you make it really hard to be Catholic. I mean, the more I think about it, the more I don't see the benefits. It's like, why should I work so hard at being good when everyone else is doing their thing and having a great time, and basically we're all in the same boat in the end? It's not like the more I pray the more I'm rewarded. It's the opposite. I'm worse off now than I ever was, and I've prayed a LOT. What I want to know is, what do you want from me? You don't seem to want love. Pain and suffering are the only things that seem to get your attention.

To Dad, God had little to do with love. Love was beside the point. Modern Christians wanted love. "Hurray! Jesus loves me!" he'd say, when we passed the hand-clapping kind of church. To Dad, God was not love. God was justice. And God was mercy. But not some wimpy American-style justice and mercy. An infinitely harsher style.

"Who was responsible for Jesus' suffering?" he said once. "Not the Jews who accused him (although they were the immediate cause), or Judas who betrayed him, or Pilate who condemned him, or the soldiers who crucified him, or even the devil who incited them all. It was God, his own beloved father, who was responsible."

Perhaps Dad took his role as father in the biblical sense. Perhaps he felt that to be just and merciful meant a father must persecute his children. If love had nothing to do with the relationship between a creator and his creation, then cruelty made sense. And if that was the case, then Dad was right to kick me out. Otherwise, I couldn't account for my exile.

I'm just a soul to him. Not a person. He doesn't want a person for a daughter, he wants a perfect soul that he can hand off to God and say, "Look what I made, God. A perfect soul, just for you." He doesn't see me. He doesn't ask me my opinion. He doesn't know me. He packages me up in a dress and says, "Follow the program," and now . . . one screwup and I'm left to die out here. He might as well have punched my faith out of me with his fist.

By this time my stomach was feeling pinched and was making gurgling noises and I knew I had to steal some food from somewhere, so I waited until it was past midnight, stashed my bag in some bushes, trotted through the shadowy streets to my house, and crawled through my bedroom window. My room was just as I'd left it. Strangely, I'd expected it would be different somehow. Sitting on my bed, I listened to the house. It gave off the sound of sleep. When the grandfather clock struck one, I tiptoed into the kitchen. Using my shirt as a hammock, I filled it with cookies, Hostess Twinkies, and a Coke, went back into my room, and feasted. When I was finished, I lay down. I smelled my pillow. I pulled the blankets over me and closed my eyes. *I'm dead to my family*, I thought. *I'm a ghost. I'm not here. I don't exist.* How strange it was to be dead to others but not to myself. My bed was comfortable and I soon drifted off. Then at about four-thirty I sat up, surprised by the sound of the shower going. Dad always hit the road by five o'clock to miss rush-hour traffic. Against the drumming of my heart, I climbed silently out the window, and made a dash for the back fence.

For three days I stayed at the park, taking shelter in the pipe at night, sneaking back home to steal food after midnight, and returning to the park before dawn. Then, on the fourth day, I looked up from the shade of my tree by the picnic area and saw Mom in the distance. With Lyle's hand in hers and baby Bernard straddling her hip, she marched across the wide lawn toward me with the hurried but orderly step of a nurse responding to a call from intensive care. I stood up and held my breath. I didn't know whether to run away from her or toward her. I held my ground. My heart was thrashing wildly. I thought, *I knew she'd come.*

And there she was, standing before me, her eyes taking me in with one swooping glance as if to confirm I was in one piece. My chest began to overinflate again and I felt ready to explode with sobs, or maybe it was laughter, but I held it in, wanting Mom to make the first sound. Her freckles were almost buried in pink and her eyes looked tired.

"Are you all right?" she asked. I nodded. "I've been looking for you everywhere."

"I was here."

"Do you know where Terry is?"

"At Hugo's house."

"Where is Hugo's house?"

"By Heather Farms Park. Behind the supermarket."

"Get in the car, you're coming home."

"Right now?"

"Right now."

Grabbing my bag, I followed Mom to the car, and she drove the short distance home. We didn't speak, but I understood she'd been hurting as much as I had and had been warring with Dad. The woman who'd always supported him had said no. I knew Mom. She was a fighter. She was a mother. Her job was to keep the family together. Even if Dad was intent on destroying it, she wouldn't let him.

Mom went looking for Terry. I don't know how she found her. She must have knocked on a lot of house doors—there were hundreds in that neighborhood. I heard Terry come into her room and drop her bag on the floor and fall onto her bed. I waited a few minutes and then leaned close to her curtain. "Knock, knock."

"Go away."

"Can I talk to you?"

"No."

I went inside anyway. "I *had* to tell Mom where you were. She *made* me. I didn't know what else to do."

"I said, *Go a-w-ay*."

"Okay."

That night we all gathered as usual in the living room for the rosary. When Dad entered, he didn't look at us. He knelt down, clutched the rosary in both hands at his back, and began the *Credo*. My heart turned under the oceanic weight. I didn't lean against the armchair. I knelt tall and straight. I held my pink crystal rosary behind my back, just like Dad, and felt the crucifix tickling my calves. I made my voice loud, so Dad would hear it over the tops of the other voices. When the rosary was over, he stood up and left the room. My heart sank deeper in its grave. The decision for us to come home had been all Mom's. Not his.

So I was right about him, I thought. *He would have been glad to see us die. I shouldn't have come home. I should have walked away and kept walking.* But then, after the kids were down for the night, I heard Dad's voice outside my blanket-door. "Terry? Ronnie?"

We emerged from our rooms, and the three of us stood in the low light of the porch. Dad looked embarrassed. He cleared his voice and looked at his shoes and sighed as he searched for words. "Listen . . . I sent Mom looking for you because—well—I couldn't bear knowing you were out there. And Mom, she's been crying for days." He looked up and met our eyes and my heart rose like a bubble out of the mud. "I was wrong to banish you. I did it out of anger. I love you both . . . very much . . . and I don't want you to leave." His face was the color of a ripe strawberry. I'd never seen Dad blush before. I wished I could hug him and put him at ease, but I hadn't hugged Dad in years. Not since puberty. "That doesn't excuse your behavior," he continued sternly. "But if you two will go to confession, and renew your efforts to live in the state of grace, and take my guidance in matters of faith . . . I will defend you both . . . forever . . . to the death."

To the death! Like a knight! Like a martyr!

No more park. No more pipe dwelling. I had my family back. I was home. My emotions ran wildly, but my mind slowed and came to a halt. *If.*

If . . . I live in the state of grace. *If* . . . I took Dad's guidance in matters of faith. That *if* stopped me like barbed wire. It snagged. It cut. It dared me to attempt to cross through. All my life I'd followed Dad's guidance. And where was I? Distant from God, empty of faith, lacking inspiration, doubtful of my future, and resentful toward the counter-revolution. I thought about those nights I'd spent in the park. They were some of the worst nights of my life. What had they been worth? My place in Dad's heart was not a given. It was contingent on my obedience to his religious teachings. I was not to think for myself. I was not to question his rules. I was to go along with the program the way I always had. I was to accept what he told me as truth.

But now I knew that was not possible. Those nights in the pipe had changed me. I'd learned to debate what I'd always taken for granted—to question what had always been unquestionable. No *if* of Dad's could undo that debate. No carefully fashioned lure could fool me into forgetting what I now understood as the beginnings of a whole new dialogue.

THAT SUNDAY BEFORE mass at the Veteran's Hall, I knelt for confession in the front office where the priest sat in a plastic foldup chair with his back to me. As I made the sign of the cross and said, "Bless me, Father, for I have sinned," and began the routine almost unthinkingly, my eyes trailed over the decorations in the room—the California state flag, framed photos of dignitaries, some military awards—and I thought about the California grizzly bear, and remembered hearing that there were none left in the wild, the last one being shot and killed in the 1920s, and I thought what a shame that was. Then, when the priest said, "Go ahead," I rattled off what I'd come to say: "I had sexual relations with a married man." It was a lie. The biggest lie I ever told. And I was telling it to a priest, and I was telling it to a priest so that he would forgive me for a sin I didn't commit. Marshall was gone. When I'd told him over the phone that Dad knew about us, he'd packed up his kids and moved to Seattle, leaving no forwarding address. I was taking the brunt for Marshall. I was angry. I was ashamed. But not for the sin. And not for lying to a priest. I was ashamed for betraying myself.

Back in Holy Innocents, I sat in the small cinder-block room and listened to Mr. Fontz recite the Latin declensions and to Father Kathrein mumble about the physics of weight and matter. At home I said the daily rosary, and wore my scapular and skirts. At the Veteran's Hall I read the missal, received Holy Communion, and followed the post–Vatican II politics. I did everything as I'd done before, only now I did it with the knowledge that I was doing it more for Dad than for my soul.

It was around that time that Dad's older sister Judy, a thrice divorced lapsed Catholic, left her current live-in boyfriend, reconverted, and came to live at our house. We hadn't spent much time with Judy over the years because Dad had disapproved of everything she did. If her name came up, he'd frown, roll his eyes, shake his head, or go silent. It seemed he couldn't forgive her for straying from the faith in the first place, and then staying away so long. I had only one memory of going to Judy's house. We'd been to the beach with Judy's son David, who was my age, and had come to drop him off, and when he got out of the car David accidentally shut the door on my thumb. I can still remember sitting on Judy's sofa overcome—not by my thumb throbbing in a bowl of ice cubes, but by the smell of incense in the house, and Judy's long frayed hair and colorful muumuu, and the glassy beads hanging in the doorways and windows, and the crocheted pillows and afghans seemingly launched propeller-style in all directions. I knew that Judy's daughter Sherry, who was only a year older than Terry, lived part time with her boyfriend, and that David spent most of his time at Grandma's house. That made their family exotic to me, and no less so when Judy quit her job as a switchboard operator at Pacific Bell, sent David to The Group, and moved into our garage to wait for the *Bagarre*.

One of Judy's goals in living with us seemed to be to force-feed me a daily regimen of spiritual counseling. Talk to her, look at her, make a comment to her, walk by her, ask her a question, catch her eye, and I'd get a lecture calculated to put me straight.

"How do you make your long hair into a bun like that?" I asked once.

She lit a cigarette and waved the match dead. "Remember, Ron, vanity is a terrible thing. I'm only telling you this because I love you and I think you need to hear it. I don't wear my hair like this to attract attention. I wear it like this because it's practical. Beauty— *real* beauty—is in the soul. That's the only beauty you need to worry about. Give in to vanity, and you'll end up doing what I did, wasting your life on drugs and free love and self-gratification, and not stopping there. I know what I'm talking about, Ron, 'cause I did it *all*, believe me, every dirty, rotten, stinking, filthy, corrupt thing there was. I slept with whomever I wanted, *whenever* I wanted, and worked in shitholes with a lot of immoral sob's who had no respect for anyone, including themselves (not that I respected myself, either, because I *didn't*). When you live for the world with no thought to your eternal soul, you lose respect for yourself. And let me tell you, Ron, it's that way for every single living human being—not just me and you. Live for the world and you'll find out it's an empty, soulless place. There's nothing *there*. The only *there* is in the Holy Catholic Church. You have no idea how lucky you are to be receiving the sacraments and keeping in the state of grace. You won't have to go through the *crap* I went through."

Since Judy had enjoyed all of life's experiences, she considered it redundant that I investigate a single one. I did not, of course, argue with her. "I know what you're thinking, Ron," she'd say. "It might be fun to go to the disco and dance all night with a lot of good-looking boys. Well, trust me, chickie babe, it *is* fun. It's so much fun you'll give away your *eternal soul* to do it. And after a while dancing will lead to sex. And sex will lead to drugs. And drugs will lead to addiction. And where does it stop? It doesn't. That's the devil's plan. If he can get you on that dance floor, he'll be halfway to winning your soul. If you want my advice, stay away from discos. I've *been* to them. I *know*."

Since Judy had gone to confession and was in the state of grace, Dad developed a new bond with her that hadn't existed since they were kids. They agreed on everything so completely they practically tripped over each other expressing their consensus.

"Have you read the paper today?"

"Not yet."

"Wait till you see the latest . . ."

"I can't wait."

"On second thought, don't read the paper. It'll just make you sick."

"I'm already sick."

"The CIA admitted the White House knew about the Soviets' plans to invade Afghanistan and did nothing to stop it."

Judy, who'd adopted The Group's Brazilian mannerisms, slapped her hands, tops to palms, back and forth. It was an expression that meant *I wash my hands of this disgusting mess*. "All I can say is Our Lady's message at Fatima will be fulfilled."

"You'd better believe it."

"I *do* believe it."

"And an earthquake in Algeria just killed more than forty-five hundred people."

"Do we need any more evidence that the *Bagarre* is here, *right now*, in our very own day and age?"

"Meanwhile J.P. II goes to Germany to compound the lies about the coverup of the Third Secret by saying he chose not to reveal the contents in order to avoid creating *sensationalism*. What kind of an excuse to ignore the wishes of Our Lady is that? The Holy Church has been stabbed by the lance of modernism and is gushing water and blood from the wound and dying a fast and painful death and J.P. II doesn't want to create *sensationalism*?"

That year our church at the Veteran's Hall split in two. On the one side were the sedevacantists (*sede vacante* meaning "the chair being empty"), who believed that the chair of Peter had been empty since 1962 since every pope since then had been a heretic, and wanted out from under the diocese to start their own parish. On the other side were the SSPX people, who maintained that the pope was valid even though the heresies he'd committed had made separation necessary, and wished to remain within the fold of Bishop Lefebvre. Both sides were adamant on their positions, and after several emotional meetings the Veteran's Hall people went back to having mass in their garages and living rooms. Dad didn't join any of the groups. They were all "false right" anyway (as The Group would later become).

Dad said to Judy, "Catholicism has been reduced to herds that form into small tribal groups that become decentralized, self-managing coteries."

And Judy said, "Just like corporate America. Reminds me of my years at Ma Bell. The stress was unbearable. You get driven to booze and pot. You never recover."

That month we began attending the Ukrainian Catholic Church of the Immaculate Conception, a uniate church in the Portola district of San Francisco. Rolling into the outskirts of the big city was like rafting in the wake of a giant steamer that had recently plowed through the steep, twisty downtown districts. Here the low hills rose and fell in smooth, measured slopes, gently lifting and dipping in rounded crests under the static homogeneous fog. The houses, stiff and blockish in their pastel pinks and greens, rode the surfaces evenly like upright buoys, and the shops—Ling Ling Dry Cleaners, Hoy Sun Restaurant, and Shun Yuan Grocery—linked hands in a line to connect San Francisco to China. As we drove, Dad gave us a quick tutorial. "In 1054, Constantinople refused to recognize the pope and split with Rome for a period of about five hundred years. Then, in the year 1596, the Ukrainian Catholic Church acknowledged the supremacy of the pope and was reunited with Rome. (Thus the word *uniate*, which is a Latin word that means "in union with.") It's one of the few traditionalist branches of the Catholic Church resisting the tide of sewage in the wake of Vatican II."

His voice was friendly to show how there were no hard feelings since he'd accepted Terry and me back into the fold of the counter-revolution, but I kept my eyes trained out the window.

"With the cease-fire, Rome allowed the Ukrainians to keep their historical liturgies and practices. The Ukrainian Catholic Church of the Immaculate Conception performs the Liturgy of St. John Chrysostom. It's very *Old World*. You'll see."

On Silliman Street we pulled up in front of a stucco church-like building and threaded ourselves inside, filling a quarter of the pews. As a newcomer, I felt obliged to sit perfectly still and remain perfectly quiet: a hard task since the silence in that room was so absolute it had the effect of magnifying every cough, blink, sniff, and swallow, and because I'd had only a glass of water that morning I dreaded that my stomach might growl and upset the stillness of the room. To fend off such embarrassing impulses, I concentrated on the religious artwork, which was so different from the typical Roman Catholic imagery.

All around, on large wooden panels, bronze-faced saints and angels, in long robes with deep shadowy folds, their figures tall and unsteady, their necks tilted at painful-looking angles, gazed out from past centuries and extended weak, fine-fingered hands in the ancient gesture of supplication or pity. Golden haloes shaped like perfect disks encircled the saintly heads, and a stiff, stern-faced baby Jesus perched awkwardly on his mother's arm to bless the poor, sad-eyed faithful who prayed with such intense stillness. I examined the parishioners. In contrast with the straight-backed, high-shouldered, fresh-faced SSPX'ers, these people had an Old World look to them: tired faces and eyes, bad teeth, and heavy postures. The difference, I supposed, was unavoidable, and had to do with a schism that happened a millennium ago, compared with one that was just starting. Would the SSPX people look like these people in another couple of decades?

I was grateful when Father Maikida, a rugged-looking priest with a large frame, thick wrestler's hands, and a deep, command-ing voice, entered the altar wearing a thick husk of glittering gold and white vestments and an Imperial Margarine–style crown, and began the liturgy in Old Slavonic—a guttural, tangled language made up of thudding consonants that lulled and throttled your ears at the same time.

Like the parishioners who attended his mass, Father Maikida exuded the hardships of past dictatorships. Dad had told us about him on the way to mass. Captured by the Nazis during World War II, he'd been forced to serve in the German army until he managed to escape, only to be captured by the British and imprisoned by them. When World War II ended, he was released by the British and emigrated to the United States, where he was ordained a uni-ate priest.

When you entered a Ukrainian church, you kissed an icon on a table called the tetrapod. During the mass you crossed yourself from right to left rather than left to right, with your fingers joined at the thumb, index, and middle to represent the Trinity. Through-out the mass, the priest and his deacon walked in and out through the doors of the iconostasis—a wall that separated the altar (the household of heaven) from us in the world (the laity). My missal alluded to parts of the mass completely unfamiliar to me. The Proskomidia (preparing the bread and wine), the Trisagion, the Insistent Litany.

Trying to follow the Liturgy of St. John Chrysostom in my small paperback missal, I could not avoid the feeling that this church, and Father Maikida's memories, and the dark, unknown stories of the parishioners and the ancient traditions they observed belonged to them and not to us. To come here, a native Californian, dressed in my flowered dress and white scarf, never having known war or starvation or death, my knowledge of religion a simplistic system of do's and don'ts straight out of *The New St. Joseph Baltimore Catechism*, and participate in such a foreign ceremony— it seemed presumptuous. I felt like a benchwarmer for the visiting team: I wore the jersey but I couldn't possibly play the game. Mom and Dad played the game. But they had age on their side, and spiritual resources I could not draw from.

As it turned out, we would attend the Ukrainian Church of the Immaculate Conception for only six months before Father Maikida was transferred and a progressive priest took his place. When we began attending Our Lady of Fatima Church, which was a Russian Byzantine Catholic church in the residential Richmond district of San Francisco, whose priest, Father Patzelt, a Jesuit and an exorcist, delivered the liturgy in his native language.

Góspodi pomíluj. Góspodi pomíluj. Tebi, Góspodi. Amin. (Lord have mercy. Lord have mercy. To you, O Lord. Amen.)

The Russian rite was, if possible, even more foreign and exotic than the Ukrainian one, especially during the consecration of the Eucharist, which the priest performed in secret behind the holy doors of the image screens, and then served in a spoon (the Eucharist was a cube of real bread soaked in strong white wine). But the mass was the same in that many of the parishioners had the same tired faces, the same look of loss and suffering, the women in black scarves and shawls, the men in dark jackets and old sweaters, and we were like the visiting team trying to fit in with their code of behavior.

Our Lady of Fatima Church was not to last, either. After several months, Father Patzelt died, and Dad decided to give the SSPX another try. A priest named Father Desoto had recently arrived from Italy, and was holding the Tridentine Mass in Danville. Now, instead of driving west over the Bay Bridge, we drove east through the open spaces of Alamo, where the grasses grew yellow and tall between bunches of oak and manzanita along the foothills of Mount Diablo. Now "church" was in a Citibank building. Putting on our scarves, we filed through a bulletproof door, down a hall, and into an air-conditioned boardroom. The group inside was small and bleak. Nine parishioners, apart from my family of twelve, sat hunched and disconnected in their metal foldup chairs, their eyes lowered as their fingers slowly turned the pages of their missals. In strange contrast, Father Desoto, with his birdlike eyes and rapidly gesticulating hands, marched in small circles and shouted his objections to Vatican II in high-pitched, strongly accented English. As small and slender as a jockey, he could have passed for a boy when his back was turned. When it came time for the sermon, however, he seemed to grow large and muscular with all his pent-up emotions. Bringing newspaper clippings, magazine articles, and notes he'd taken during the week, Father Desoto read highlighted portions out loud, and then flew into diatribes that stretched what could have been a half-hour mass to an hour or longer.

"The mass used to be a ceremony with a sermon tacked on," I murmured to Terry during a particularly long one. "Now it's a sermon with a ceremony tacked on."

"Do you think all Italian men are that small?"

Getting through mass had never been so difficult. But it was not the sermon—which could sometimes be entertaining—that did me in so much as the boardroom (I thought of it as the *bored room*). There was nothing to look at. No art to absorb, no music to contemplate. The place had the character of a vacuum cleaner, the way the air whistled in through one vent and out another, its low-pile carpet bathing your eyes with the pale gray color of dust, its white acoustic ceilings with their fluorescent paneled lights filling every crevice with light, washing away shadows, reflecting on the dials of old people's eyeglasses, drying out the moisture of your eyes, and blinding you with brightness. The large promotional posters that advertised banking services mixed with Father Desoto's sermon and filled your head with amorphous fuzz.

"Dogmatic constitution . . ."

"Variable APR!"

"Divine right of the pope . . ."

"Mortgage solution."

"Sacred liturgy . . ."

"FDIC insured."

"*Novus Ordo*."

"No minimum balance."

"Passion on the Cross."

"Consolidate now!"

I'd managed to get through the mass in other soulless places, but at Citibank I found it impossible to pray. My body expressed no will to move. I slouched when I sat. I slumped when I stood. I knelt on one knee instead of two. Mom frowned at me. Her expression said, *Concentrate! Don't act so depressed!* She tapped her missal. She shook her rosary. I sighed and renewed my effort. But my mind was vacant. I might as well have been in a coma.

Once Dad said, "I believe that True Catholics can detect the aura of Catholicism where it exists. I have detected it, but only rarely, in those Catholic oases that exist amid the burning and life-less deserts of the New Church."

The Citibank church was not an oasis. It was an empty bat-tleground after our army's defeat. And we were like the reserves arriving too late for the fight. The medics had already cleared away the bodies. Nothing was left but flies and tourists. What were we going to accomplish? Terry slipped further into dreaminess. Jen-nifer started rocking (a childhood habit she still hadn't broken). Vinny closed his eyes. Mary and Bernadette sank to the floor and fell asleep. Only Mom and Dad still prayed, their eyes locked on the crucifix, their lips actively dancing with the prayers in their heads. The last of the wounded demanding another war.

15

a death of sorts

TERRY'S BELLY BEGAN to rise like dough, her breasts to swell.
The rigid frame of her posture softened. Her eyes blinked sleepily.
Her lips lounged into a gestation-drunk smile of contentment. All
kinds of changes were happening to Terry, inside and out, but they
didn't include me. They included Mom, who loaned her maternity
clothes, drove her to doctor's appointments, counted out her vita-
mins, suggested naps, and spent hours helping her fold doll-sized
clothes. And they included Dad, who treated her with quiet defer-
ence now that she'd gone to confession and received Holy Communion, and discussed the baptism with her, and was careful to
give her privacy, space, and extra time in the bathroom. And they
included everyone else, who looked into the empty bassinette and
imagined a tiny niece or nephew in there and imagined themselves
being called by their new names—Aunt Mary, or Aunt Bernadette, or Uncle Lyle. Terry's baby brought a new dimension and a
new happiness to the family.

But not to me.

I was immune to the thrill of new motherhood. I couldn't account for Terry's surrender to it. If it had been me who'd gotten pregnant, I would be devastated, depressed, furious at myself. I would rather have come down with a terrible disease and *died*. To be shackled forever with a *kid* . . . What could be worse than that? I knew I was thinking selfishly, but pregnancy seemed to necessitate the most selfish of standoffs. I didn't understand how Terry could be so merrily accepting of such a disastrous fate. Had she thought it through? Was I the only one searching frantically for an alternative? One day, in her first trimester, as we sat alone in the backseat of Dad's car waiting for him outside an old Baptist church after an SSPX mass, I couldn't stand the misgivings anymore and turned to her. "Did you ever consider? You know . . ." I rolled my eyes. She bugged her eyes at me. "What? An abortion?" I nodded sheepishly. After all, it seemed to me, once the deed was done all she had to do was confess it and be genuinely sorry and promise not to do it again and then start over with a clean slate, and no one had to know except God, and under the circumstances, God would understand. It wasn't like Jesus would have to die on the Cross all over again. Terry stared back at me, clearly appalled. "No *way*. I couldn't do *that*." I looked down at my lap and felt like a monster. So it was only me who thought of the pregnancy as a problem and not as a gift. Of course she couldn't murder her own baby. "I meant . . . adoption," I said, but we both knew what I'd meant. She frowned and looked out the window. "I could never give my own baby away." Terry was obviously made of more heroic stuff than I was. I thought of myself first; Terry thought of what was right. She was in this for the long haul, and she wasn't looking back.

That May, with Mom at her side, Terry gave birth to a baby girl she named Rebecca after the mysterious character in her favorite novel. Eight months later, Mom gave birth to Rebecca's uncle, whom she named Charles after the great king Charlemagne. With the noise in the house at a peak, I would now spend entire days behind my blanket-door, lying on my slip of a mattress, feeling cut loose from the chaos, miles outside the margin of responsibility, and think about myself and where I was headed in life. The prognosis was grim. I was seventeen. I had no friends. No job. No talents. No vocational calling. No special gift that I knew about. No big idea. No real education. No hidden aptitude. No prospects. No boyfriend. No self-esteem. No ace in the hole. No shocking revelations. No dreams. No hopes. Nothing to show for myself. Who was I? A girl in a bedsheet dress waiting for the Apocalypse.

I talked to myself out loud.

"Number one: I've got to get out of Holy Innocents. That place is killing me. Number two: I've got to get a job, and *not* a babysitting job; something that pays. Number three: I've got to save my money. I can't do anything without money in the bank. Once I do all those things, I'll be set. The *Bagarre* can come or not come, it won't matter. I'll be independent."

For a week I prepared my speech to Mom and Dad, and when I judged it the right time, I cornered them in the kitchen and delivered it, adopting the aggressive tone Dad employed when he was imparting the unpalatable truth.

"First off, high school is a waste of time. Okay? There are no two ways about it. Unless you are actually going to use what you learn there, there's really no point in going. Tell me, how am I going to use math and physics? Huh? And biology? Let's face it, I'm not going to be a scientist or a mathematician or a linguist or whatever, so what's the point in me sitting at a desk all day pretending to absorb facts that are totally irrelevant to me? It's not like I'm headed to *college*. Anyway, the *Bagarre* is coming. And while I may need a lot of things when the *Bagarre* comes, I certainly won't need a *diploma*."

I'd saved the best point for last, and to my astonishment it worked. Mom and Dad looked at each other and their expressions showed admission to my logic. Mom murmured that of course she could always use an extra set of hands at home, and Dad admitted he didn't get a high school diploma before he joined the Marines. And they both agreed that a diploma would be useless once the *Bagarre* got here, truth be told.

I did not register that year for senior high.

The school hurdle crossed, I faced the job hurdle. You need money to survive. I mean, why have a car if you can't put gas in the tank? And what about insurance? And repairs? Only a dork drives around without some kind of paperwork. Dad said, "I hate to see you sell yourself to the vulgarity of a minimum-wage job," but stopped short of forbidding it, and Mom, an advocate of self-reliance, rolled her eyes to look the other way, and although we all agreed that money would be useless when the *Bagarre* came, it still had its uses *now*.

So I got my first real job making french fries at a McDonald's.

Working at McDonald's, I realized how the rest of the world saw me: as a Christian. The only employee who would talk to me was the assistant supervisor, Stan, a nerdy Evangelical who played Jesus songs for his church on the electronic keyboard. Stan's eyes followed me longingly from behind his glasses all shift long. To impress me, he made tapes of his songs and dedicated them to me, waited for me in the parking lot, and sometimes left obsessive notes on the VW windshield. *You barely said one word today. Are you mad at me?* I had to get away from Stan, so after three months I quit that job, and worked as a clerk at a 7-Eleven. This time my paramour was the assistant manager: a twentysomething Lithuanian man, who would trap me inside the walk-in fridge as I was stocking products and try to kiss me. "You are beautiful to me," he'd say.

"I want to introduce you to my mother. She will like you. She will think you are beautiful, too." A customer, a middle-aged Korean man, would sit in his car in the parking lot and wait until the store was empty. Then he'd come in and give me presents—like a long-stemmed rose, or a charm for a bracelet. He, too, wanted me to meet his mother. Lloyd, a balding weightlifter from a nearby gym, asked, "I don't get you. What *are* you? Some kind of flower child or something?" He too asked me out on a date. I was relatively sure his mother would not be invited.

To deflect Christians, desperate foreigners, and body builders, I began wearing thick black eye makeup, which I would apply in the rearview mirror of my car, and tight jeans, which I would stash under the backseat of the VW and pull on while driving to work. When I came back home, I'd dress back into my skirt, steering the car with my knee while I buttoned up, and wipe off as much of the makeup as I could. I still wore my scapular and medal under my blouse, but I was going to make damn sure that nobody could peg me for a Christian.

I worked full time, and over the months socked the money away until I had more than a thousand dollars. Life at that point became interesting. What does a seventeen-year-old do with a thousand dollars? A smart one doesn't do anything with it. She earns another thousand and puts them together, which is what I did. I wanted buying power. I was saving up for something big. The only question that tormented me was, *What am I going to spend it on?* The *Bagarre* could come, and then all bets would be off. I finally ended the torment by making a decision. I knew what I wanted to do with my money.

It is an irony that lives with me to this day, literally. At the time, I thought of it as an adventure: an impulsive and thrilling adventure, if a little harebrained. Now I know the adventure for what it was: a distraction. What I did, I did out of boredom—with myself and with my life—and because of the hopelessness I felt toward my future. And also because I needed a catalyst for change, in thinking and direction, and must have subconsciously understood that. At any rate, one day, after thinking it through carefully, and without discussing it with Mom, I withdrew all my money from the bank, went out, and got myself a baby. That is, I purchased an expensive pet: a nine-month-old, hand-raised parrot (a blue and gold macaw).

I'd been opposed to Terry having a baby, and now I had one. Like a baby, Gideon was active and noisy, quickly getting into trouble when I wasn't looking, making constant screeching sounds, and demanding as much or more than any human baby. Within hours of bringing him home, I realized what I'd done. Gideon wanted attention at all times, and if he didn't get it, he'd belt out a scream that sounded like someone being tortured to death. His message was a peremptory *Come back immediately!*, and my response was to oblige him.

I mothered him in tenuous harmony for months. And then my baby decided to take off. It happened in a flash. We were crawling around on the front lawn when he flapped his wings a few times, caught an updraft, gained height, and soared off, flying high over the city. I was stunned; horrified; brokenhearted. Not only was my baby gone, I'd managed to lose the one thing that stopped me from facing myself (not to mention fourteen hundred bucks plus tax). I climbed onto the roof and sat on the apex, and scanned the powder-blue horizon for a streak of cobalt-blue. Mom shouted up to me, "What are you doing on the roof? Post signs. Get out there and hunt him down!" So I made signs and posted them all around the city, then climbed back onto the roof and prayed to St. Francis, the patron saint of animals, to help me find him.

My rooftop vigil lasted four days. On the fifth day, a kid walking home from school spotted him high in a tree and called me on the phone. After pulling on a pair of jeans under my skirt, I sprinted the eight blocks to the tree, and peered to where the boy pointed. Gideon was so high I could barely make him out, but I caught a glimpse of his sword-shaped tail at the peak of the towering spire. I began to climb. The boy's mother yelled after me, "Shouldn't we call the fire department?"

Soon, I was out of speaking range. The briery sap-soaked branches poked out like rungs on a ladder, one above another, as if measured for the purpose of climbing. I didn't pause to look down, but continued fast, until I made it to the top. When I reached the highest branch that could carry my weight, I clung to the trunk. Gideon watched me from his post on the far tip of a branch. "Hello," he said. I looked down. I was higher than the top of a telephone pole. "Gideon. It's time to come home. Come here right now. I mean it." He danced back and forth and preened his feathers, but made no move to come. He wasn't like a dog. He didn't obey orders. It was up to me to go to him. So I gradually inched toward him, using the thin, flexible branches above me as guides. When I was a few feet away, I put my arm out. "Hop on, Gid. *Please* . . . If I fall, I'm *dead*." He plucked a twig and dropped it, turning his head sideways to watch it fall. He looked back at me. "Hello." I sighed. *Okay. One more step*. I put my foot out, and at that moment I heard a *snap*, and the tree shot upward.

I'd fallen twenty-nine feet before and survived. Falling fifty feet, I might not be so lucky. This was the real thing, and I knew it. I was hurtling uncontrollably toward probable death. As a kid, I'd been warned about situations like this: You get hit by a car. Your life flashes before your eyes. You've got seconds to live. What do you do? The obvious answer: Save your everlasting soul by reciting a perfect Act of Contrition. That, however, is not what happened. For one thing, my life did not flash before my eyes. But something else happened. As the air whistled through my hair, and the pine needles hissed past my ears, and the bark nipped off chunks of my skin, my mind sped past me. In fact, it flew so fast it overtook the speed of my fall, like an envoy racing ahead in order to assess the damage in advance in order to report back. And it did report back, and its report was remarkable. Entering my death, a few seconds hence, it found a prevailing sense of calm there. A purity. A quiet. And I knew that death was good. And God was good. The knowledge was instantaneous, more an impression than a thought, but the impression was clear-cut and unambiguous because my conscience didn't have time to mess around. It had barely enough time to acknowledge its near termination before—

I hit solid ground. My bones crashed like cymbals inside me. My teeth locked. My legs bent like staples. My back buckled. My lungs gurgled out their last breath. Pain charged into my body like a locomotive. I did not know I could absorb a locomotive, but I absorbed it. My vision went white. I vibrated with light. I was dying. Half-expecting an angel to appear, take my hand, and fly away with me, I waited to feel the sensation of flying. I did not fly. No angel came. Flesh-and-blood paramedics came. They asked questions I couldn't answer. They put oxygen tubes into my nose. They cut my leather boots off my legs with scissors. They mummified my body inside a balloon cast. Four pairs of hands lifted me up, moved me through space, and encased me in an ambulance. Every movement caused excruciating pain, but I couldn't cry out. The ambulance rolled off, its siren blaring. And I knew Death was gone. It had been held off by the paramedics. *The paramedics were stopping me from dying.* Their tank of oxygen was stopping me. If I could speak, I would tell the paramedics to let me go. I wanted to die. I knew now that it was okay. Death wasn't a bad thing. It was a *good* thing, and I was prepared to go. God was good. I was good. We were all good.

The next time I opened my eyes, Mom was looking down at me. Mom, who'd remarked more times that I could count, "When your time's up, your time's up, and there's nothing you can do about it," wore a strange look—part terror, part relief, part joy, part blame. "Are you wearing your scapular?" she asked, which was a silly question because except for a thin white sheet I was naked on the gurney and my scapular was strung across my neck. I gave the slightest nod. She wiped a tear, took a visible breath, and held my hand. "Why'd you do it?" she asked, as if it had been a suicide attempt. "Why'd you take the risk?" I didn't have the breath to speak. If I did, I wonder what I would have said.

The doctor took X rays, and listed my injuries: a compression fracture of six vertebrae, a collapsed lung, a fractured foot, shock. He crossed his arms. "I won't lie to you," he said to Mom. "Your daughter should be dead. Or at least a quadriplegic for life." Mom smiled confidently. "I'll have you know that Ronnie's guardian angel works overtime."

Gideon came back on the third day of my recuperation and was captured on a neighbor's roof. That day, KGO Talk Radio called to interview the girl who'd fallen fifty feet and survived. The next day *The Contra Costa Times* knocked on our door. Mom let them in because we were subscribers. Terry did the interview for me, softening the truth a little since I was such an embarrassment to her. Then she brushed my hair and I smiled with Gideon for the photographer. The next day, a large color photo of me lying in bed with my bird standing on my chest appeared on the front page. The headline read: *Parrot Can Fly, Owner Can't*. Ha ha ha.

And then the attention died down and I was alone with Gideon, who sat on the back of the chair beside me. My most frequent visitor was Vinny, who sat for hours in a chair at my bedside, his eyes blinking over thoughts that he rarely divulged, and who cared for me like some kind of self-elected butler, delivering my meals, clearing the dishes, emptying my bedpan, and straightening the blankets.

"Are you afraid of dying?" I asked him one day.

"A little," he said.

"Well, don't be. It's not what you think. It's different. Less scary. I'm not afraid one bit."

Vinny contemplated that for a minute, and then turned to look at me. "Wonderful," he said.

"See, I have a new theory. I think the true God is above petty vengeance. He isn't a scorekeeper or tally-up kind of God who counts up your sins, weighs them against the prayers you've said, finds you in the red, and checks you off heaven's guest list. God is interested in a different kind of outcome altogether, a simpler, more logical one that benefits everyone involved. Know what I mean?"

"I think so."

"I mean . . . There I was . . . *falling*. You know? And suddenly I thought, *Uh-oh, I'm in trouble. I'm going to die and go to hell*—since I haven't gone to confession in a while and I'm not in the state of grace."

"You sinned?"

"Yeah . . . just stupid stuff, like . . . uh . . . never mind."

Vinny rolled his eyes and smiled, a look of sheer bliss on his face.

"And then just as suddenly I wasn't afraid. I knew I wasn't going to hell—"

Vinny bit his lower lip. "Want me to close the door?" he asked.

"—Or even heaven, really . . . I know it sounds weird, Vinny, but God isn't what we think. Death isn't what we think. Heaven and hell aren't what we think. What lies after death is unknowable. I'm no authority on what lies after it, but what I do know is that we're not going to burn for eternity. How do I know this? I don't know how I know. I just *know* that I *know*. Know what I mean? Just like I know how to ride a bicycle, or tie my shoes, or run. I can't explain how I know, only that *I know*."

"Want me to close the door?"

"Think about it. Suffering for an eternity is like . . . come on . . . a *disproportionate* punishment for a goddamned *sin*. I mean, if you did something bad and Mom got mad at you for doing it and chopped your head off, what would she be accomplishing? What kind of a God makes all these souls just to fling most of them into hell? That's called premeditated torture. If God did that, He'd make Hitler seem saintly in comparison. And what about Mary? No mother I know can stand it when her kids are suffering. Moms aren't like that. They *care*. Look how Terry bolts across the house to pick up Rebecca at the smallest whimper and smothers her with kisses. Could a heavenly mother enjoy spending an eternity in heaven knowing that all those souls were suffering for eternity in hell with no chance of going home? I don't think so."

"Want me to close the door?"

"Nah, it's okay. I'm done talking about it. Unless *you* want to talk about it."

"Want some ice cream?"

THAT MONTH, DANNY called home from Brazil to tell Dad that The Group was a cult and they were brainwashing him and programming him to be a warrior monk against his will and that he wanted to quit and come home. Dad's response was a resounding *no*. "First of all, you're exaggerating," he said. "They're not brainwashing you. Where'd you get such a foolish idea? Second of all, you have *Thau*. You belong there. You're not coming home." Danny begged. "Dad, you don't understand. You don't see the stuff I see. Plinio escaped the SS and started a cult. These guys are a bunch of Nazis. I'm telling you." Dad said, "You're wrong! They're *anti*-Nazi. I don't know who's putting this stuff in your head but it's *wrong*. As your father, I'm commanding you to stay." Danny fought back. He said Nick was homesick and walking around like a zombie, and if Dad didn't fly them both home to California they'd disappear in São Paulo and Dad would never hear from them again. Dad was furious. His son was defying him. His sons were apostates. Especially Danny. He had the *Thau* and was rejecting his vocation. Trapped, he bought the tickets. But he refused to speak to either of them when they came home.

I had just begun to take short walks around the house with my cast and crutches and back brace when I saw my brothers. This homecoming was different from the last. Mom picked them up alone while Dad was at work, and there was no feast with cakes and pies. This time Danny didn't greet me with "Salve Maria," or call me a *fasuda*, or talk about hell and eternity. They threw their suitcases in the back room and made themselves sandwiches. In the evenings they didn't lead Grace and counsel us on the *Bagarre*. Instead, they took their plates of food to the picnic table in the backyard. I followed. Out there, Danny poured wine. Nick lit up a joint, and we passed it around in the soft moonlight. Up in the oak trees the owls hooted their tunnel-throated song. In the house our family went on with business, creating a low roar. Danny did most of the talking.

"You don't know what it's like. They get you. I was mesmerized. As an apprentice I had to wear the brown tunic and the knee-high black boots. I had to march. We all did. The courtyard was lit with blue ambient lights. The hooded monks wore red sashes around their arms, and shiny chains with seven links around their waists. They did the goose step with the leg straight out, Hitler-style, only they slid each foot. Slide, left leg kick, right arm snap salute. Swivel in perfect unison. Marching and chanting about Dr. Plinio being a prophet, about his mother being a saint. We marched for hours in preparation of Plinio's visit. When he came, the others kissed his feet. I refused. They took me aside, tried to brainwash me. I knew what they were up to. They think they're chosen, an elite group who carries the truth and is responsible for leading the faithful out of the darkness."

He sipped from the glass, then took a drag from the joint and blew the smoke straight up toward the moon. The lamp's soft glow encased us in our own nimbus, leaving the rest of the world in darkness.

"I was confused. Malnourished. That's how they break you down. The hierarchy eats steak and potatoes on porcelain plates, and drink wine out of crystal glasses, and the apprentices eat beans and rice. In New York we raised money on the streets selling magazines, and campaigning outside churches. When we saw Hasidic Jews, we hissed and pinched our noses. We said they were dirty pigs, the curse of world, behind the corruption of planet, the downfall of civilization. Blacks were the same. They came from the cursed son of Noah. We said all this stuff because it made us feel superior."

Nick flicked the dead ash from the joint, sucked at the tip, and held his breath. He grinned, smoke curling from his nostrils, and passed the joint to me.

"They forced us to go on caravans from house to house and state to state asking for donations from people. I was always in trouble, stealing cars, buying beer, and eating pizza. Finally, Mr. Capito called home. He said, 'There is a problem and Danny is the problem.' That's when Dad got on the phone with me and said, 'Pack your bags. You're going to Brazil. Nick is going to Canada to be apart from you.' So I went to Brazil, and lived in the compound-monastery, surrounded by gated walls, armed guards, and attack dogs. The dogs belonged to the cook, and the cook was hired from the outside, so I knew if I made friends with the cook I could get past the dogs. The cook said, 'Rub your hands all over this meat. Now give a piece to the dogs. Let them smell you so they remember you. They know you now. You can escape.' He was a life-saver. Every night I slipped out, and Thomas, who lived at another compound a mile away, linked up with me. He knew São Paulo well and took me to bars, cheap restaurants, and underground movie theaters to see X-rated movies. We wandered everywhere. Transvestites hit on us in the parks. The nightlife was a whole weird scene, but it didn't hurt us. We could deal with it. It was a freak show. We went to the parks on purpose just to look at the freaks. One night I got drunk, staggered home late, and didn't hear the morning bell. When they woke me up, they realized I was drunk. That's when they tried to break me."

"How?"

"They put me in a room and made me do the Chapter of Faults. That's where you lay prostrate on the floor in form of a cross, surrounded by monks with torches. The monks are the witnesses. Each one gives his testimony of what your faults are. Mr. Salgado sat on a chair at the end; he was the judge. The monks—six on each side—were the jury. I laid facedown, prostrate, forehead on floor, while they said things about me. 'I saw him jump the wall' . . . 'I saw him in town drinking beer ' . . . 'He went to movies ' . . . 'He is going the way of the world' . . . 'He isn't doing the rituals' . . . 'He isn't going to church, or meetings.' When I heard what they said, I realized I was being followed. But I didn't care. Mr. Salgado said, 'We heard the testimonies, and we are going to make an exception. We can make you a warrior monk right now if you change your position. You must take the vow.'"

"Jesus Christ," I said. "And I thought I had it bad."

"I vibrated when he said, 'Take the vow.' My mind was shouting inside, saying, 'Get out. Get out.' So I stood up, and I said, 'I gotta go.' Everyone stared as I walked outside into the daylight. Mr. Salgado followed me. He slithered up to me like an eel and put his hand on my shoulder. He said, 'Daniel, Daniel, Daniel. You can't do this. You have *Thau*. Reconsider.' I said, 'No. I want to go to California.' And he said, 'But your vocation!' And I said, 'If you try to stop me I'll go to the press and tell them you kidnapped me against my will, and Nick too.' And he said, 'Daniel. You don't have to do that. Think of Nicholas.' Yeah, right. By that time Nick had come to Brazil, too, and had let them shave his head because my head was shaved. He didn't want to stay. He was homesick and crying every day and walking around like a zombie. So that day I told Nick, 'I'm leaving. They can't stop me.' And Nick said, 'I'm leaving, too.' So I called home and Dad bought the tickets and we went to New York, and from there to California. Dad was furious. He's *still* furious. He doesn't want to hear what I have to say. He says I'm lying. He says the pathway to hell is paved with the heads of monks that have apostatized."

I looked at Nick and he nodded silently, which was his way, and I didn't ask him any questions. He concentrated on relighting the joint and drawing the final mouthful of smoke from the last burning strands of marijuana. It was safe out there in the backyard. We all felt it. Across the yard our house was solid-packed with people and noise and dishes and laundry and babies and toys and dogs and cats and cocktails and neighbors and prayers and candles and foreboding and fear and worry and resentment and agitation and self-pity and of course the anxiety that comes from not-talking-about-what-really-matters. I thought there was not enough space inside a baseball stadium for this amount of turmoil, let alone in one small house, which was ripping at the seams. All told, fifteen Arnolds were living under one roof, sharing one bathroom, one dining table, one narrow floorspace, and one belief system. To walk through the kitchen, you had to wait for a space to open up and then missile through. If you needed a shower, you'd better announce it an hour in advance to give everyone a chance to use the toilet or have people banging on the door or tripping the lock, and you'd better do it between laundry cycles or there'd be no hot water. Bathroom emergencies got sent to the Fontanas' bathroom next door, or to the far end of the backyard where the weeds were thick. Once I had to rinse Vinny down with the garden hose after a poop accident because someone forgot to announce a shower. Jennifer shared the middle bedroom with three siblings and put on her training bra under her blanket. Nick built a shed in the backyard, installed a woodstove, used a lantern for light, and slept there. Danny alternated between sleeping in a tent and curling up on a mat in Nick's shed.

I renovated a section of the back porch. Rolling up the old bamboo fencing, I bought a stack of two-by-fours, Sheetrock, compound, tape, and a door with a handle that locked. Nick, who'd always been good at carpentry and would soon be making his living at it, helped me drill a plank into the pavement, frame a wall, and hang the door. I hammered the Sheetrock on the walls and ceiling. Applied compound and tape. Painted the walls. Hung curtains. I considered hanging a sign: *Keep out. No trespassing. Private. Womb.* I decided against a sign. The lock would be my sign.

In my room I was as good as gone. Behind my locked door I could lie in bed and watch the sunlight crawl slowly across the wall like an unhurried silverfish, and hear the racket of my family through the back window of the house, and feel my heart plow ahead on its blind journey toward the unknowable beyond. On the other side of the wall there were dishes to be done, laundry to be folded, children to be fed, the rosary to be said. But on my side of the wall, routines failed to stir a breath in the air. Mary could bang with both fists on my door screaming to come inside. I didn't respond. I was unreachable.

I WAS GRIPPED by reverie—depression by another name. Mom bustled, bolstered, trumpet-sounded, and took me to task. "Curtains open! Up and at 'em! If you're not going to finish high school, you're going to volunteer at Vinny's school. I told the principal you'd start right away." In the mornings I boarded the special bus with Vinny and spent the day at Strandwood reading stories, mopping up glue, and handing out snacks. I knew Mom's goal in sending me there was to get me to stop feeling sorry for myself. Compared with some people, I had it pretty damn good. In my journal I gave up prose and expressed my appreciation for my life in poetry:

> Life is a swirling, sucking eddy of despair
> With short moments of false hope
> In an ever-blackening universe.

Mom didn't let up. She took me to physical therapy for my back. She cooked magnificent meals, built cheerful fires in the fireplace, played Vivaldi on the stereo, and taught Gideon how to talk. "What's the matter?" Gideon would say at strangely appropriate times. My answer was either a blank stare or something that even a bird could grasp.

"Life is the matter, Gideon. *Life*. It just keeps *going*."

Judy applied for a job at 7-Eleven and was soon working alongside me—acting as my guardian angel in disguise. No more pants. No more heavy black makeup. No more perusing the porn mags when there were no customers. No more drinking stolen beer as I stocked the freezer. Against the piped-in easy listening music, I was back to being a Trad weirdo in an orange and yellow polka-dot uniform and knee-length skirt. Only now I had Judy overseeing me.

"Don't pretend you didn't notice that creep checking you out," she'd say knowingly, after a customer left with his purchase. "I spotted him the second he walked through the door. I knew he'd come here to buy a porn magazine. I know his type. Next time he comes in, don't flatter him with eye contact. He's only after one thing. Believe me."

> *The brutality of noon.*
> *I am cold and dark and godless inside.*

Writing had a calming effect on me. It was a way of rebelling without actually rebelling. I was innocent because I wasn't *doing* anything. I was only writing ideas about doing things. Sort of.

> *I am a top losing its spin. I am a top losing its spin. I am a top losing. I am a top losing. I am a top. I am a. I am . . . I*

I yearned for change but had a terrible fear of change. I didn't want to upset the boat. I seemed to have found an okay balance between religion, work, family, and self, and I worried that if I tilted one way or the other the boat would flip over and I'd fall in. Into what, I didn't know. I only knew it would be cold and dark and very deep, and that I might drown.

> *What is life? It is somethingness. What is death? It is nothingness. What is God? Nothingness nourishing itself on somethingness.*

By writing, I told myself, I was *embracing reality*. I suspect, however, that I was doing the opposite. I was leaving reality behind— my reality, that is. The Trad-girl-at-a-dead-end reality. Writing gave me a sense of being apart from the day-to-day. It lifted me above ground. It gave me a wide-angle view. I told Mom I wished I could exist as pure thought. Mom's reaction was, "For crying out loud. You and your father!"

> *Catholic girl, age eleven,*
> *Her soul sits three pews back.*
> *So aware there's nothing there*
> *But wants to go to heaven.*

What began as a short poem, written every week or so, evolved into longer poems written every day. Some of the poems were grandiose. They appeared to say so much while at the same time saying very little. Some were simple, just a thought. Either way, I didn't understand them. I only wrote them, and continued to write them.

> *Cogito ergo sum's the thing*
> *That keeps me always wondering.*
> *I can't know God but I might find*
> *That I can easily know my mind.*

I didn't notice it right away. But over time, as the journal filled with poetry, the ghost of an idea began floating around in the chambers of my imagination. The idea was little more than a lightly shimmering slip of a suggestion sliding through the corridors and cracks, a thing as quiet as a wink, as soft as a whisper, the gentlest of touches, a glimmer caught by my peripheral vision. Because I couldn't make it out very well, much less capture it with my hands and hold on to it, I waited for it to come out of the darkness and show itself in plain, full view.

The idea might have been put there by God, I thought. Or perhaps the idea *was* God. But not the traditional God. A god of self-will. A god of language and ideas. An internal voice god. Me, in other words. The idea was to stop what I was doing. Backtrack. Start from scratch. Think independently. Take control.

> *A frantic nerve, electrified*
> *Raced up my back and down my side*
> *It struck me hotly with fire and bite*
> *Giving me options: fight or flight.*

Waking up early one morning, I slipped from bed, rolled a pair of pants under my skirt, crept out the door of my room, and climbed over the back fence. Stashing my skirt behind the blackberry bushes, I trotted toward the bus stop. Boarding a bus with a sign that read *Diablo Valley College*, I took a seat at the far back as the bus roared slowly up Contra Costa Boulevard. My heart dribbled like a basketball against my rib cage and my armpits stung with pricks of perspiration. What was I afraid of? I told myself I was just a regular teenager going to check out the local community college, not a counter-revolutionary ignoramus on a dead-end mission like I felt.

Getting off the bus at the entrance to campus, I walked up the front steps. In my head, a voice mocked me. *Get a load of who's coming to college!* Laughter and finger-pointing rotated around and around my head stereophonically. *Look! Ronnie Arnold wants to go to college! Ronnie Arnold wants an education!* I saw myself from a low camera angle, head backed by a bright sky, hair blowing, mouth set, eyes level. *She's that girl who fell from that tree, remember? The Trad girl who never finished high school.*

I followed the signs to Administration, and entered a carpeted room with a counter. I moved toward a wall where a dozen or so brochures rested in slots and took one of each. The lady behind the counter watched me. I must have looked like I didn't know what I was looking for, so she asked, "May I help you?" I looked down at my handful of brochures and back at her. "Uh . . . Yes. Thank you. I'm—I'm—thinking of applying."

She asked a couple of questions, and before I knew it I was spilling the whole truth—that I had no diploma, and less than an eighth-grade education. That I was depressed. Hopeless. That my brothers were in the same boat, and Jennifer had just quit school too, and Mary had already run away once and probably would again, and Terry was a mother at eighteen. I didn't say all this had happened because we were waiting for the Apocalypse. I said I didn't know what to do with my life, where to go, who to talk to, how to begin.

"There are ways around diplomas," the lady said, and went on to give me all kinds of useful information about tests and grants. As she talked, I could feel a lump of excitement rising in my throat. *College.* I thought. *College!*

I thanked the lady and practically sprinted back to the bus stop. I wanted to get home before anyone noticed my absence. I didn't want to have to explain where I'd been or be discovered carrying all those brochures. But as I climbed back over the fence, who should be standing in the backyard waiting for me but Terry. "I know what you're up to," she said, her arms crossed. I froze, trusting in Terry's intuition completely. She knew I'd been to college. She knew I was on a fast track to losing my faith.

"Who are you sleeping with?" she asked.

I laughed shortly. "Shane."

She rolled her eyes. "Come on. You've been out all night. Who are you sleeping with?"

I told her my plan. That I was going to study for the California High School Proficiency Exam. The library had all the study materials I needed. All I had to do was get a library card. Then, once I passed the test, I could register for classes at a junior college. The classes would be remedial, but they would prepare me for what came next: accredited units that would add up to a two year degree. And then . . . I could transfer to a university.

"A *university*," I said, my eyes almost tearing.

Terry looked stunned. She asked why I wanted to do such a thing. I said I honestly didn't know. Then she asked if I was going to tell Dad. "He'll understand," she said. "After all, he went to college." I said, *no way*. I didn't want to discuss this with anyone, especially not Dad. I didn't want to hear his opinion. I didn't want to see the look on Mom's face. I didn't want to contend with Judy. I wanted to do this on my own.

"You've got to swear you won't tell," I said.

She shrugged. "Have it your way."

And our eyes met, and, well . . . there was a connection there, if a fragile one. I thought I detected the slightest hint of respect, but I might have been wrong. I knew I detected envy. And I felt a sense of regret for her. I wished things had been different. I wished we could go to college together. It would be like old times, but better. Better than getting drunk at a Holy Innocents barbecue and shocking everyone by singing "Get Down, Make Love." Better than dropping shrooms in the garage and hallucinating over the dishes while The Group was in the other room. Better than sneaking off to smoke pot with Hugo and his new friend Alex. I mean, that was all great fun, but wouldn't it be fun to go to *college*? I was sorry Terry was going to miss out on such a great adventure, but she'd made her choice, and I wasn't going to let her or anyone else hold me back.

16

a birth of sorts

IN MY FAMILY history, my paternal grandfather always stood out to me as a kind of rebel pioneer. The second youngest of ten siblings growing up in Salem, Oregon, Grandpa had just turned twelve when he ran away from home to get away from his father, Elvin Arnold, an abusive alcoholic who would later be institutionalized in an asylum. After spending a year trapping bobcats on his brother's farm in Nevada, Grandpa packed it up there, too, and hitchhiked all the way to Florida, where he was hired as a paid driver for a new breed of land dealers that had sprung up in the state, including Bill Dozier (who eventually went on to Hollywood to produce the *Batman* television series) and William Jennings Bryan, a three-time Democratic nominee for U.S. president who was lecturing on the virtues of the Florida climate for fees from a land promoter. In between his driving duties, Grandpa sat in the bleachers and listened to Bryan's pitch. Not surprisingly, he picked up enough knowledge to make a go in land dealing and earn himself a fortune—a fortune he would later lose in a bad deal that got him arrested.

When I was young, Grandpa was making a modest living selling hearing aids, but he never failed to fascinate me with all the surprises he had up his sleeve. Coin tricks, card tricks, the tale of a pet fish he trained to breathe, the unearthly physical strength to squeeze water out of a rock. Grandpa was a handsome, big-hearted, and generous character, but a cocky and slippery one too, who was (as Dad put it) "a larcenist at heart." I'm sure he made his mistakes in life, but I always thought of him as someone who took risks and did things his way, and I admired him for that. It was a goal I set for myself.

To achieve the greatest distance between my father and me, I attended college. For the first semester I crept over the back fence in the early morning and returned before anyone noticed I was missing. From the college library I brought home books—some on the English course reading lists and some not. I read authors without knowing who they were or what they were talking about, but sensing their nonconformity much as I sensed my own within my poems. The authors seemed to welcome me into their dialogue, and to respect my opinion and invite me to reciprocate. It was like a club of ideas, and I was an honored guest. I'd never experienced respect for my mind before, and it was a wonderful thing.

Being in that club gave me enough self-confidence to come clean with Dad. I said, "I want you to know I've been going to college, and that I intend to keep on going. It's not a choice for me. It's something I *have* to do. I hope you understand. If you forbid me to go, I will pack my bags and move out." Dad's reaction surprised me. He said he was proud of me for choosing "the intellectual life." He said college was a good road for someone like me—although dangerous. He said he would buy a little camper and put it on blocks in the driveway to serve as a quiet place for me to study. He recommended books. "Read *Politics*, by Aristotle," he said. "And *Soul of the Apostolate*, by Dom Chautard. Those'll get you on the right track." Mom, too, was proud but wary. "My mother went to college," she said. "And she was a bitterly unhappy woman who never should have had children. I don't want that to happen to you. Go to college if you have to. But try to keep your head on straight."

It was the beginning of a long period of growth and change for me, and ultimate withdrawal from the Catholic Church—something I sensed would happen from the very start. Faith cannot be force-fed. It seems to come either naturally or not at all. To believe in a dogma, you must be trusting, and compliant, and willing to take the word of someone else as to what life is all about, whether or not it contradicts logic. You must allow truth to be told to you, and not attempt to arrive at it by independent thought and experience. For me, education and religion proved incompatible. I could not simultaneously free my mind to think differently and confine it within a set of ideological principles. I chose to free it in order to follow my plan. *Backtrack. Start from scratch. Think independently.* I had to search for my own *Weltanschauung*. Everyone does.

I often remember a quote by Bertrand Russell that influenced me back in those early years of college:

> *Men fear thought as they fear nothing else on earth—more than ruin—more even than death. . . . Thought is subversive and revolutionary, destructive and terrible. Thought is merciless to privilege, established institutions, and comfortable habit. Thought looks into the pit of hell and is not afraid. Thought is great and swift and free, the light of the world, and the chief glory of man.*

My parents fought hard to keep me in the Church, and then they let me go. They've had to let most of their children go. There was no way to keep us all from thinking independently. Feelings were raw, and still are. We don't agree on many issues—our dad and us. When I told my dad I was writing this memoir, and he asked what it was about, I said, "It's about how our family was torn apart by religion." His response was, "Boy, are you ever right about that. The Catholic Church really did a number on us."

To him, this is true. To him, Vatican II was "the greatest crime in history apart from the Crucifixion" and was responsible for everything that happened to us since 1962. To him, Vatican II was the rotten apple that spoiled the whole crate of us. Will he still believe that after he reads this book? I can say with complete confidence that yes, he will. My father is still one of the "two percent" of people on the planet that knows the "real truth." He is still waiting for the Apocalypse and fighting for the Catholic counter-revolution with his whole heart. The rest of us lost the will to fight that battle. Only one of his eleven kids is still a practicing Catholic. And the other ten of us . . . We aren't fighting for the One Holy Catholic and Apostolic Church, but we still have heart. And that heart is for the family. For keeping it intact. For keeping it whole. And despite everything, I thank Mom for that.

epilogue

I DO NOT wish to leave readers with the impression that my family's story is a tragedy. Large families are like epics: they grow and evolve and have adventures that go on and on, seemingly without end. For those interested, the years brought many changes and improvements. Nick built an addition onto the house, and Danny fixed up what had been a mortifying eyesore in the neighborhood, landscaped the garden, put in patios, windows, a fireplace, and floors. Even Pleasant Hill experienced a face-lift. Terry (who now spells her name Tarri) eventually did go to college and graduated with a degree in art. Judy bought a house in Sacramento and moved there with her son David. Mom, the inexhaustible pillar of the family, went on to see all of her children through myriad phases and hardships, supported us all in our directions in life, gave us a permanent home to come back to, and refused to let religion come between her and us. Even Dad, who we've had to accept "is who he is and will never change," eventually made amends with all of us and confessed to many regrets. He now writes full time for *Tra-*

dition in Action and is on his second book. As for our split with Catholicism, he is disappointed but considers it a "victory with a capital V" that none of us belong to the modern Catholic Church and wrote his own book explaining his radical views called "Radical Catholic." If there is a sad chapter to our epic, it is the one in which our mother died, on March 2, 2007, after a short battle with pancreatic cancer. She will be mourned for the rest of our days.

acknowledgments

MY DEBT TO others extends miles. Foremost I would like to thank my husband, John, who did everything short of changing the weather to set my ship afloat. Without his madminded determination to build me a desk, upgrade my computer, rally the kids, shop for groceries, and dutifully defend my daily writing schedule, an impossible enterprise would never have become possible. To a man who prefers to remain anonymous, thank you, my love. You are my champion. I would also like to express my deepest gratitude to the magnanimous author Michael Lewis, who so kindly went to bat for me in the early beginnings; to Star Lawrence (a man of many pens) for his high standards and quiet guidance; to Winifred Golden for her charismatic council and faithful arbitration; to Molly May, Nydia Parries, and Erin Sinesky-Lovett for their labors behind the scene; to Lucy Hilmer, my comrade and soul sister, for loaning her creative self to me in the pursuit of art; and to the singular Sarah Kerruish for her inimitable talent for bringing people and their purposes together. Huge thanks to the fantastic Poole family—Noreen, Teri, Tami, Dixon, and Michelle—for their ongoing friendship and extraordinary sense of humor, to artist Jane Hambleton for her graphic arts support (and daily dose of irony), and to the stoical workhorse Ray Day for his charitable off-hours industry. I extend my sincerest appreciation to fellow writers Suzanne LaFetra, Kathy Briccetti, Annie Kassof, Sybil Lockhart, Lynn Goodwin, and Rachel Sarah for their invaluable feedback at every juncture, and to patrons of the arts Jane Hambleton, Shawn Lovell, Sarah McGrath, Betsy Joyce, and Natalie Trujillo, who put up with spontaneous readings and kept me constantly laughing. Big thanks to Filipa Veselko and Sérgio Leandro for their hospitality on my return trip to Portugal, and for help with translation. No less thanks (and even bigger apologies) are long overdue to my sons, Daniel, Cameron, and Kyle, who've suffered through the endless telling and retelling of family-related stories and repeated complaints of how hard I had it compared with them—not to mention the many spoiled dinners caused by writing-related activities (writers should not cook and write at the same time). And finally, and with all my heart, I wish to thank my father, Lyle Arnold Jr.; my sisters, Tarri, Jennifer, Mary, Bernadette, and also Rebecca; my brothers Danny, Nick, Vincent, Lyle III, Bernard, and Charles; and my aunt Judy and cousin Dave, for giving me the unconditional freedom to tell the truth.